Greening Growth in Pakistan through Transport Sector Reforms

DIRECTIONS IN DEVELOPMENT
Infrastructure

Greening Growth in Pakistan through Transport Sector Reforms

A Strategic Environmental, Poverty, and Social Assessment

Ernesto Sánchez-Triana, Javaid Afzal, Dan Biller, and Sohail Malik

THE WORLD BANK
Washington, D.C.

© 2013 International Bank for Reconstruction and Development / The World Bank
1818 H Street NW, Washington DC 20433
Telephone: 202-473-1000; Internet: www.worldbank.org

Some rights reserved

1 2 3 4   16 15 14 13

This work is a product of the staff of The World Bank with external contributions. Note that The World Bank does not necessarily own each component of the content included in the work. The World Bank therefore does not warrant that the use of the content contained in the work will not infringe on the rights of third parties. The risk of claims resulting from such infringement rests solely with you.

The findings, interpretations, and conclusions expressed in this work do not necessarily reflect the views of The World Bank, its Board of Executive Directors, or the governments they represent. The World Bank does not guarantee the accuracy of the data included in this work. The boundaries, colors, denominations, and other information shown on any map in this work do not imply any judgment on the part of The World Bank concerning the legal status of any territory or the endorsement or acceptance of such boundaries.

Nothing herein shall constitute or be considered to be a limitation upon or waiver of the privileges and immunities of The World Bank, all of which are specifically reserved.

Rights and Permissions

This work is available under the Creative Commons Attribution 3.0 Unported license (CC BY 3.0) http://creativecommons.org/licenses/by/3.0. Under the Creative Commons Attribution license, you are free to copy, distribute, transmit, and adapt this work, including for commercial purposes, under the following conditions:

Attribution—Please cite the work as follows: Sánchez-Triana, Ernesto, Javaid Afzal, Dan Biller, and Sohail Malik. 2013. *Greening Growth in Pakistan through Transport Sector Reforms: A Strategic Environmental, Poverty, and Social Assessment*. Directions in Development. Washington, DC: World Bank. doi:10.1596/978-0-8213-9929-3. License: Creative Commons Attribution CC BY 3.0

Translations—If you create a translation of this work, please add the following disclaimer along with the attribution: *This translation was not created by The World Bank and should not be considered an official World Bank translation. The World Bank shall not be liable for any content or error in this translation.*

All queries on rights and licenses should be addressed to the Office of the Publisher, The World Bank, 1818 H Street NW, Washington, DC 20433, USA; fax: 202-522-2625; e-mail: pubrights@worldbank.org.

ISBN (paper): 978-0-8213-9929-3
ISBN (electronic): 978-0-8213-9930-9
DOI: 10.1596/978-0-8213-9929-3

Cover image: Pakistani trucks are true works of art. They are often referred to as folk or public art. © Ameer Hamza / Getty Images. Used with the permission of Ameer Hamza / Getty Images. Further permission required for reuse.
Cover design: Naylor Design, Inc.

Library of Congress Cataloging-in-Publication Data

Sánchez Triana, Ernesto.
 Greening growth in Pakistan through transport sector reforms : a strategic environmental, poverty, and social assessment / Ernesto Sánchez-Triana, Javaid Afzal, Dan Biller, and Sohail Malik.
       pages cm. — (Directions in development)
    Includes bibliographical references.
 ISBN 978-0-8213-9929-3 (alk. paper) — ISBN 978-0-8213-9930-9 (ebook)
    1. Freight and freightage—Environmental aspects—Pakistan. 2. Transportation and state—Pakistan. I. Title.
    TD195.T7S26 2013
    388.095491—dc23   2013015882

Contents

Foreword xi
Acknowledgments xiii
About the Authors xv
Abbreviations xvii

Overview 1
    Introduction 1
    Methodology 2
    Sector Challenges and Proposed Reforms and Interventions 2
    Poverty Issues Associated with Freight Transport 4
    Priority Social Issues Associated with Freight Transport 5
    Environmental Aspects Associated with Transport 7
    Sectoral Reforms for Socially and Environmentally
        Sustainable Trade and Transport 9
    Social and Environmental Reforms for Socially and
        Environmentally Sustainable Trade and Transport 11
    Notes 13
    References 13

Chapter 1   **Introduction** 15
    Objective 15
    Methodology 17
    Contents of this Report 20
    Notes 21
    References 21

Chapter 2   **Sector Status and Trade and Transport Policy Reforms** 23
    Freight Transport Sector 24
    Trade Facilitation 35
    Trade and Transport Reforms 35
    Notes 37
    References 37

Chapter 3   **Priority Issues Associated with Freight Transport Reform** 39
    Spatial Transformation 39

	Effects of Productivity Enhancements of the Transport Sector	44
	Summary	51
	Notes	52
	References	53
Chapter 4	**Priority Social Issues Associated with Freight Transport**	**55**
	Freight Transportation and Social Conflicts	56
	Connectivity and Migration	61
	Spatial Transformation and Urban Sprawl	65
	Impact on HIV/AIDS	72
	HIV and Freight	74
	Resettlement and Displacement	74
	Summary	76
	Notes	77
	References	80
Chapter 5	**Priority Environmental Issues Associated with Freight Transport**	**83**
	Air Pollution	83
	Noise Pollution	90
	Road Safety	92
	Hazardous Waste Transportation	98
	Climate Change	99
	Habitat Fragmentation and Natural Resource Degradation	101
	Notes	104
	References	105
Chapter 6	**Policy Options for Environmentally and Socially Sustainable Trade and Transport**	**107**
	Multimodal Transport System	108
	Railways	111
	Modernization of the Trucking and Port Sectors	112
	Redefining the Role of Government and the Need for Private-Sector Participation	114
	The Way Ahead	116
	Notes	119
	References	120
Chapter 7	**An Agenda for Environmentally and Socially Sustainable Trade and Transport Reforms**	**121**
	Addressing Priority Social and Poverty Issues	122
	Addressing Priority Environmental Issues	128
	Addressing Institutional Change	132
	Notes	134
	References	135

Appendix A	Key Issues for the Institutional Analysis of the Freight Transport Sector	137
Appendix B	Pakistan's Environmental Regulatory Framework	157
Appendix C	Overview of Methodology	167
Appendix D	Technical Notes Regarding Methodology	177
Glossary		201

Box

| 4.1 | NACP Mapping of HIV Risk Behavior among Truck Drivers in Pakistan | 75 |

Figures

O.1	Ranking of Selected Developing Countries on Quality of Transport Infrastructure	3
2.1	Ranking of Pakistan's Infrastructure out of 142 Countries	24
2.2	Changes in the Market Share of Road and Rail Freight, 1955–2009	29
2.3	Growth Rates in the Aviation Sector, 1995–2005	33
2.4	Pakistan's Five Priority Development Themes	36
3.1	Relative Road Density in Punjab, 1992–93 versus 2005–06	44
3.2	Poverty Incidence in Districts where Road Upgradation Is Planned or Currently Undertaken	45
3.3	Poverty Incidence in Districts where Road Construction Is Expected	46
4.1	Social Conflict Events in Pakistan, 1989–2010	58
4.2	Urban Sprawl and Road Freight Transport Development in Pakistan, 1990–2005	68
5.1	Legally Binding Sulfur Content in Diesel in Selected Countries, and Average PM_{10} Concentrations in Urban Centers, 2006	84
5.2	Number of Registered Vehicles in Pakistan, 2000–10	85
5.3	Carbon Monoxide Emissions from Vehicle Fleet ($MtCO_2$), 2000–06	85
5.4	NO_x Emissions from Vehicle Fleet	86
5.5	Suspended Particulate Matter from Vehicle Fleet	86
5.6	Particulate Emission Damage in Selected Asian Countries, 2001 and 2007	90
5.7	Annual Cost of Environmental Health Effects	92
5.8	Estimated Number of Road Traffic Deaths per 100,000 Inhabitants, 2007	93
5.9	Correlation between Total Road Traffic Deaths and Several Explanatory Factors	94

5.10	Number of Road Accidents, Fatalities, and Injuries in Pakistan, 1998–2008	95
5.11	Evolution of Total Accidents, Road Length, Vehicles on Road, and Population in Pakistan, 1998–2008	95
5.12	Evolution of Accidents per Inhabitant, Rate of Paved Roads, Traffic Density, and Road Passengers in Pakistan, 1998–2008	96
5.13	Number of Accidents and Fatalities per 100,000 Inhabitants in Pakistani Provinces, 2007–08	97
5.14	Percentage of Fatal Accidents and Number of Deaths per Accident in Pakistani Provinces, 2007–08	97
5.15	Estimated GHG Emissions (TgCO$_2$eq) by 2025 under Different Policy Options	100
5.16	Estimated Diesel Consumption (Billions of Liters per Year) by 2025 under Different Policy Options	100
5.17	Average Environmental Costs of Different Transport Modes	101
6.1	Comparison of Economic Cost between Trucks and Railways	110
6.2	Comparison of Tariffs between Trucks and Railways	110
D.1	General Structure of a Social Accounting Matrix	178
D.2	Effect of Increase in Total Factor Productivity on Economic Surplus	185

Maps

2.1	Pakistan Road Map Depicting Proposed Links	27
2.2	Proposed New Rail Links and Rehabilitation Measures	32
3.1	District-Level Employment Shares in Pakistan's Manufacturing Sector, 2005–06	40
3.2	Spatial Disparities in Road Density in Punjab, 2005–06	42
3.3	Spatial Disparities in Road Density in Khyber Pakhtunkhwa, 2005–06	43
4.1	Map of Pakistan's Security Landscape in 2010	57
4.2	Karachi Urban Sprawl	70
4.3	Social Groups in Influence Area of Urban Transportation Infrastructure in Karachi	71

Tables

O.1	Policy Options to Manage Poverty and Social Priority Issues Associated with Freight Transportation Sector Reforms	11
O.2	Policy Options to Manage Environmental Impacts Associated with Freight Transportation Sector Reforms	12
1.1	Stakeholder Identification	20
2.1	Select Trade and Infrastructure Rankings for Asian Countries	25
2.2	Pakistan Railway Traffic	30
2.3	Earnings of Pakistan Railways	30

2.4	Arrival Performance for Runs during March 2008 from Karachi to Lahore	31
2.5	Pakistan's Port Efficiency Relative to Comparable Benchmarks	34
3.1	Poverty Incidence by Province	44
3.2	Distribution of Population and Incidence of Poverty by Household Groups, 2007–08	47
3.3	Impact of a 10 Percent Increase in TFP of All Transport Subsectors on Household Income by Household Groups	48
3.4	Households and Associated Population Being Adversely Affected by Simulated Improvement in TFP of Transport Subsectors	48
3.5	Impact of a 10 Percent Increase in TFP of Rail and Road Sectors on Sectoral Value Added	49
3.6	Impact of a 10 Percent Increase in TFP of All Transport Subsectors on the Value Added and Price of these Subsectors	50
3.7	Impact of a 10 Percent Increase in TFP of Rail and Road Sectors on Macroeconomic Indicators	50
4.1	International Migration	62
4.2	Inter- and Intramigration in Pakistan, by Province, 2009	63
4.3	City Population of Urban Agglomerations 2000–20	65
4.4	HIV Prevalence by City and High-Risk Group	73
5.1	Comparison of Pakistan's Draft National Air Quality Standards with WHO, EU, and U.S. Air Quality Guidelines	87
5.2	Estimated Health Impacts of Urban Air Pollution from Particulate Matter in Pakistan	87
5.3	Environment and Competitiveness in Pakistan, 2004–08	88
5.4	Noise Levels in Major Cities in Pakistan	91
5.5	Road Traffic Deaths, Population, and Road Traffic Death Rate in the South Asia Region	93
5.6	Projections of Freight Transport Demand and GHG Emissions	99
5.7	Potential Environmental and Social Effects on Priority Environmental Issues	103
6.1	Approximate Road Distances in Pakistan	109
7.1	Policy Options to Manage Poverty and Social Priority Issues Associated with Freight Transportation Sector Reforms	127
7.2	Policy Options to Manage Environmental Impacts Associated with Freight Transportation Sector Reforms	132
A.1	Recommended Actions for Improving Pakistan's Institutional Framework for Management of Trade and Transport	155
B.1	Recommended Actions for Improving Pakistan's Environmental Framework	165
C.1	Stakeholder Identification	171
C.2	List of Communities Visited	172
C.3	List of Persons Interviewed	172

C.4	Key Features of Social Analytical Tools	174
D.1	Social Accounting Matrix Accounts	179
D.2	Poverty by Agro-Climatic Zone, 2005–06	180
D.3	National Trade Corridor (NTC) Districts	181
D.4	Districts Falling in Agro-Climatic Zones	182
D.5	Poverty Bands by Agro-Climatic Zone	183
D.6	Basic Facts Regarding Pakistan's Transport Sector	184
D.7	Population, Poverty Rates, and Monthly Expenditures by Household Groups	187
D.8	Composition of the Total Income by SAM Household Group	188

Foreword

The answer to the question of how Pakistan can maintain steady medium-term economic growth has continued to be at the forefront of the development agenda for the country's policy makers for a while. Part of the answer lies in making the best use of the country's infrastructure stock and improving it for continuous future use. This is recognized by the Government of Pakistan's 2011 Framework for Economic Growth, which seeks to place the country on a sustained high economic growth path by reducing the cost of doing business, improving the investment climate, and strengthening institutions.

Trade and transport reforms are central to achieve the Framework's goals. The transport sector constitutes 10 percent of Pakistan's gross domestic product (GDP) and provides 6 percent of the employment in the country. The sector plays an important role as an enabler of other sectors in the economy via facilitating agglomerations, contributing to both domestic and international trade, and helping facilitate spatial transformation. However, present patterns in transport and trade logistics generate inefficiencies that are costing Pakistan's economy roughly 4–6 percent of GDP per year, which is a major constraint on the aspirations set out in the Framework.

This report examines the poverty, social, and environmental aspects associated with trade and transport sector reforms aimed at increasing the freight transport sector's productivity to meet the Framework's goals. This report is organized as follows. Chapter 1 provides the objectives and methodology of this work. Chapter 2 discusses the sector status and the trade and transport policy reforms. Chapter 3 establishes the priority issues associated with freight transport reform, and chapters 4 and 5 focus on the social and environmental aspects of the reform, respectively. Chapters 6 and 7 conclude the report by discussing policy options to promote environmentally and socially sustainable trade and transport and an agenda to advance environmentally and socially sustainable trade and transport reforms in Pakistan.

As Pakistan transitions to a new political administration, trade and transport are likely to play a more significant role in the country's economy and with its renewed desire to foster greater regional integration. We hope this report also stimulates dialogue on greening growth in the country through trade and transport reforms.

John Henry Stein
Sector Director
Sustainable Development Department
South Asia Region
World Bank

Acknowledgments

This report is a result of the fruitful collaboration between the Planning Commission of the Government of Pakistan and the World Bank.

This report was prepared by a team led by Ernesto Sánchez-Triana (SASDI). The core team included Javaid Afzal (co-TTL), Santiago Enriquez, Cecilia Belita, Ghazal Dezfuli, Dan Biller, and Sohail Malik. The extended team included Asif Faiz, Zia Al Jalaly, Amer Zafar Durrani, Hasan Zaidi, Zafar Raja, Jean-Noel Guillossou, Fernando Loayza, Rahul Kanakia, Paula Posas, Hammad Raza, Bjorn Larsen, Elena Strukova, Marie Florence Elvie, Stan Wanat, Ashma Basnyat, Aude-Sophie Rodella, Stefanie Sieber, Safiya Aftab, Hina Nazli, Wajiha Saeed, Sara Rafi, Shehreyar Rashid, Hiba Zaidi, Kulsum Ahmed, and Innovative Development Strategies (IDS). Valuable guidance was provided by peer reviewers Sonya Sultan, Fernando Loayza, Catherine J. Nove-Josserand, Leonard Ortolano (Stanford University), Daniel Slunge (University of Gothenburg), Jack Ruitenebeek (IUCN), and Rob Verheem (Netherlands EIA Commission). Editorial and manuscript preparation support was provided by Stan Wanat and Ashma Basnyat. Several colleagues also provided helpful advice and detailed contributions, particularly Asif Faiz, Shahzad Sharjeel, and Amer Zafar Durrani. Jeff Lecksell amended the maps to match World Bank guidelines.

The Government of Pakistan, mainly through the Planning Commission and the National Trade Corridor Management Unit, provided key feedback during the preparation of the study and participated actively in the production of diverse parts of the report. The team is indebted to Dr. Nadeem Ul Haq, Deputy Chairman, Planning Commission, and various Secretaries of the Planning and Development Division for their valuable guidance and patronage of the study. The team also recognizes the important contribution of the following government officials: Dr. Raja Aurangzeb Khan, Chief (Environment), Planning Commission; Sysed Tanweer Hussain Bukhari, Project Director, NTCMU; and his team, Malik Muhammad Akram and Ghulam Mohayuddin Marri, Members Infrastructure, Planning Commission.

The team is particularly grateful to the governments of Australia, the Netherlands, Norway, and Finland for their support to fund some of the studies that underpin this report.

About the Authors

Javaid Afzal is a Senior Environment Specialist at the World Bank's Islamabad office. His responsibilities include moving the environment development agenda forward with client government agencies. He also task manages operations in water resources and the environment, and he provides environmental safeguards support for the South Asia Region. Prior to joining the World Bank he worked at a leading consulting company in Pakistan. He has traveled extensively for his work. He holds a PhD in water resources management from Cranfield University, U.K., as well as master's and bachelor's degrees in agricultural engineering from the University of Agriculture, Faisalabad, Pakistan. He has published in a number of peer-reviewed journals on the topics mentioned above.

Dan Biller is the Sustainable Development Lead Economist for the World Bank's South Asia Region. Previously, he was Lead Economist for the East Asia and Pacific Region, and Environment and Natural Resources Program Leader at the World Bank Institute. He was also a senior economist at the Organisation for Economic Co-operation and Development (OECD, France), and has taught at the Fundação Getúlio Vargas (Getulio Vargas Foundation—FGV, Brazil) and the Universidade Santa Úrsula (Saint Ursula University—USU, Brazil). Dr. Biller received his PhD and MS in economics from the University of Illinois at Urbana-Champaign, and a BS in economics with a minor in geophysics from the University of Kansas. He has published extensively on topics such as economic development, natural resource and environmental economics, sustainable consumption, urban/rural linkages, infrastructure, climate change, and social development issues.

Sohail Jehangir Malik is Chairman, Innovative Development Strategies, and Visiting Senior Research Fellow at the International Food Policy Research Institute. During the late 1990s, he was the Poverty Cluster Coordinator for the World Bank's Operations Evaluation Department. He has held Chairs of Econometrics at the Universities of Faisalabad and Sargodha in his native Pakistan, and has widely consulted for international organizations such as the UNDP, FAO, and WTO. He has published extensively in national and international journals on issues of poverty assessment and economic development. Dr. Malik holds a PhD in econometrics from the University of New England, Australia, and master's degrees in agriculture development economics from the Australian National University, Australia, and in economics from the Quaid-e-Azam University, Islamabad in Pakistan.

Ernesto Sánchez-Triana holds MS and PhD degrees from Stanford University, and an engineer degree from Universidad de los Andes, Colombia. He joined the World Bank in 2002 after service as a government officer and university professor. He has led the preparation of numerous policy-based programs, investment projects, technical assistance operations, and analytical works. From 2006 to 2012, he worked in the South Asia Region, where he led multiple operations, including "Greening Growth in Pakistan through Transport Sector Reforms." He is currently the Lead Environmental Specialist for the World Bank's Latin America Vice-Presidency. Dr. Sánchez-Triana has numerous publications in the areas of environmental economics, energy efficiency, poverty reduction, strategic environmental assessment, pollution management, and green growth.

Abbreviations

CAA	Civil Aviation Authority
CES	constant elasticity of substitution
CGE	computable general equilibrium
CMI	Census of Manufacturing Industries
CO_2	carbon dioxide
DALY	disability-adjusted life year
DWT	deadweight tonnage
EALS	environment, afforestation, land, and social
EIA	environmental impact assessment
ESCAP	United Nations Economic and Social Commission for Asia and the Pacific
ET	environmental tribunal
EU	European Union
FGD	focus group discussion
FSW	female sex worker
GDP	gross domestic product
GHG	greenhouse gas
GoP	Government of Pakistan
HSE	health, safety and environment
IBBS	Integrated Biological and Behavioral Surveillance
IDU	injecting drug user
IFPRI	International Food Policy Research Institute
JICA	Japan International Cooperation Agency
KAIRP	Katchi Abadi Improvement and Regularization Program
KICT	Karachi International Container Terminal
KP	Karachi Port
KPT	Karachi Port Trust

LES	linear expenditure system
LFS	labor force survey
LPI	logistics performance index
LUMS	Lahore University of Management Sciences
MoCC	Ministry of Climate Change
MoE	Ministry of Environment
MoF	Ministry of Finance
MoI	Ministry of Industries
MoPNR	Ministry of Petroleum and Natural Resources
MSW	male sex worker
NACP	National AIDS Control Program
NEET	not in education, employment, or training
NEQS	National Environmental Quality Standards
NGO	nongovernmental organization
NHA	National Highways Authority
NLC	National Logistics Cell
NTC	National Trade Corridor
NTCIP	National Trade Corridor Improvement Program
PACCS	Pakistan Customs Computerized System
Pak-EPA	Pakistan Environmental Protection Agency
PEPA	Pakistan Environmental Protection Act of 1997
PIA	Pakistan International Airlines
PM	particulate matter
$PM_{2.5}$	particulate matter less than 2.5 microns
PM_{10}	particulate matter less than 10 microns
PPM	parts per million
PPP	public-private partnership
PQA	Port Qasim Authority
PR	Pakistan Railways
PS&QCA	Pakistan Standards and Quality Control Authority
PSIA	poverty and social impact analysis
QICT	Qasim International Container Terminal
ROW	rest of the world
SAM	social accounting matrix
SEA	strategic environmental assessment
SEPSA	strategic environmental, poverty, and social assessment

STI	sexually transmitted infection
TAP	Turkmenistan-Afghanistan-Pakistan
TEU	twenty-foot equivalent unit
TFP	total factor productivity
UNHCR	United Nations High Commissioner for Refugees
WHO	World Health Organization

Overview

Introduction

The Government of Pakistan's (GoP's) 2011 *Framework for Economic Growth* (GoP 2011b) seeks to place Pakistan on a sustained high economic growth path of 7 percent per year through measures to reduce the cost of doing business, improve the investment climate, and strengthen institutions. Trade and transport reforms are central to achieve the *Framework's* goals. The transport sector constitutes 10 percent of Pakistan's gross domestic product (GDP) and provides 6 percent of the employment in the country (GoP 2011a).[1] The sector plays an important role in linking other sectors in the economy, contributes to both domestic and international trade, and helps facilitate the spatial transformation occurring in Pakistan. However, present patterns in transport and trade logistics generate inefficiencies that are costing Pakistan's economy roughly 4–6 percent of GDP per year, which is a major constraint on the aspirations set out in the *Framework*.

This analytical work on strategic environmental, poverty, and social assessment (SEPSA) of trade and transport sector reforms examines poverty, social, and environmental aspects associated with reforms that would increase the freight transport sector's productivity to meet the *Framework's* goals. It focused on the following areas:

- SEPSA's methodology and aims;
- Description of key challenges in Pakistan's freight transport sectors, including the road, trucking, railway, port, and aviation sectors, as well as trade and transport interventions and reforms proposed by the GoP and other stakeholders;
- Identification of stakeholders, particularly the most vulnerable groups that could be affected by reforms aimed at increasing freight transport productivity, and analyzing the priority poverty issues associated with freight transport in Pakistan;
- Identification jointly with stakeholders of priority social and environmental issues associated with freight transport, and analyzing such issues;

- Examination of potential freight transportation social and environmental policy options for enhancing positive effects or reducing adverse effects associated with increases in freight transport productivity; and
- Identification of options to strengthen governance and the institutional capacity of agencies to manage the environmental, social, and poverty priorities associated with Pakistan's freight transportation.

Methodology

SEPSA follows the methodologies developed for policy or institutionally based strategic environmental assessment (SEA)[2] and poverty and social impact analysis (PSIA).[3] These methodologies are not traditional environmental impact assessment methodologies used for projects and programs. The GoP and the World Bank held a series of workshops during 2009 to scope out the studies that would be completed using the SEA methodology. These stakeholders helped to identify the priority environmental, poverty, and social issues that the analytical work assessed. Each of the studies was prepared in close consultation with relevant stakeholders. Some studies explicitly incorporated structured and semi-structured interviews and focus groups to obtain feedback from a broader range of stakeholders, including vulnerable groups.

Sector Challenges and Proposed Reforms and Interventions

According to the logistics performance index (Arvis et al. 2010), Pakistan's performance on most logistics indicators, including the quality of trade and transport infrastructure, is worse than that of other Asian countries. The transport supply chain system is not providing the value-added services that have become the hallmark of modern logistics, such as multimodal systems that combine the strengths of different transport modes into one integrated system. While the transport sector is functional (figure O.1), it suffers from low quality, long traveling times, and poor reliability (particularly rail transport), which hinder the country's economic growth. In addition, increased motorization and poor urban planning have resulted in significant pollution and traffic congestion in urban areas. Congestion in urban areas reduces the competitiveness of the country's exports, increases the cost of doing business, and constrains Pakistan's capability to integrate into global supply chains.

Geography endows Pakistan with the potential to reap huge economic gains from becoming a hub for regional trade that will have spillovers for economic growth. Central Asia, China, India, and Iran are among the dynamic economies that Pakistan could connect. However, the GoP's decided action will be crucial to capitalize on this opportunity. For example, the recent granting of "Most Favored Nation" status to India needs to be followed up with practical steps for an efficient payment system, a sensible trade policy that avoids excessive (and unfair) injury to Pakistan's industry, trade facilitating government services, a sensible visa regime, and transport networks.

Figure O.1 Ranking of Selected Developing Countries on Quality of Transport Infrastructure (out of 142 Countries)

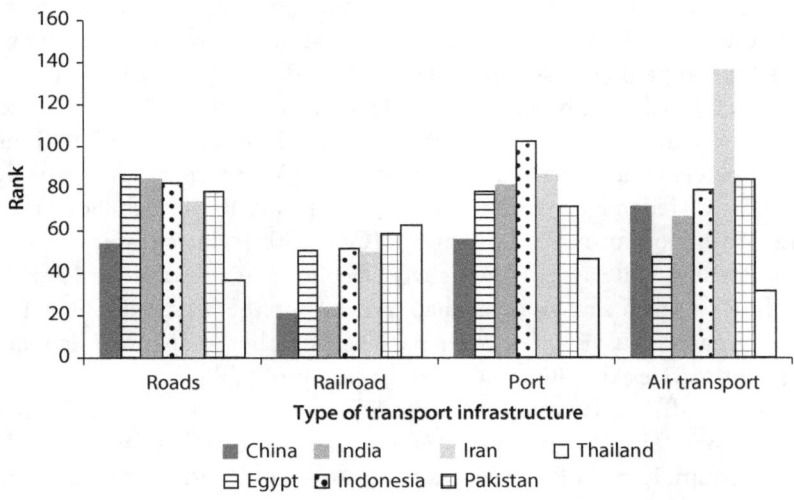

Source: World Economic Forum 2011.

Different organizations have suggested investments in road and railway construction, rehabilitation and upgradation, as part of efforts to facilitate trade with Pakistan's neighbors. However, most of the proposed investments still have not been justified on technical and economic grounds. Some analysts have proposed evaluating roads and railway links as private-sector investments under long-term concessions. Other analysts propose giving priority to improving road/rail access to seaports and dry ports through urban road/highway improvements and removal of trade bottlenecks such as inefficient container handling and freight clearance procedures. The former argue that inefficient urban transport raises freight transport costs and increases unreliability.

The trucking sector carries 96 percent of the total freight traffic (GoP 2009). The presence of a small fleet of owners—who generally own fewer than five vehicles—characterizes the trucking sector. The bulk of trucking companies is centered in the port city of Karachi, where trucking tends to be concentrated within an ethnic community (IDS 2011). According to the GoP, by 2007, inefficiencies of the trucking sector were estimated at US$2.62 billion per year, consisting mainly of (i) US$1.04–US$1.57 billion per year in extra fuel costs and diesel subsidies, (ii) US$0.52–US$0.61 billion per year in additional road user costs, and (iii) a US$0.44 billion per year contribution to the infrastructure deficit (GoP 2007). Over the past 20 years, revenues per kilometer have decreased in real terms by 1.4 percent on average per year (World Bank 2006b). Many trucks operate long hours and carry excessive loads while traveling at low speeds of 20–25 kilometers per hour compared to 80–90 kilometers per hour in Europe. Road freight takes an average of 3–4 days between ports and the north of the country (a distance of

1,400–1,800 kilometers), which is twice what it takes in some other countries of Asia and Europe (GoP 2007).

Railways used to be the predominant mode of transportation in Pakistan. At their peak between 1955 and 1960, railways handled 73 percent of freight traffic, compared to less than 4 percent by 2011. Between 1990–91 and 2010–11, total rail track length decreased by 11 percent, from 8,775 to 7,791 kilometers. Total freight and passengers carried decreased from 5,709 to 3,925 million tons (31 percent) and 84.9 to 58.9 million (31 percent), respectively. During 2005–10, federal expenditure on railways was Rs 45.5 billion, compared to Rs 155 billion for national highways (GoP 2009). Currently, it takes 21–28 days for Pakistan Railways (PR) to deliver upcountry at a distance of 1,800 km, which is four to seven times slower than in the United States and China, respectively. PR's main focus is on serving passengers rather than providing high-quality freight services, despite freight being more profitable.

Port traffic in Pakistan increased 6 percent annually during the period from 2000 to 2005, with container traffic realizing the highest growth at 15 percent per annum. Karachi Port handles the majority of Pakistan's seaborne trade traffic (38.7 million tons in 2008–09). The bulk of the remainder of freight traffic—25.2 million tons—is handled by the Port Qasim Authority. The newly constructed Gwadar Port had not been able to attract any significant traffic until 2008, when the government diverted imports of bulk cargoes of wheat and fertilizers to the port, which handled 1.3 million tons during January–June 2009. Growth of dry cargo at Pakistan's ports has been high, averaging 11 percent per year in the five years up to 2008–09. Growth in bulk cargoes—namely coal, fertilizers, wheat, rice, cement, and clinker—has been even higher. Productivity per ship-hour was found to be just slightly below the average for ports in the region. However, shipping lines handled speeds of 55–60 containers per ship-hour for the two ports, which is below the speeds of up to 100 containers per ship-hour in the region. Major impediments include post-customs delays and lack of rail services and logistical facilities to take containers out of the port. Ship-shore container-handling speeds are up to international levels, but on-shore container processing times are more than twice as long as at efficient international ports (World Bank 2006a).

Poverty Issues Associated with Freight Transport

Pakistan's largest agglomerations are located around the metropolitan cities of Karachi and Lahore. Localization economies (within-industry externalities) and agglomeration are fundamental to industrial competitiveness, as they promote (i) knowledge and information spillovers and innovative ideas among firms, (ii) labor-market pooling, and (iii) input-output linkages. Industrial agglomerations form in districts with good market access, low transportation costs, and a skilled labor force.[4] The spatial geography shows that domestic markets are not able to connect with industrial clusters in urban areas because of high transport costs (which include the costs resulting from inefficient urban transport and poor maintenance of existing provincial and local roads). Deficient urban transport and congestion significantly reduce the connectivity between industrial clusters and domestic and international markets.

According to economic analysis using a computable general equilibrium (CGE) model, a 10 percent increase in total factor productivity (TFP) in transport would increase income of all households. Rural agricultural laborers and the urban nonpoor can realize the largest benefits of such an increase, with their incomes increasing by 1.4 and 1.2 percent, respectively. However, an increase in the TFP in rail or road reveals that nonfarm households and the urban poor can potentially be made worse off. Overall, the CGE estimates that improvements in TFP in transport could adversely affect approximately 40,000 households in the rural nonfarm nonpoor sector, 12,500 households in the rural nonfarm poor category, and 42,000 households in the urban poor category.

Efficient rail and road sectors can increase both imports and exports, thus playing a critical role in increasing revenue from indirect taxes. A 10 percent increase in the TFP of road and rail transport has a positive impact on economic indicators. In addition, economic simulations reveal that improvements in the TFP of the transport sector and its respective subsectors (rail, road, air, and ports) have positive impacts on sectoral value added and household income.

Priority Social Issues Associated with Freight Transport

The scale and the sectors concerned with envisioned reforms in the freight transport sector can be expected to have an impact on social tensions. In the case of ports and shipping, ethnic tensions have already arisen from the perception that recent recruitments favored one ethnic group from communities in and around Karachi to the detriment of other groups. In the case of the trucking industry, an ethnic group from Southern Khyber Pakhtunkhwa owns, manages, and works as employees of this industry even in areas outside the province of Khyber Pakhtunkhwa, making it the main group concerned by the reforms.

In the case of reforms in the port, shipping, and trucking sectors, there is a risk that youth (particularly from nonfarm households and urban poor households) could be directly affected either through direct retrenchment or indirect loss of jobs, as well as through the loss of job prospects they had envisioned and invested in through the *Ustad Shagird* arrangement (Master Apprenticeship). The importance of starting off right is particularly important for young people, since it is the initial transition to the labor force that is a significant determinant of the future economic (and social) well-being of the individual and, if taken collectively, in determining the level of development in Pakistan. Without the proper foothold to start out in the labor market, young people are less able to make choices that will improve their own job prospects and those of their future dependents, thus perpetuating the cycle of insufficient education, low-productivity employment, and poverty from one generation to the next.

Reforms in the freight transport sector can be expected to influence migration flux, patterns, and composition at the national, regional, and international levels by facilitating connectivity. Evidence indicates that migration can help to integrate leading and lagging regions within a country; however, it also has the potential to drive other social impacts, such as social conflict, HIV, or urban sprawl.

While the benefits of urbanization (including intra-industry spillovers) are significant, a number of externalities, such as congestion and pollution, can offset them. Pakistan's urbanization, largely fueled by migration, has accelerated over the last decades, during which the urban growth rate has been twice that of population growth. Indeed, the share of Pakistan's urban population has continued to increase since 1996, and it is estimated that 35.9 percent of the country's population lived in urban settings in 2010 (UN HABITAT 2011, 208). With economic motivations dominating rural-to-urban migration, it is not surprising to find Lahore and Karachi, the two most highly concentrated districts in large-scale manufacturing employment, among those facing the most challenges with regard to growth and urban sprawl.

The expected improvements in road infrastructure and freight transport policy reforms and investments are likely to increase job creation mainly in the manufacturing and service sectors. Although poor migrants are typically not qualified for the better-paid jobs in the manufacturing and service sectors, the creation of formal and higher-paying jobs in urban centers results in an increased demand for low-paying jobs for which many of them are qualified. These types of lower-paying jobs in the informal economy will lure people living in rural areas who will likely populate new or expanded shantytowns located on the outskirts of large urban areas, or slums in the downtown areas, where they would likely find friends and relatives.

Urban sprawl in Pakistan is partially correlated with road transportation. The observed expansion of slums along the main roads and highways is the result of the concentration of informal economic activity associated with road transportation. In most cases, local authorities lack the ability to anticipate population growth, which in turn may constrain their ability to provide land for the urbanizing poor. Another contributing factor is the issue of land rights and tenure security, which tend to be denied to the urban poor, driving people to the periphery of towns and further contributing to urban sprawl. Recent estimates suggest that there was a deficit of 6 million housing units in Pakistan in 2005, and the sustained flux of rural-to-urban migration is likely to accentuate this situation. In urban areas, informal housing units largely meet the deficit, as available data indicate that there are about 3.5 million housing units in informal settlements, housing 24.5 million people (Hasan and Raza 2009). Informal settlements, which lack access to basic services and infrastructure, do not fall under the realm of responsibility of city administrations and, as such, tend to be un-serviced or critically under-serviced.

The greater degree of connectivity, migration, and urbanization, fostered by trade and transport sector reforms, can also be expected to affect the status of HIV/AIDS in Pakistan. Pakistan remains a country with a concentrated epidemic, with prevalence levels consistently reported to be greater than 5 percent among injecting drug users and cross-dressed sex workers. Long-distance truckers, assistants, and sex workers constitute a major vector of HIV/AIDS in Pakistan. Truck drivers, cleaners, and assistants remain engaged on long trade routes for several weeks. When they make stopovers and take breaks during such periods, a high prevalence of sex providers, both male and female, frequent their stops. Such services mushroom and grow in tandem with the expansion of trade. The drivers may also sexually exploit the young cleaners who take care of and clean the trucks.

Involuntary resettlement could become a priority issue in the construction of new roads or railways for transportation.[5] Resettlement action plans are made and implemented for projects supported by international financing organizations or by donor agencies, as required by those organizations. However, lack of a unified national policy means that implementing agencies follow a range of different guidelines when devising resettlement plans for different donor-funded projects, or worse, draw up inadequate plans or no plans at all when working with public funds.

Environmental Aspects Associated with Transport

Ambient air pollution is one of Pakistan's most serious public health problems (World Bank 2006a, 2011). A 2006 World Bank report found that more than 22,600 deaths per year are directly or indirectly attributable to ambient air pollution at the national level (World Bank 2011). A more recent analysis concluded that outdoor air pollution in 2009 in Sindh had a cost equivalent to 0.9–2.2 percent of the province's GDP and was responsible for more than 10,000 premature deaths, with roughly 80 percent of them happening in Karachi. Analytical work by the World Bank provides solid evidence that particulate matter, especially fine and ultrafine particulate matter, is the most important ambient air contamination problem to be addressed in Pakistan.

Although trucks represent a minor fraction of Pakistan's vehicle fleet, they emit pollutants of local and global concern. Estimates based on limited available information suggest that mobile sources (including two- and three-wheel vehicles, cars, trucks, and buses) contribute a significant percentage of emissions of fine and ultrafine particles. These vehicles run on fuels that have high sulfur content, a main ingredient in the formation of particulate matter. Most fuel in Pakistan has a sulfur level of 5,000–10,000 parts per million, a level much higher than Euro II, Euro III, or Euro IV emission standards, which have already been adopted in some South Asian countries (World Bank 2006b). The GoP has adopted a plan to reduce sulfur content in fuels; however, various reasons have delayed it.

Noise levels in most urban locations are well above the World Health Organization (WHO) recommended limits. According to the Pakistan Environmental Protection Agency, there is no national monitoring system of environmental noise levels in cities. Analytical work carried out by the World Bank found that the mean annual cost of noise pollution in 2008 in Punjab was Rs 8 billion, while road traffic noise had a cost of Rs 25.8 billion in Sindh. About 58 percent of this cost is associated with morbidity and 42 percent with premature mortality.

According to estimates by WHO, in 2007 there were 41,494 road fatalities in Pakistan. This implies a rate of 25.3 deaths per 100,000 inhabitants. In contrast, the observed rates in industrialized countries range between 5 and 10 fatalities per 100,000 inhabitants. In the rest of South Asia, the observed rates range from 12.6 to 18.3. According to official data, the general trend over the last decade has been rather stable, with around 10,000 accidents per year and an average of 5,200 fatalities per year. Since traffic has increased over this period, the accidents per million vehicle-kilometer of travel and per 1,000 vehicles have been decreasing. However, available data are not fully reliable, and there is evidence of significant underreporting.

In addition to pain and suffering, road accidents generate significant economic costs. A study conducted under SEPSA estimated that, in 2009 in Sindh, road accidents (associated with all kinds of vehicles) caused 1,800–2,200 deaths, 5,400–6,600 cases of permanent disabilities, 59,000–105,000 other serious injuries, and 423,000–474,000 minor injuries. The cost stemming from these accidents is equal to Rs 50 billion per year or 1.4 percent of the province's GDP. The largest costs are those related to permanent disability (Rs 23.4 billion), fatalities (Rs 9 billion), and serious injuries (Rs 7.7 billion). The limited information that is available suggests that a significant share of road accidents and fatalities in Pakistan involved a truck, even though these vehicles comprise only around 3 percent of the vehicle fleet (World Bank 2006b). The record for trucks might be better than buses and cars, but it is still extremely poor.

By stimulating trade and economic growth, freight transport reforms will contribute to the acceleration of the industrialization process in Pakistan, and also increase the use of many types of chemicals and the transport of other hazardous products. Many industrial sectors (such as leather processing, and pulp and paper) are heavily dependent on many chemicals during production, and some of them are very dangerous to public health. Despite the risks associated with transporting hazardous substances, there is very little reliable data on this subject in Pakistan. Poor management of environmental waste leads to serious environmental implications. An example of a deadly accident involving transport of hazardous materials in Pakistan was the leakage of poisonous chlorine gas on January 8, 1997.

Pakistan's ecosystems already face significant threats, and the expansion of transport infrastructure could aggravate them. Pakistan faces the highest annual deforestation rate of Asia, at 2.1 percent. Deforestation is highest in the Indus Delta mangroves, with an annual rate of 2.3 percent. Wetlands are particularly important, as they provide livelihoods to communities and offer protection against floods, which recurrently affect the country, as evidenced by the severe floods of 2010 and 2011. The potential effects of the expansion of transport infrastructure on ecosystems include habitat fragmentation, wetland destruction, and induced increases in deforestation as roads facilitate access to these natural resources. Areas that would be particularly susceptible to increased deforestation include the Indus Watershed and its tributaries, as well as its affluents' gallery forests and wetlands. In the past, wetlands have also been drained and destroyed to build dikes. Degradation and destruction of these ecosystems would have significant implications, including heightening Pakistan's vulnerability to extreme weather events.

The effective and efficient use of environmental impact assessment (EIA) could inform decision making and identify alternatives to reduce or mitigate the negative effects of transport infrastructure development, including those related to habitat fragmentation or deforestation. However, despite its use for more than 20 years in Pakistan, EIA still faces a number of shortcomings, including problems in screening and scoping, insufficient public participation, poor quality of environmental assessment reports, and weak capacities of environmental authorities to review environmental reports and monitor compliance with the conditions of the environmental authorization.

Pakistan's greenhouse gas (GHG) emissions are relatively small, but have been growing and are anticipated to increase at high rates over the coming years. In 2007–08, the transport sector contributed 21 percent of the energy sector's emissions. Most of the sector emissions originate from road transportation, which consumed about half of the country's total petroleum products during 1997–98 to 2006–07. GHG emissions from railways were only 0.17 percent of total transport carbon emissions in 2006–07. Road transport emits an average 0.17 $TgCO_2eq$ per billion ton-kilometers, compared with railway transport's emissions of 0.02 $TgCO_2eq$ per billion ton-kilometers. Estimates based on future GDP projections suggest that transport demand for freight will increase steadily in the coming years and will hence increase GHG emissions. The results clearly indicate that in future years, the road sector will generate the lion's share of emissions. For example, in 2030–31, total $TgCO_2eq$ emissions for road transport are anticipated to be 90.17, compared with 3.05 for rail. An assessment of different scenarios indicates that shifting toward investments in rail would most reduce GHG emissions and diesel consumption.

Sectoral Reforms for Socially and Environmentally Sustainable Trade and Transport

Pakistan's freight transport system needs to shift toward one based on the integration and complementarities of rail and trucking to improve efficiency and decrease environmental impacts. Rail freight generally has a competitive advantage and lower costs over road freight transport via trucks for longer distances. The adoption of a multimodal freight transport system—one that uses rail for long hauls and road freight for shorter distances—is a strategy for enhancing the sustainability of freight transport. Given that rail is more environmentally sustainable than road, the case for integrating rail more significantly into freight logistic itineraries for goods is critical. Failure to integrate a multimodal transport system would have adverse consequences for Pakistan, including lack of competitiveness and increased social and environmental costs.

Adopting a multimodal transport system and modernization of the trucking sector will help reduce negative *environmental* externalities generated by the trucking sector. Under the multimodal system, a reduction in the number of long-distance truck drivers; substituting newer models for existing obsolete, poorly maintained trucks; and modal shift to railways are anticipated, which would help decrease road congestion, improve air quality, reduce GHG emissions, decrease the probability of road accidents and fatalities, and reduce noise pollution and the risk of hazardous material spills.

Also, adopting a multimodal transport system and modernization of the trucking sector will help mitigate a number of negative *social* impacts. A modernized trucking system and increases in rail freight transport would help reduce HIV transmission risks. Long-distance truck drivers (who spend substantial time away from home) and sex workers who work along major transport routes are identified as highly vulnerable groups at the greatest risk for HIV. The modernization of the transport sector and modal shift to railways could lead to the reduction in the long-distance trips carried out by truck drivers, and thus, to a decrease in the risk of HIV transmission.

To allow for rail to operate on a commercial basis, PR might be split into two different organizations: one responsible for freight and the other for passenger services, without any sort of subsidization.[6] This would allow PR to be relieved of costs of operating the large noncommercial network of lines and services. PR should, over time, separate core and noncore activities with a view to having the company focus on its core function of providing rail transport rather than on management of its nonoperational land assets, such as factories and workshops. Investment in new rail lines for freight transport should be made based on public-private partnerships sharing risks and using the highest economic, financial, social, and environmental standards.

To remedy inefficiencies in the trucking sector (which arguably generates the lion's share of environmental and social problems in freight transport), the GoP might accelerate implementing its 2007 National Trucking Policy. The overall objective of modernizing the trucking sector is to encourage the use of large and modern fleet trucks that meet minimum European emission standards and can meet Pakistan's freight transport demand at a lower cost. This reform is particularly important for the transport of heavy and bulk commodities.

Increasing freight transport productivity requires private-sector participation. Due to federal budget constraints, bringing in private participation (particularly in rail and aviation) is required. To provide a level playing field, the government might consider developing a regulatory framework for ensuring market competition in the rail and air transport sectors, including provisions for entry and exit of private operators. This regulatory framework could facilitate intermodal connectivity and private-sector participation. The regulatory structure should include responsibilities on cross-cutting issues such as the following: environment and social management, project and concession contract development, and monitoring and evaluation. An apex regulatory organization could take over responsibilities such as regulatory policies and promotion of private-sector participation.

Social and Environmental Reforms for Socially and Environmentally Sustainable Trade and Transport

Stakeholders and experts in Pakistan identified the priority potential social issues associated with reforms in the freight transport sector. The main social issues identified by stakeholders include social and ethnic conflicts, migration and urbanization, urban sprawl, disease transmission (particularly HIV/AIDS), and involuntary resettlement and displacement. Table O.1 summarizes the policy options that the GoP might consider to manage the priority poverty and social issues associated with reforms in the freight transport sector.

Freight transportation reforms might consider a number of environmental policy options to enhance the positive effects and mitigate the negative

Table O.1 Policy Options to Manage Poverty and Social Priority Issues Associated with Freight Transportation Sector Reforms

Priority social issue	Description	Policy option
Social conflict in urban centers	Ethnic groups could be particularly affected.	Ensure adequate engagement of potentially affected groups in the design and implementation of proposed policies.
Urban poor and nonfarm households affected by increase in transport productivity	Urban poor and nonfarm households might lose their livelihoods as a result of reforms in the trade and transport sector.	Promote structural change to raise the contribution of industrial manufacturing to the economy, boost employment, and increase fiscal revenues. Strengthen connectivity linking industrial clusters to domestic and international markets.
Urban sprawl	Creation of economic opportunities in urban areas may increase "pull" migration, increasing the demand for housing and public services.	Give priority to upgrading slums and service delivery in urban settings. Build capacity of at least two tiers (provincial and district) of government to better design and implement urban development strategies that respond to Pakistan's spatial transformations.
Small operators in the trucking sector have a probability of losing business to new and larger enterprises due to trade and transport reforms	Truckers largely operate in the informal sector and have little or no contact with government agencies. Urban poor and nonfarm households might lose their livelihoods as a result of reforms in the trade and transport sector.	Direct programs for assisting truckers to reach out to a variety of truckers' associations, which cover truck manufacturers, drivers, adda owners, and goods companies. Involve community development organizations, which typically have experience in advising communities on small-scale enterprise development, in design and implementation.
HIV/AIDS transmission	Growth in the road transport sector, under a business-as-usual scenario, is associated with increased spread of sexually transmitted infections, including HIV/AIDS. At the same time, increasing railway's participation and modernizing the trucking sector could significantly reduce the risk of HIV/AIDS transmission.	Strengthen the National AIDS Control Program in the freight transportation sector, including information campaigns targeting vulnerable groups.
Involuntary resettlement	Potential involuntary resettlement due to construction of freight transport infrastructure.	Create and implement a national resettlement policy that is enforced effectively and uniformly in all provinces and federal territories, with adequate grievance-redress mechanisms.

Table O.2 Policy Options to Manage Environmental Impacts Associated with Freight Transportation Sector Reforms

Priority environmental problem	Description	Policy option
Air pollution	Pakistan urban centers rank as some of the worst with regard to particulate matter air pollution. Burning of high sulfur fuel leads to high quantities of fine and ultrafine particulate matter, harming public health.	Stricter standards on sulfur content in diesel should not be delayed beyond January 2014. Purchase low/ultralow sulfur fuels from different suppliers, as such fuels are available in international markets. Strengthen the Pakistan Environmental Protection Agency and provincial environmental protection departments and build their capacity to enforce recently adopted ambient air quality standards and vehicular emission standards. Accelerate implementation of the 2007 National Trucking Policy, particularly the replacement of obsolete, poorly maintained, highly polluting trucks with larger and modern trucks.
Noise pollution	Excessive noise levels in urban areas cause ear damage, sleep disturbance, psychiatric conditions, and cardiovascular disorders.	Develop a regulatory framework and enforcement capacity to control environmental noise pollution.
Road safety	Pakistan ranks as one of the most dangerous countries in the world in road safety.	Develop a regulatory framework and enforcement capacity on road safety.
Hazardous waste transportation	With further investment in trade and transport, and greater commerce, movement of hazardous materials and the probability of spills and other emergencies might increase.	Design and implement a national framework to manage the transportation of hazardous materials, based on international best practices.
Habitat fragmentation and natural resource degradation	Pakistan faces the highest deforestation rate in South Asia. Increases in the road infrastructure could exacerbate this.	Strengthen the environmental impact assessment system to improve decision making for the development of freight transport infrastructure.
Climate change emissions of greenhouse gases	Models showed that some modal shift from road to rail would significantly reduce GHG emissions.	Provide greater emphasis on railroads and on using existing railroads.

consequences of trade and freight transport reforms. Table O.2 summarizes the policy options that the GoP might consider to manage the priority environmental issues associated with reforms in the freight transport sector.

The lack of environmental and social planning capacity at transport agencies should be rectified with a program of institutional strengthening and capacity building. Environmental and social units should be established in all organizations that still lack them. These units should be integrated into the planning and decision-making process of their organization, so they possess the ability to influence construction and operation in such a way as to take into account environmental and social considerations (particularly early on in the planning process, when such considerations can be dealt with more efficiently).

As a result of the 18th Amendment to the Constitution, Pakistan's Ministry of Environment (MoE) was formally dissolved in June 2011. The recently created

Ministry of Disaster Management will be given a mandate to carry out the functions of the former MoE. These functions are likely to include developing national environmental policies, engaging in international environmental negotiations, dealing with transboundary environmental issues, and promoting interprovincial coordination. The apex environmental agency should also be given responsibility for coordinating the institutional strengthening and capacity building of provincial EPAs and environmental units to be created within transport agencies.

Notes

1. In many developed countries, transport contributes between 6 and 12 percent of national GDP; see Rodrigue et al. (2009). In India, the transport sector contributed between 5.7 and 6.4 percent of GDP between 1999 and 2005 (Singru 2007).
2. SEPSA's SEA was based on the strategic environmental assessment in policy and sector reform approach developed by
   - OECD DAC (Organisation for Economic Co-operation and Development, Development Assistance Committee); see OECD DAC 2006.
   - World Bank; see World Bank 2005.
   - World Bank, University of Gothenburg, Swedish University of Agricultural Sciences, and Netherlands Commission for Environmental Assessment; see World Bank et al. 2010.
3. SEPSA's PSIA was based on the approach developed by the World Bank in 2002 (www.worldbank.org/psia). The general elements of the PSIA approach, as outlined in the User's Guide, were adjusted and tailored to the political, social, cultural, economic, and security situation in Pakistan at present and to the situation in the trade and transport sector in particular. For the World Bank PSIA User's Guide, see http://web.worldbank.org/WBSITE/EXTERNAL/TOPICS/EXTPSIA/0,,contentMDK:20454976~menuPK:6145452~pagePK:148956~piPK:216618~theSitePK:490130~isCURL:Y~isCURL:Y~isCURL:Y~isCURL:Y~isCURL:Y~isCURL:Y,00.html.
4. A description of the econometric analysis can be found in the consultant report prepared by LUMS (Lahore University of Management Sciences) for the World Bank; see LUMS 2011.
5. Work on the Faisalabad-Khanewal section of the E-4 motorway is currently ongoing with support from the Asian Development Bank, but the bulk of the investment component has yet to be undertaken.
6. The analyses of passenger transport in general and train passenger services in particular are beyond the scope of SEPSA.

References

Arvis, Jean-François, Monica Alina Mustra, Lauri Ojala, Ben Shepherd, and Daniel Saslavsky. 2010. *Connecting to Compete 2010. Trade Logistics in the Global Economy: The Logistics Performance Index and Its Indicators*. Washington, DC: World Bank. http://siteresources.worldbank.org/INTTLF/Resources/LPI2010_for_web.pdf.

GoP (Government of Pakistan). 2007. National Trucking Policy. National Trade Corridor Improvement Programme. Islamabad. http://www.ntcip.gov.pk/.

———. 2009. *Pakistan Economic Survey 2008–2009.* Ministry of Finance. Islamabad. http://finance.gov.pk/survey_0809.html. Accessed March 28, 2010.

———. 2011a. *Pakistan Economic Survey 2010–2011.* Ministry of Finance. Islamabad. http://finance.gov.pk/survey_1011.html. Accessed November 15, 2011.

———. 2011b. *Pakistan: Framework for Economic Growth.* Planning Commission. Islamabad.

Hasan, Arif, and Mansoor Raza. 2009. "Migration and Small Towns in Pakistan." Working Paper Series on Rural-Urban Interactions and Livelihood Strategies, No. 15. London: IIED (International Institute for Environment and Development). http://books.google.com.pk/books?id=U7imPH4KVJUC&printsec=frontcover#v=onepage&q&f=false.

IDS (Innovative Development Strategies). 2011. *SEPSA: Poverty and Social Impact Assessment.* Consultant report, Islamabad: World Bank

LUMS (Lahore University of Management Sciences). 2011. Abid A. Burki, Kamal A. Munir, Mushtaq A. Khan, M. Usman Khan, Adeel Faheem, Ayesha Khalid, and Syed Turab Hussain. *Industrial Policy, Its Spatial Aspects and Cluster Development in Pakistan.* Consultant report by the Lahore University of Management Sciences for the World Bank. Lahore, Pakistan.

OECD DAC (Organisation for Economic Co-operation and Development, Development Assistance Committee). 2006. *Applying Strategic Environmental Assessment: Good Practice Guidance for Development Co-operation.* Paris: OECD Publishing.

Rodrigue, Jean Paul, Claude Comtois, and Brian Slack. 2009. *The Geography of Transport Systems.* 2nd edition. New York: Routledge. http://books.google.com/books?id=afRodkxRoCsC&printsec=frontcover#v=onepage&q&f=false.

Singru, Narendra. 2007. *Profile of the Indian Transport Sector.* Manila: ADB (Asian Development Bank). http://www.iptu.co.uk/content/trade_cluster_info/india/indian-transport-profile.pdf.

UN HABITAT. 2011. *Global Report on Human Settlements 2011: Cities and Climate Change.* Oxford, U.K.: Earthscan.

World Bank. 2005. *Integrating Environmental Considerations in Policy Formulation: Lessons from Policy-Based SEA Experience.* Report 32783. Washington, DC: World Bank.

———. 2006a. *Pakistan Strategic Country Environmental Assessment.* Washington, DC: World Bank. http://web.worldbank.org/WBSITE/EXTERNAL/COUNTRIES/SOUTHASIAEXT/0,,contentMDK:21459418~pagePK:146736~piPK:146830~theSitePK:223547,00.html.

———. 2006b. *Transport Competitiveness in Pakistan: Analytical Underpinnings for the National Trade Corridor Improvement Program.* Report No. 36523-PK. Washington, DC: World Bank.

———. 2011. *Pakistan Transport Sector.* Washington, DC: World Bank. http://go.worldbank.org/A0D9IJ5SH0.

World Bank, University of Gothenburg, Swedish University of Agricultural Sciences, and Netherlands Commission for Environmental Assessment. 2010. *Strategic Environmental Assessment in Policy and Sector Reform: Conceptual Model and Operational Guidance.* Washington, DC: World Bank.

World Economic Forum. 2011. *Global Competitiveness Report 2011–2012.* Geneva: World Economic Forum.

CHAPTER 1

Introduction

Objective

Pakistan's development efforts are guided by the *Framework for Economic Growth* (GoP 2011), which proposes a new strategy to address the country's volatile economic growth, declining long-run growth, and stagnation of per capita income levels. The new strategy aims to depart from the country's past growth policy based on public-sector projects and arbitrary incentives, subsidy, and protection. Instead, the thrust of the new strategy is to focus on the "software" of economic growth (such as economic governance, institutions, and incentives) to enable an environment in which the "hardware" of growth (physical infrastructure) can be expanded and made more productive. A key goal of the new strategy is achieving an annual gross domestic product (GDP) growth rate above 7 percent, which is the rate needed to incorporate Pakistan's growing youth into the labor market.

The *Framework* recognizes that improving connectivity to spur commercial activity is crucial to achieve its goals. The transport sector plays an important role in linking other sectors in the economy, contributes to both domestic and international trade, and helps facilitate the spatial transformation occurring in Pakistan. Transport is essential for industrial growth and the economy in several ways—for example, in bringing raw materials to industries, moving final outputs from one industry to another, distributing different commodities to various distributors and wholesalers, and distributing imported and domestically produced goods to consumers. However, Pakistan's transport and trade logistics sector is currently plagued by inefficiencies that are costing Pakistan's economy roughly 4–6 percent of GDP per year (World Bank 2006), which is a major constraint on the aspirations set out in the *Framework for Economic Growth*.

To help fulfill Pakistan's development objectives, the Government of Pakistan (GoP) has requested the World Bank's assistance to build the capacity of the agencies responsible for managing Pakistan's trade and transport programs (World Bank 2009a). Key areas to be supported include reforms that would

- Lead to modern and streamlined trade and transport logistics practices, to a modern customs system, and to reduce the costs for port users and enhance port management accountability;
- Create a commercial and accountable environment in Pakistan Railways and increase private-sector participation in the operation of rail services;
- Modernize the trucking industry and reduce the cost of externalities for the country;
- Sustain delivery of an efficient, safe, and reliable National Highways system; and
- Promote and ensure safe, secure, economical, and efficient civil aviation operations and boost air trade.

The World Bank's analytical work on strategic environmental, poverty, and social assessment (SEPSA) of trade and transport sector reforms supports the GoP's analysis of alternatives for sustainable freight transportation that takes advantage of location economies. The World Bank's analytical work aims to identify cost-effective opportunities for improving the efficiency of the freight transport system to meet the goals of enhancing export competitiveness, promoting spatial transformation for poverty alleviation, and reducing environmental degradation. This analytical work is different from a traditional environmental and social impact assessment; it does not aim to conduct an ex-ante evaluation of specific programs or projects proposed by GoP agencies. Instead, it begins by recognizing that the overall objective of the GoP's reform agenda is to enhance the competitiveness of the trade and transport sector as a means of spurring economic growth. It then identifies the main costs and benefits that would arise from the sector's increased productivity, as well as how these would be distributed among different stakeholders. This is followed by an examination of policy proposals that would not only increase the sector's competitiveness, but would also reduce its environmental and social externalities, protect vulnerable groups from adverse effects, and contribute to Pakistan's fight against poverty.

This analytical work focuses on

- Analyzing the policy and institutional adjustments required to address environmental, social, and poverty aspects of increased transportation efficiency;
- Identifying policy options to better serve the population, to enhance social cohesion, and to foster equitable benefit sharing with low-income or other vulnerable groups;
- Developing a broad participatory process to give a voice to stakeholders who could be affected by enhancements of freight transport productivity; and
- Making robust recommendations to strengthen governance and the institutional capacity of agencies to manage the environmental, social, and poverty consequences of freight transportation infrastructure.

The GoP also holds the view that enhancing the country's competitiveness will only be sustainable if environmental and social considerations are mainstreamed into transport policy reforms and investment programs. The World Bank's strategic country environmental assessment indicated that environmental degradation costs Pakistan at least 6 percent of GDP, or approximately Rs 365 billion per year. More recent estimates by the World Bank indicate that environmental degradation in Sindh represented around 15 percent of the provincial GDP in 2009, even using conservative estimates (Larsen and Skjelvik 2012). Pakistan's *Framework for Economic Growth* acknowledges the importance of minimizing the negative environmental effects of development activities and improving the business climate through the adoption and enforcement of environmental requirements. In this context, the GoP is committed to strengthening the institutional framework for environmental management as a means of increasing productivity, reducing regulatory burdens, orienting agriculture and industrial sectors toward higher value markets, reducing the pressure of productive sectors on the natural resources base, and taking advantage of new business opportunities in global markets. The GoP's policies also stress the need for engaging a broad range of stakeholders to address inequalities, foster inclusive growth, and competently manage the country's economic and political transformations.

Methodology

The analytical work incorporated methodologies developed for strategic environmental assessment (SEA),[1] poverty and social impact analysis (PSIA), and analysis of spatial disparities and industrial cluster development. Specifically, the SEPSA methodological framework combines the *two key elements of PSIA*[2]— namely, analysis of distributional impacts and engagement of stakeholders in policy making—with the *key elements of the SEA approach*: analytical work that would provide a foundation for meeting SEPSA's objectives, and public discussions to ensure meaningful exchange among relevant stakeholders. The PSIA, more specifically, is intended to assist policy makers to enhance the positive impacts of reforms and minimize their adverse impacts through

- Understanding the impact of policy reforms on poverty and social outcomes;
- Analyzing intended and unintended consequences of policy interventions (ex-ante, during implementation or ex-post);
- Considering trade-offs associated with reforms by assessing opportunities, constraints, and risks; and
- Designing appropriate mitigation measures and risk management strategies, and building country ownership and capacity for analysis and implementation of policy reforms.

The analysis included a compilation of trade and transport reforms and interventions proposed by different stakeholders and governmental organizations. The analysis focuses primarily on transport reforms because they have stronger linkages with Pakistan's environmental, poverty, and social priorities. Data collection efforts permitted the mapping of the different interventions and proposals on railways, roads, ports, and airlines. Based on these efforts, SEPSA collected and organized systematically not only the main reform proposals, but also the key infrastructure investments planned by various governmental organizations, which this document publicly presents for the first time.

Discussion among Key Stakeholders

The objectives of the stakeholder consultations are twofold. They not only raise public awareness and support for reforms in the trade and transport sector, but they also allow participation and involvement of unorganized or voiceless groups in the planning and implementation of such reforms. One means to achieve the second objective is to use the consultations to let stakeholders identify priorities for the sector's environmental and social development objectives and interventions.

To ensure meaningful discussion among key stakeholders in the identification of specific sustainability criteria that would be incorporated into transport reforms, the GoP and the World Bank held a series of workshops during 2009 to scope out the studies that would be completed using the SEA's methodology. The opinions and inputs provided by representatives from federal and provincial governments, as well as by nongovernmental organizations, were incorporated into SEPSA's concept note. These stakeholders helped to identify the priority environmental, poverty, and social issues that were assessed in the analytical work. In addition, each of the studies mentioned above was prepared in close consultation with relevant stakeholders. The methodology of some studies explicitly incorporated tools to obtain feedback from a broader range of stakeholders. In particular, structured and semi-structured interviews were carried out as part of the PSIA and the gender analysis to obtain feedback from vulnerable groups (IDS 2011). A major effort to reach additional stakeholders will be carried out to discuss the key findings and policy recommendations of SEPSA, including a series of workshops that will take place during the second half of 2013.

Analytical Work as a Foundation for Meeting the GoP's Economic Objectives

To provide the analytical underpinnings for policy reform, SEPSA included a series of studies that address the environmental, social, and poverty implications of enhanced freight transport productivity. The environmental management component of SEPSA focused on the environmental aspects of investments and reforms in the freight transport sector. The potential environmental consequences of three strategic alternatives were analyzed: (i) business as usual, in which no sectoral productivity increases are envisioned; (ii) efficiency increases in the road freight sector; and (iii) policies that emphasize reforms and investments in the rail freight sector. Each alternative was evaluated based on the set of priority issues identified jointly with stakeholders (climate change, air quality, transport of hazardous materials, road and railway safety, urban sprawl and accessibility, and environmental management systems) to assess their potential environmental and social implications.

The PSIA[3] was prepared to identify possible ex-ante social and distributional impacts of transport sector reforms on stakeholder groups. The analysis focused on answering the following three questions:

- Which groups will be affected, how, and to what extent over the short and long term?
- What will be the distributional impacts on the well-being of social groups?
- How will Pakistan's freight programs correlate with social cohesion and inclusion in Pakistan?

The PSIA employed a computable general equilibrium model, which is a model that uses actual economic data to estimate how an economy might react to changes in policy or other external factors. To estimate how Pakistan's economy might react to the reforms proposed by the GoP for the transport sector, the model was run for a 10 percent increase in total factor productivity (TFP). This variable refers to the efficiency and intensity with which such inputs are utilized in production, rather than to the portion of output that is explained by the *amount* of inputs used in production. The model therefore incorporates the proposed reforms' aim of removing bottlenecks and thereby enable a more efficient and intense use of inputs, and thus help increase economic output. The PSIA identified the main social consequences of increased TFP, and developed a menu of options to incorporate social development and poverty alleviation measures into the design of transport reforms and projects.

A study prepared by the Lahore University of Management Sciences (LUMS) assessed existing spatial disparities and industrial cluster development in Pakistan (LUMS 2011). Economic research has shown that production tends to become spatially concentrated as countries grow from low to high income. Many countries have been able to institute policies that facilitate the economic integration of high economic growth regions with domestic and international markets, and thereby promote the convergence of living standards across space (World Bank 2009b). The LUMS study assessed the geographic concentration of economic activity, income, social infrastructure, and other relevant variables in Pakistan, and provided insights on the ways in which Pakistan's spatial transformation might strengthen the competitiveness of the transport sector and also contribute to the economic integration of the country's lagging and leading areas.

Vulnerable Groups and Stakeholder Identification
As part of the PSIA and stakeholder discussions, efforts were made to identify the groups that would be affected (directly, indirectly, positively, negatively) by the program, and to assess their interests, concerns, and influence in relation to transport policies. As part of the PSIA, the first step in this regard was to identify stakeholders within each freight transport sector (ports, aviation, highways and trucking, and rail). Within each sector, a number of stakeholder groups were identified as possible sources of information or groups to be contacted for interviews and discussions (table 1.1). Substantial information has been generated

Table 1.1 Stakeholder Identification

Sectors	Stakeholders
Ports	Port authorities at Karachi, Gwadar, and Qasim Ports
	Pakistan Customs
	International and local terminal operators
	Federal Board of Revenue
	Karachi Dock Labor Board (working at Karachi Port) and other employee associations at the ports
	Private-sector stevedoring companies
	Logistics and freight forwarding companies as well as clearing agents
	Exporters and importers, in addition to the business community in general
	Fishing communities
Highways and trucking	National Highway Authority
	Owners and employees of trucking companies (many are sole proprietorships)
	Owners and employees of auxiliary services
	Families and communities where the road transport sector is a major employer
	Logistics and freight forwarding companies as well as clearing agents
	Dry ports
	Trucking manufacturing industry
	Standards and Quality Control Authority
	Exporters and importers, in addition to the business community in general
Railways	Pakistan Railways
	Railway Workers Union
	Logistics and freight forwarding companies as well as clearing agents
	Exporters and importers, in addition to the business community in general
Aviation	Civil Aviation Authority
	Pakistan International Airlines
	Management of at least one private airline
Cross-cutting	Communities living along the main trade corridor
	Families of those employed in the trade and transport sector (including women and children)

throughout the course of the PSIA that identifies the range of stakeholders (both organized and unorganized groups) that reforms are likely to affect.

Contents of this Report

This report comprises seven chapters. Chapter 1 provides an introduction to SEPSA, including its methodology and aims. Chapter 2 describes the main challenges in the freight transport sectors of Pakistan, including the road, trucking, railway, port, and aviation sectors. Chapter 3 examines the priority *poverty* issues associated with increased productivity in freight transport in Pakistan, including linkages with spatial transformation. Chapter 4 discusses the priority *social* issues associated with freight transport, including impacts of reforms on spatial transformation, HIV/AIDS, displacement, and women. Chapter 5 describes the priority *environmental* issues associated with transport in Pakistan, including air and noise pollution, road safety, transport of hazardous materials, and climate change. Chapter 6 presents policy options that can enhance environmental and social sustainability in the transport sector. Chapter 7 identifies social policies that safeguard the welfare of groups likely to be negatively affected by increases in transport freight efficiency, while at the same time enhancing positive social impacts. This report subsequently identifies environmental reforms that can help manage environmental priority problems associated with transport on air quality, noise pollution, road safety, transport of hazardous materials, climate change, and urban sprawl. The policy options are then contextualized in light of Pakistan's *Framework for Economic Growth* and its strategic objectives. Appendixes A–D present additional background information, describe the economic and institutional analyses employed, and provide details regarding methodology.

Notes

1. SEPSA's SEA was based on the strategic environmental assessment in policy and sector reform approach developed by
    - OECD DAC (Organisation for Economic Co-operation and Development, Development Assistance Committee); see OECD DAC 2006.
    - World Bank; see World Bank 2005.
    - World Bank, University of Gothenburg, Swedish University of Agricultural Sciences, and Netherlands Commission for Environmental Assessment; see World Bank et al. 2010.
2. SEPSA's PSIA was based on the approach developed by the World Bank in 2002 (www.worldbank.org/psia). The general elements of the PSIA approach, as outlined in the User's Guide, were adjusted and tailored to the political, social, cultural, economic, and security situation in Pakistan at present and to the situation in the trade and transport sector in particular. For the World Bank PSIA User's Guide, see http://web.worldbank.org/WBSITE/EXTERNAL/TOPICS/EXTPSIA/0,,contentMDK:20454976~menuPK:6145452~pagePK:148956~piPK:216618~theSitePK:490130~isCURL:Y~isCURL:Y~isCURL:Y~isCURL:Y~isCURL:Y~isCURL:Y,00.html.
3. The PSIA was undertaken using the World Bank's PSIA sourcebook as a guiding framework; see World Bank 2007. *Tools for Institutional, Political, and Social Analysis of Policy Reform: A Sourcebook for Development Practitioners.* Washington, DC: World Bank. https://openknowledge.worldbank.org/handle/10986/6652.

References

GoP (Government of Pakistan). 2011. *Pakistan: Framework for Economic Growth.* Planning Commission. Islamabad.

IDS (Innovative Development Strategies). 2011. *SEPSA: Poverty and Social Impact Assessment.* Consultant report prepared for the World Bank. Islamabad.

Larsen, Bjorn, and John Magne Skjelvik. 2012. *Environmental Health Priorities in the Province of Sindh, Pakistan.* Consultant report prepared for the World Bank. Washington, DC.

LUMS (Lahore University of Management Sciences). 2011. Abid A. Burki, Kamal A. Munir, Mushtaq A. Khan, M. Usman Khan, Adeel Faheem, Ayesha Khalid, and Syed Turab Hussain. *Industrial Policy, Its Spatial Aspects and Cluster Development in Pakistan.* Consultant report by the Lahore University of Management Sciences for the World Bank. Lahore, Pakistan.

OECD DAC (Organisation for Economic Co-operation and Development, Development Assistance Committee). 2006. *Applying Strategic Environmental Assessment: Good Practice Guidance for Development Co-operation.* Paris: OECD Publishing.

World Bank. 2005. *Integrating Environmental Considerations in Policy Formulation: Lessons from Policy-Based SEA Experience.* Report 32783. Washington, DC: World Bank.

———. 2006. *Transport Competitiveness in Pakistan: Analytical Underpinnings for the National Trade Corridor Improvement Program.* Report 36523-PK. Washington, DC: World Bank.

———. 2007. *Tools for Institutional, Political, and Social Analysis of Policy Reform: A Sourcebook for Development Practitioners.* Washington, DC: World Bank. https://openknowledge.worldbank.org/handle/10986/6652.

———. 2009a. "Second Trade and Transport Facilitation Project. Project Appraisal Document." Report 48094-PK. Sustainable Development Unit, Pakistan Country Management Unit. Washington, DC: World Bank.

———. 2009b. *World Development Report 2009: Reshaping Economic Geography.* Washington, DC: World Bank. http://www-wds.worldbank.org/external/default/WDSContentServer/IW3P/IB/2008/12/03/000333038_20081203234958/Rendered/PDF/437380REVISED01BLIC1097808213760720.pdf.

World Bank, University of Gothenburg, Swedish University of Agricultural Sciences, and Netherlands Commission for Environmental Assessment. 2010. *Strategic Environmental Assessment in Policy and Sector Reform: Conceptual Model and Operational Guidance.* Washington, DC: World Bank.

CHAPTER 2

Sector Status and Trade and Transport Policy Reforms

There is growing recognition within the Government of Pakistan (GoP) that the sustainability of economic growth is strongly linked to the efficiency of the transport system.[1] The transport sector constitutes 10 percent of Pakistan's gross domestic product (GDP) and provides 6 percent of the employment in the country (GoP 2011a). However, while the transport sector is functional (figure 2.1), it suffers from low quality, long traveling times, and poor reliability (particularly rail transport), which hinder the country's economic growth. In addition, increased motorization and poor urban planning have resulted in significant traffic congestion in urban areas, while provincial roads that connect much of the traffic flowing into the National Highways network have received comparatively little governmental attention. Both congestion in urban areas and poor rural roads constitute bottlenecks for Pakistan's road sector. These factors reduce the competitiveness of the country's exports and internal trade, increase the cost of doing business, and constrain Pakistan's capability to integrate into global supply chains. The inefficient performance of the transport sector costs Pakistan's economy 4–6 percent of GDP every year.[2]

The transport supply chain system is not providing the value-added services that have become the hallmark of modern logistics, such as multimodal systems that combine the strengths of different transport modes into one integrated system. In general, logistic services provided by freight forwarders are simple, because of the simple structure of the supply chain, which does not always utilize the most efficient mode of transport for the movement of goods. For example, rail freight generally has a competitive advantage over road freight for longer distances and for the transport of bulk commodities. Integrated logistics services are mainly offered by local offices or representatives of large international companies, with the latter making up half of the logistics market (World Bank 2011). According to the logistics performance index (LPI; Arvis et al. 2010), Pakistan's

---

This chapter draws from the following three reports: IDS 2011, LUMS 2011, and World Bank 2006.

Figure 2.1 Ranking of Pakistan's Infrastructure out of 142 Countries

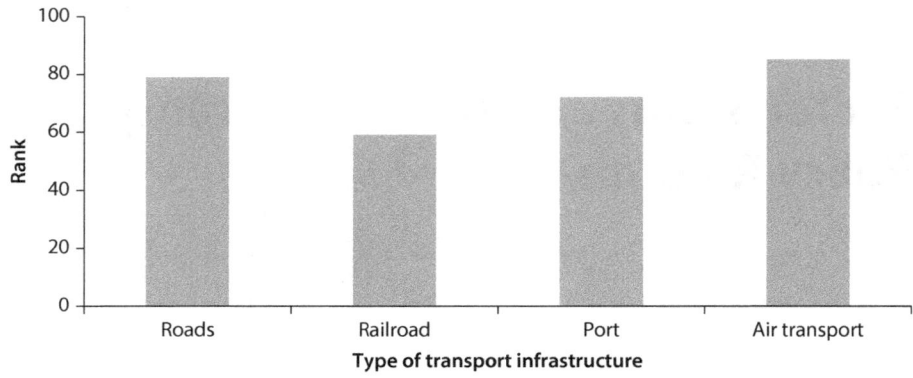

Source: Salai-i-Martin et al. 2012.

performance on most logistics indicators, including the quality of trade and transport infrastructure, is worse than that of other countries from South and East Asia. Pakistan's rankings in the LPI worsened in 2009 and 2010. Pakistan fell from an overall global LPI ranking of 68th to 110th. South Asia's regional average is low because of the poor performance of various countries (Afghanistan, Bhutan, Nepal, and Sri Lanka); yet, Pakistan's score is below the regional average for South Asia in all but two categories. The country's Customs are ranked 134th in the world—even lower than Afghanistan Customs. The World Economic Forum *Global Competitiveness Report* identifies inadequate supply of infrastructure as one of the most problematic factors for doing business in Pakistan (Salai-i-Martin et al. 2012; see table 2.1).

Freight Transport Sector

This chapter describes the major inefficiencies in transport and logistics issues in the following areas: (i) highways and trucking, (ii) rail, (iii) aviation, and (iv) ports and shipping. This analysis will provide the basis for developing a holistic and integrated approach that will help increase the efficiency of Pakistan's trade and transport practices and procedures, with a view toward removing infrastructure bottlenecks, supporting sustained economic growth, and improving competitiveness, a subject further discussed in subsequent chapters in this report.

Highways

In Pakistan, road transportation is the most important means for moving goods within the country and to neighboring countries. Roads handle roughly 96 percent of total freight traffic (GoP 2010). The National Highways and Motorways network constitutes 4.2 percent of the total road network and carries more than 90 percent of Pakistan's total traffic (96 percent of freight and 92 percent of passenger traffic). The majority of traffic moves along the north-south 1,760 kilometers of the N-5 Highway, which is Pakistan's longest highway

Table 2.1 Select Trade and Infrastructure Rankings for Asian Countries

	Bangladesh	China	India	Malaysia	Pakistan	Sri Lanka	Thailand
Logistics performance index (ranking out of 150 countries)[a]	79	27	47	29	110	137	35
Customs (ranking out of 150 countries)[a]	89	32	52	36	134	143	39
Infrastructure (ranking out of 150 countries)[a]	72	27	47	28	120	138	36
International shipments (ranking out of 150 countries)[a]	61	27	46	13	66	118	30
Logistics competence (ranking out of 150 countries)	96	29	40	31	120	141	39
Tracking and tracing (ranking out of 150 countries)[a]	92	29	52	41	93	142	37
Timeliness (ranking out of 150 countries)[a]	72	36	56	37	110	124	48
Quality of overall infrastructure (ranking out of 133 countries)[b]	125	66	89	27	87	63	41
Quality of roads (ranking out of 133 countries)[b]	95	50	89	24	65	60	35
Quality of railroad infrastructure (ranking out of 133 countries)[b]	65	27	20	19	51	44	52
Quality of port infrastructure (ranking out of 133 countries)[b]	113	61	90	19	73	43	47
Quality of air transport infrastructure (ranking out of 133 countries)[b]	116	80	65	27	76	64	26

Sources: a. Arvis et al. 2010; b. World Economic Forum 2009.

and runs from Karachi to Torkham. The N-5 Highway carries 65 percent of intercity traffic[3] and connects the key industrial centers in Punjab and neighboring Afghanistan with international markets through the southern Karachi area ports. It serves over 80 percent of Pakistan's urban population, and contributes to 80–85 percent of GDP (Pirzada 2011).

Geography endows Pakistan with the potential to reap huge economic gains from becoming a hub for regional trade that will have spillovers for economic growth. To the northeast is China, with a population of over a billion and the world's fastest growing economy, increasingly engaged in the development of its Western frontier that lies close to Pakistan. To the northwest and west lie resource-rich economies of Central Asia and the Islamic Republic of Iran, eager to combine their mineral wealth with skills to generate higher income for their citizens. To the East is India, growing at 8 percent per annum, with large pools of skilled labor and savings looking for gainful employment and investment avenues. To reap economic benefits in this neighborhood of growing opportunities, Pakistan needs to play its historical role of a connector of markets that lie in the North (China) and the West (Central Asia and the Islamic Republic of Iran), to markets in the East (India). This requires liberalizing the highly restricted trade with India that has stunted cross-border legal trade, encouraged smuggling, and prevented investment and technology exchange between the two countries.

The recent announcement granting "Most Favored Nation" status to India is a welcome development. It needs to be followed up with practical steps for an efficient payment system, a sensible trade policy that promotes trade but also avoids excessive (and unfair) injury to Pakistan's industry, trade facilitating government services, a sensible visa regime, and transport networks.

Different organizations have suggested investments in road construction, rehabilitation, and upgradation, as part of efforts to facilitate trade with Pakistan's neighbors. However, most of the proposed investments still have not been justified on technical or economic grounds. Some analysts have proposed evaluating these links as private-sector investments under long-term concessions. Other analysts propose increasing efficiency by giving priority to improving road/rail access to seaports and dry ports through urban road/highway improvements and removal of trade bottlenecks such as inefficient container handling and freight clearance procedures. The former argue that inefficient urban transport raises freight transport costs and increases unreliability. Map 2.1 includes the different road investments proposed by different government organizations. Most of these investments lack specific implementation plans or technical and economic justification.

The quality of the road infrastructure in Pakistan has severe capacity constraints that obstruct the facilitation and efficient movement of goods to their destination. Poor road maintenance is due to factors such as insufficient funding and overloading of vehicles. A 2004–05 survey of pavement condition on the federal network revealed that 37 percent of the road network was in poor to very poor condition. The maintenance requirement of these roads is significant, and toll revenues and government expenditures fund roughly half of it. Provincial roads, which are the primary feeder roads for the National Highways network, are at the bottom of the road hierarchy system. As a result, the government gives more priority for National Highways investment than provincial road investment (Pirzada 2011). The federal budget shows a strong bias for road development work. From 1996–97 to 2010–11, total road length increased by 13 percent to a total of 259,758 kilometers, of which 180,866 kilometers were "high-type" (paved) roads. Over the past couple of years, most low-type roads (unpaved) have been converted to high-type roads. The National Highways Authority currently has 89 road development projects with a budget demand of Rs 39,900.27 million; however, the budget allocation for projects has historically been insufficient for the timely and necessary expansion of road capacity, while accounting for the deteriorating quality of current roads (GoP 2010). In addition, increased motorization and poor urban planning have resulted in significant pollution and traffic congestion in urban areas (GoP 2011b). Congestion in urban areas constitutes a bottleneck for Pakistan's freight transport.

Trucking

The trucking sector carries 96 percent of the total freight traffic (GoP 2009). While there are 216,119 registered trucks, the GoP estimates that only 200,500 of these (93 percent) actually operate on roads. Sixty-five to seventy percent of

Map 2.1 Pakistan Road Map Depicting Proposed Links

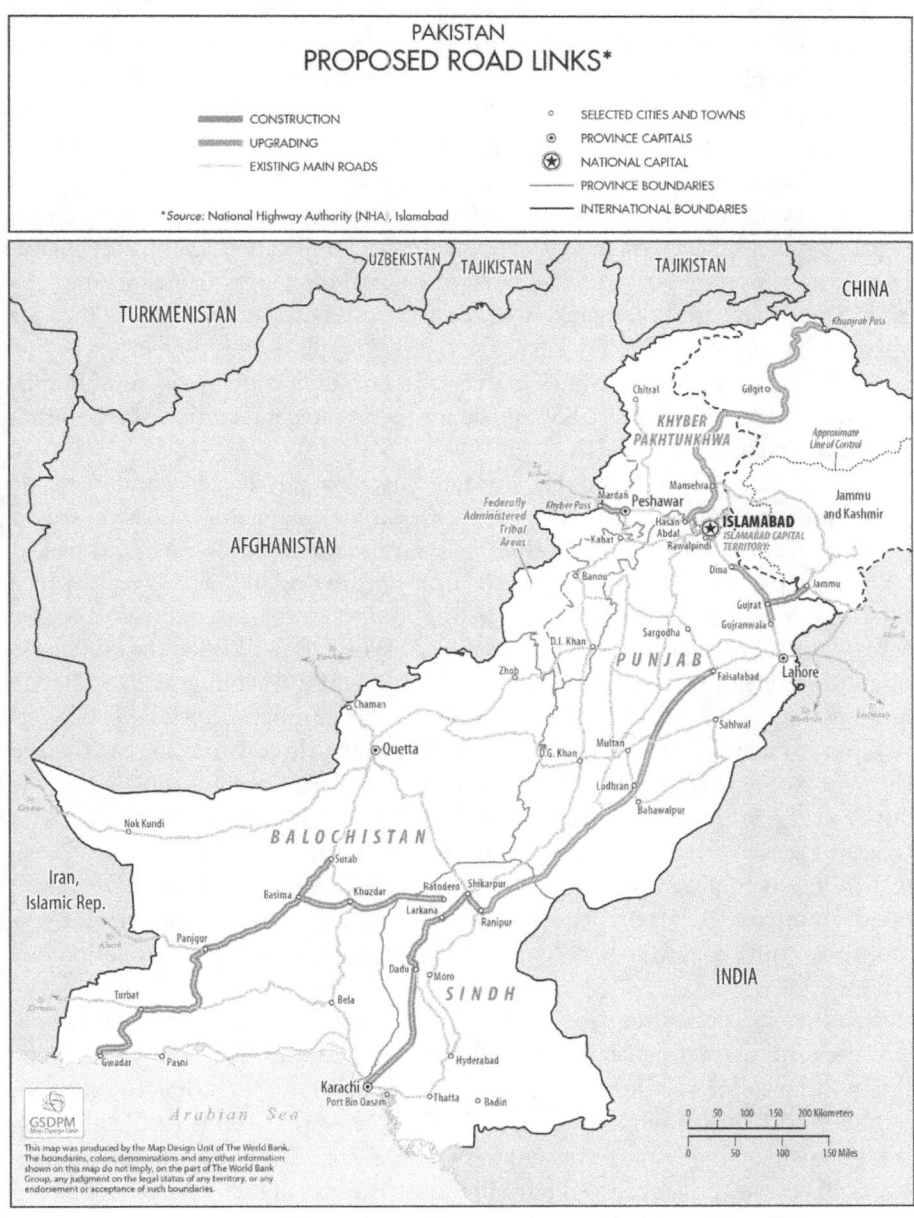

Source: This map was drafted by World Bank consultant Luis Miglino based on primary information provided by the National Highway Authority, Islamabad. The map was amended by Jeff Lecksell of the Map Design Unit to meet World Bank guidelines.

the total truck fleet consists of single- or double-axle trucks. The trucking sector is characterized by the presence of a small fleet of owners who generally possess fewer than five vehicles. The bulk of trucking companies are centered in the port city of Karachi, where one ethnic group dominates trucking (IDS 2011). The trucking sector is highly competitive, characterized by low barriers to entry, many small operators, and low freight rates.

To maintain high revenues, trucks are overloaded, which damages road quality and increases the demand for higher road investment. Lack of enforcement of regulations on safe operation, crew hours, truck modification, and trailer manufacture increase the risk of accidents. According to the GoP's Trucking Policy, by 2007, inefficiencies of the trucking sector were estimated at US$2.62 billion per year, consisting mainly of (i) US$1.04–US$1.57 billion per year in extra fuel costs and diesel subsidies, (ii) US$0.52–US$0.61 billion per year in additional road-user costs, and (iii) a US$0.44 billion per year contribution to the infrastructure deficit (GoP 2007).

The trucking fleet is largely outdated by several decades and runs on underpowered engines. High import tariffs on high-capacity multiaxle trucks protect local manufacturers producing low-capacity and low-powered trucks, and hence prevent the trucking sector from improving its fleet. Over the past 20 years, revenues per kilometer accruing to operators have decreased in real terms by 1.4 percent on average per year (World Bank 2006). Many trucks operate long hours and carry excessive loads while traveling at low speeds, ranging between 20 and 25 kilometers per hour compared to 80–90 kilometers per hour in Europe. Journeys in Pakistan take three times longer than in Europe. Road freight takes an average of 3–4 days between ports and the north of the country (a distance of 1,400–1,800 kilometers), which is twice what it takes in some other countries of Asia and Europe (World Bank 2006, 69). While it might seem unfair to compare Pakistan with these more developed countries, it is with them that Pakistan competes in global markets. Transport time is often lost by trucks needing repairs due to overloading (JICA 2006).

Road crashes occur frequently as trucks crash with other vehicles (that is, two-wheelers and three-wheelers), carts, as well as pedestrians. Pakistan ranks among the most hazardous countries in the world in road safety. According to estimates by the World Health Organization, in 2007 there were 41,494 road fatalities in Pakistan, which in relative terms implies a rate of 25.3 deaths per 100,000 inhabitants. In contrast, the observed rates in industrialized countries range between 5 and 10 fatalities per 100,000 inhabitants. Pakistan's rate is also higher than many other developing and middle-income countries around the world.

Railways

Railways used to be the predominant mode of transportation in Pakistan some decades ago (figure 2.2). Its market share shrank steadily as government-owned Pakistan Railways (PR) did little to improve its efficiency while a dynamic road sector emerged, integrated by a myriad of privately owned units competing

Figure 2.2 Changes in the Market Share of Road and Rail Freight, 1955–2009

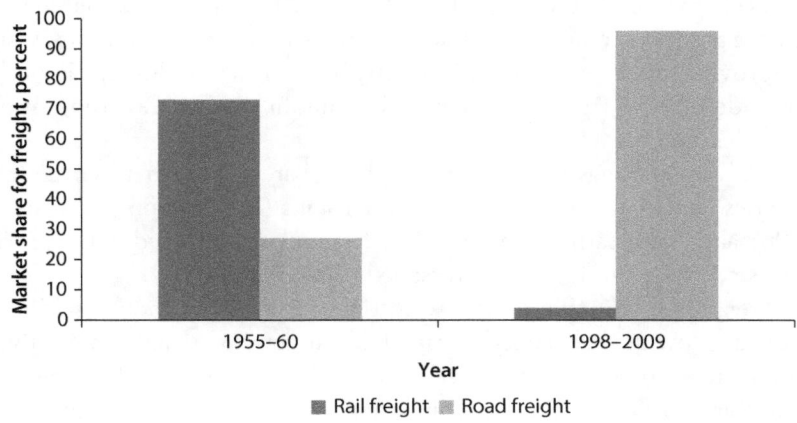

Source: World Bank 2011.

intensely in a largely unregulated environment. At its peak between 1955 and 1960, railways handled 73 percent of freight traffic; currently, railways handle less than 4 percent of the total freight traffic.

PR faces severe competition from road transport and this competition has gotten worse because of governmental priority for investment in road over rail transport, as well as PR's inability to compete due to its poor governance. Between 1990–91 and 2010–11, total rail track length decreased by 11 percent from 8,775 to 7,791 kilometers. Total freight and passengers carried decreased from 7.7 to 4.6 million tons (40 percent) and from 84.9 to 58.9 million (31 percent), respectively (GoP 2011a). During 2005–10, federal expenditure sanctioned for railways was Rs 45.5 billion, compared to Rs 155 billion for national highways (actual expenditure was significantly below the sanctioned amount; GoP 2010). Moreover, only one-third of the total rail network is used for core commercial purposes.

Railway infrastructure, technology, and equipment are obsolete, which leads to significant transport delays and safety hazards. PR owns a very small fleet of modern train wagons that can run at high speed; the majority of wagons are obsolete. Signaling and the telecommunications system are outdated and create delays as well as safety hazards. Other PR shortcomings include the following: (i) running numerous unnecessary lines; (ii) cross-subsidizing passengers from freight and the noncore network from the core network; (iii) offering supply-driven services; and (iv) failure to downsize staff, streamline operations, and reduce costs and tariffs.

PR's main focus is on servicing passengers rather than providing high-quality freight services, despite freight being more profitable. In 2009–10, PR carried 58.97 million passengers, and only 4.6 million tons of freight (GoP 2011a). Giving higher priority to freight services would make business sense for PR, as average freight revenue is higher than unit passenger revenue. However, the GoP gives priority to passenger rail services over freight rail, including train paths, more powerful and reliable locomotives, and management. As a result, freight volumes have declined almost continuously in both tons and ton-kilometers (table 2.2), and are unreliable and costly. These practices, coupled with lack of investment in locomotives, wagons, and improving track capacity and quality, have clearly reduced PR's capacity to provide reliable freight services and maintain the business reputation it held decades ago.

Railway earnings are very low and are barely enough to cover the cost of salaries (Rs 14 billion per year) and pensions (Rs 7 billion per year). Between 2008 and 2009, earnings increased by 16 percent compared to the previous year, but since then earnings have worsened (table 2.3).

Freight sector inefficiencies are costing the economy about Rs 150 billion per year, and low quality service is impeding Pakistan's regional competitiveness: the productivity of PR freight services is roughly one-eighth of Chinese Railways, one-third of Indian Railways, and half of Thai Railways (Aly et al. 2009). Currently, it takes 21–28 days for PR to deliver upcountry at a distance of 1,800 kilometers, which is four to seven times slower than in the United States and

Table 2.2 Pakistan Railway Traffic
millions

Year	Freight (tons)	Ton-kilometers
1980–85	11.2	7,380
1985–90	11.0	7,940
1990–95	7.7	5,890
1995–2000	5.9	4,370
2000–05	6.1	4,744
2005–10	6.2	5,285

Source: Aly et al. 2009, 47.
Note: Data for 2005–10 estimated from the Pakistan Economic Survey 2010–11.

Table 2.3 Earnings of Pakistan Railways

Fiscal year	Earnings (Rs millions)	Percent change
1998–99	9,310	N.A.
1999–2000	9,889	6.2
2000–01	11,938	20.7
2001–02	13,046	9.3
2002–03	14,812	13.5
2003–04	14,636	−1.2
2004–05	18,027	23.2
2005–06	18,184	0.9
2006–07	19,194	5.5
2007–08	19,973	4.1
2008–09	23,160	16.0
2009–10	22,269	−3.8

Source: GoP 2010.
Note: N.A. = not available.

Table 2.4 Arrival Performance for Runs during March 2008 from Karachi to Lahore

Performance	Number of trains	Percent
Arrived on time or earlier	3	8.57
Were late by 1–5 hours	13	37.14
Were late by 6–10 hours	12	34.28
Were late by 11–15 hours	5	14.28
Were late by 16–22 hours	2	5.71

Source: Aly et al. 2009.

China. Table 2.4 reveals statistics from the railway runs during March 2008 for trains headed to Lahore. As in the case of roads, several organizations have proposed new rail links and rehabilitation investments for Pakistan's freight transport railways. Map 2.2 depicts new rail links and rehabilitation measures proposed under Pakistan's freight transport programs, most of which lack specific implementation plans or economic and technical justification.

Aviation

The growth of air traffic has remained modest in Pakistan. The country has 42 functional airports, of which 10 serve international flights. The Sialkot International Airport has generated US$600 million of annual revenues from transport of cargo and passengers. The new Islamabad International Airport is expected to handle annual traffic of 100,000 metric tons of cargo. Jinnah International Airport in Karachi is Pakistan's busiest airport for both passenger and freight traffic; however, Lahore and Islamabad airports also handle large amounts of domestic and international traffic.

Air traffic has not kept pace with economic growth. Figure 2.3 depicts growth rates in Pakistan's aviation sector. Aviation infrastructure is not on par with international competitors. Cargo-handling facilities need major upgrading, and parking and landing facilities are inadequate and limited. No airline in Pakistan is dedicated solely to the transport of cargo for both exports and imports. Private airlines are not able to respond to the high demand in freight or passenger transport due to the government's close collaboration and protection of Pakistan International Airlines (PIA), which carries almost all domestic freight traffic.[4] Pakistan adopted an Open Skies Aviation Policy in the early 1990s, which allows private airlines to join the civil aviation industry. However, stiff competition from PIA generated heavy losses for many of these small airlines, many of which went out of business. The preference given to PIA is not only a major disincentive for other private airlines to enter the industry, but also reduces PIA's incentives to improve its efficiency and quality of services. PIA also operates as a monopoly on certain routes, such as Haj traffic.

A 2006 Pakistan logistical cost study found that air freight dwell times at airports are two to three times longer than the actual transport time because of an inadequate supply of air freight capacity on planes. There was a general

Map 2.2 Proposed New Rail Links and Rehabilitation Measures

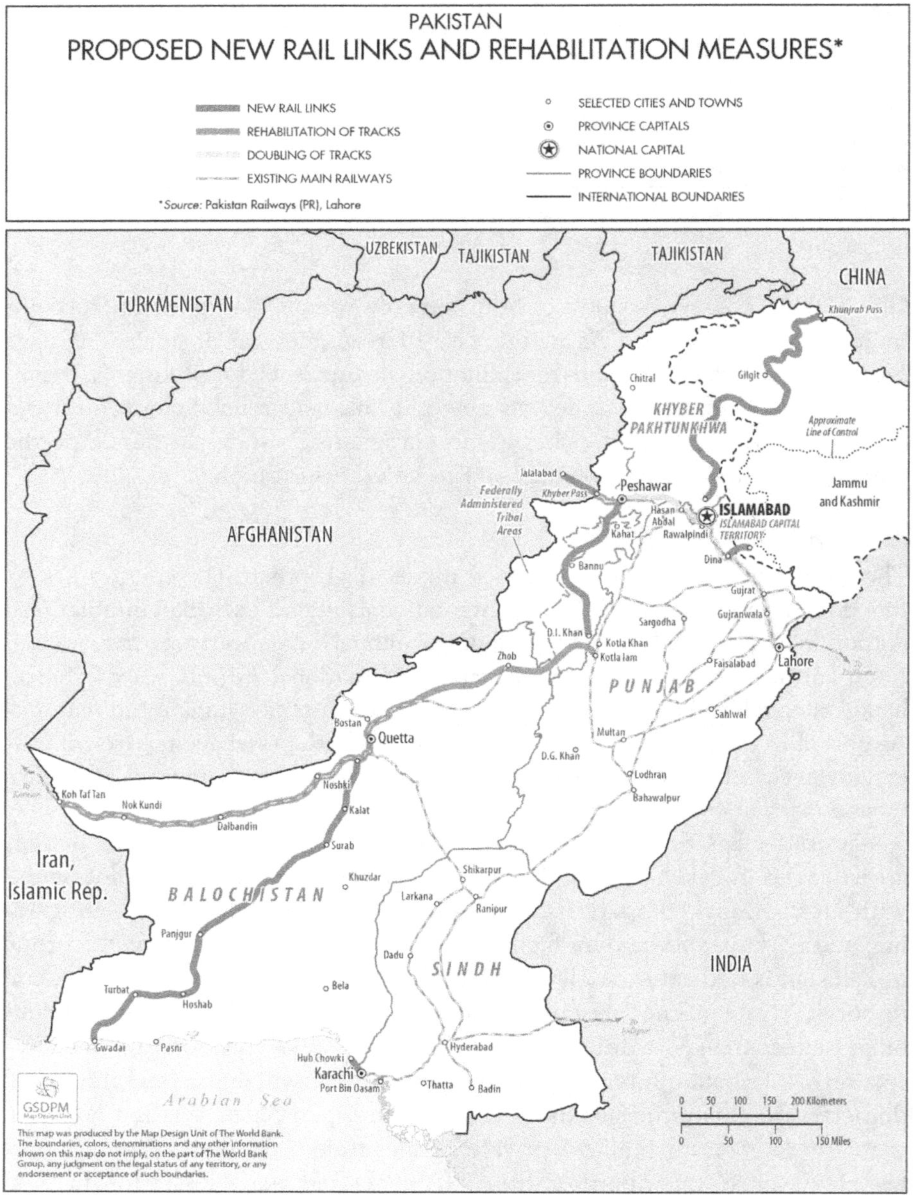

Source: This map was drafted by World Bank consultant Luis Miglino and amended by Jeff Lecksell based on primary information provided by Pakistan Railways, Lahore, 2009.

delay of 4–7 days. Additionally, the study found that Indian exporters have access to bigger air freight capacity than Pakistani exporters. For example, according to Logistics Consulting Group (2006, 78–81), the frequency of air freight transport out of all of Pakistan's international airports (which include Karachi, Islamabad, Lahore, and Peshawar) to Frankfurt is 10 flights per week.

Figure 2.3 Growth Rates in the Aviation Sector, 1995–2005

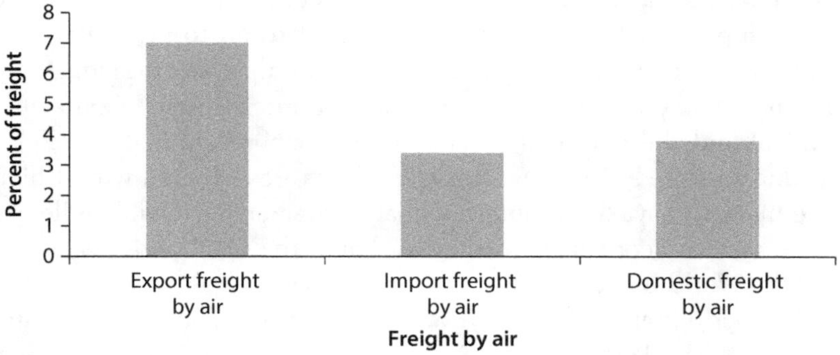

[Bar chart: Export freight by air ≈ 7%; Import freight by air ≈ 3.4%; Domestic freight by air ≈ 3.7%. Y-axis: Percent of freight (0–8). X-axis: Freight by air.]

Source: World Bank 2011.

Flights from Mumbai, India, to Frankfurt, including a MD-11 full freighter that flies three times per week, can accommodate 300 percent more freight export by air.

Ports and Shipping

Port traffic in Pakistan increased 6 percent annually during the 2000–05 period, with container traffic realizing the highest growth, at 15 percent per annum. The two major ports, Karachi Port and Port Qasim, handle 95 percent of all international trade. Gwadar Port, which was inaugurated in March 2007 and is being operated by the Singapore Port Authority, is aiming to develop into a central energy port in the region.[5] Karachi Port handles the majority of Pakistan's seaborne trade traffic (20.2 million tons in 2010–11). The Port Qasim Authority, the second busiest port in Pakistan, handles the bulk of the remainder of freight traffic—13.1 million tons. The newly constructed Gwadar Port had not been able to attract any significant traffic until 2008, when the government diverted imports of bulk cargoes of wheat and fertilizers to the port, which handled 7.05 million tons in 2009–10. Growth of dry cargo at Pakistan's ports has been high, averaging 11 percent per year in the five years up to 2008–09. Growth in bulk cargoes—namely, coal, fertilizers, wheat, rice, cement, and clinker—has been even higher. Karachi Port's traffic in these cargoes increased 18 percent per year in the five years up to 2008–09 (World Bank 2011). Positive elements in sea freight include (i) sea freight rates for container and bulk cargoes that are in line with regional and international levels and (ii) sea transit times that are slightly better to some major markets than for its competitors.

The Karachi Port and Port Qasim have satisfactory indicators for handling cargo. Containers handled per crane-hour at Karachi and Qasim average 25 and 24, respectively, which is similar to averages in India; Sri Lanka; and Hong Kong, SAR. Productivity per ship-hour was found to be just slightly below the average for ports in the region. However, shipping lines handled speeds of 55–60 containers per ship-hour for the two ports, which is below the speeds of up to 100 containers per ship-hour in the region (World Bank 2011).

Postcustoms delays represent major impediments. Other delays are attributable to the lack of rail services and logistical facilities to take containers out of the port. Ship-shore container-handling speeds are up to international levels, but on-shore container processing times are more than twice as long as at efficient international ports. At both the Karachi International Container Terminal (KICT) and the Qasim International Container Terminal (QICT), the berth occupancies are low while the stacking areas are full, even with 4-high stacking. The Indian Nhava Sheva International Container Terminal handles about three times as many containers as the KICT and the QICT, with a berth of similar length (World Bank 2006).

The performance of port operations is improving, but remains insufficient for the long term. Port charges have been reduced marginally and are still above international average levels (World Bank 2011). With the implementation of the Pakistan Customs Computerized System (PACCS), the customs clearance time has decreased from 4–5 days to less than 24 hours at KICT. PACCS was rolled out to the three other container terminals at the end of 2006. The free storage period also decreased from 7 days to 4–5 days. However, container dwell times (5–6 days on average) were still above the international standard of 3–5 days, which decreases the capacity of container terminals to less than their potential. Since 2007, the automation of Pakistan Customs has stalled, and both clearance and dwell times have gone up significantly. Tariffs for bulk and general cargo were found to be relatively low (US$4–US$6 per ton) compared to the rates in the region, but tariffs on containerized cargo were, relatively speaking, on the high side (table 2.5). Total container-handling charges in 2006 were found to be, on average, US$113 and US$105 per twenty-foot equivalent unit (TEU) at Karachi Port and Port Qasim, respectively, compared to an average of US$80 per TEU for India.[6] In addition, the ports' limited drafts of 10–12 meters prevent the most efficient ships from calling (GoP 2011b).

Table 2.5 Pakistan's Port Efficiency Relative to Comparable Benchmarks

	Karachi Port Trust	Sri Lanka, South Asia Gateway Terminals	Hong Kong, SAR	India (Nhava Sheva)
Handling charges/TEU or ton	110	150	140	80
Ship dues/ship call, 2,800 TEU ship	$30,000	$5,500	$6,000	$25,000
Container dwell times (days in the terminal)	10	5	4	6
Containers handled/ship-hour	55	70	100	65
Percentage of containers examined physically	100	<5	<5	High
TEU/meter of quay/annum	400	1,000	1,800	2,000
TEU/terminal hectare/annum	18,000	—	40,000	43,000
TEU or ton/staff member/ annum	900	1,200	1,600	3,000
Water depth (m)	10.5	13	14	12

Note: — = not available.

Trade Facilitation

While Pakistan has achieved considerable progress in simplifying its customs tariff structure and decreasing its tariff levels,[7] customs procedures are still an obstacle to trade. Customs clearances in Pakistan are lengthy, compared to only a few hours in other ports in the region. Delays are the result of the use of clearance systems characterized by numerous official signatures and verifications (GoP 2011b). Such long, cumbersome customs procedures increase congestion at the ports.

PACCS was piloted in the KICT and rolled out to the Pakistan International Container Terminal and QICT. However, the process has stalled and there are no clear prospects of a national rollout. Electronic customs declaration forms, which are available in Pakistan, can help facilitate trade activities by consolidating other information onto the form, which is in line with integrated systems in Hong Kong, SAR, and France. Its successful implementation in the aforementioned countries helped decrease congestion and improve overall transparency and accountability by providing a comprehensive, user-friendly, and interconnected electronic data interchange system (GoP 2011b).

Trade and Transport Reforms

As discussed before, Pakistan faces major inefficiencies and challenges in transport and logistics that increase the cost of doing business, and hence reduce export competitiveness. These inefficiencies and challenges include

- Poor highway conditions; underpowered, slow, and obsolete trucks; and the widespread overloading of trucks;
- Low priority for freight rail services, despite their potential for being quite profitable relative to passenger services and relative to long-run freight hauls;
- Long customs clearance times and long container dwell times at ports;
- Long air freight dwell times and poor competition in the air freight market; and
- A rudimentary supply chain system that does not combine the strengths of transport modes into one integrated system.

Although the transport sector is functional, its inefficiencies with long waiting and traveling times, high costs, and poor reliability hinder the country's export competitiveness and internal trade. Moreover, these inefficiencies increase the cost of doing business in Pakistan and limit the country's ability to integrate into global supply chains, which require just-in-time delivery (World Bank 2011).

A number of reasons explain Pakistan's worsening indicators in transport and logistics. Indications that the GoP may restore public-sector regulation of the freight forwarding industry (after allowing professional self-regulation only in 2006–07) has shaken confidence in a bright and emerging industry, resulting in an inability to focus on self-improvement and service delivery. The lack of progress on financial services available to this formal sector activity has also thwarted modernization in freight forwarding, trucking, and railway services. The loss of rail infrastructure during the 2007–08 riots and continuing downward spiral in rail freight services since, as well as the impact of heightened security measures on road infrastructure and services, are also reflected in this large drop in the LPI ranking. In addition, Pakistan Customs has failed to complete the automation at the three private terminals at the ports and has failed to undertake the planned nationwide rollout of this automation.

A number of reforms have been proposed in the last decade. Some of those reforms have been adopted, such as the National Trucking Policy, the modernization of the ports and shipping sector, and the Pakistan Customs Computerized System. Some of the reforms have been slowly implemented, such as the trucking policy. Other policies have been adopted, but have not been implemented. On May 28, 2011, the National Economic Council approved the *Framework for Economic Growth*. The *Framework* is a landmark and widely embraced reform to get the roles of government and market in balance to develop efficiency within and between the two. Among its key thrusts is an emphasis on connectivity. It states, "Commercial activity requires dense well-connected cities and communities. Connectivity is a critical stratagem of the growth framework" (World Bank 2011, 14). Connectivity has been identified as a key development theme for the country's new *Framework* (figure 2.4).

As part of the implementation of the *Framework for Economic Growth*, the Planning Commission initiated the design of a comprehensive transport policy. Meeting the goals set in the *Framework for Economic Growth*, including achieving a 7–8 percent annual growth rate, requires implementing reforms to unleash the potential of the freight transport system to enhance the country's competitiveness and increase the reliability and quality of supply chains for the transport of goods to and from industrial clusters. This analytical work, strategic environmental, poverty, and social assessment, not only develops a menu of policy options within the *Framework* target areas, but also identifies needed mitigation measures and phasing considerations to avoid and minimize negative social and environmental externalities that could undermine development gains.

Figure 2.4 Pakistan's Five Priority Development Themes

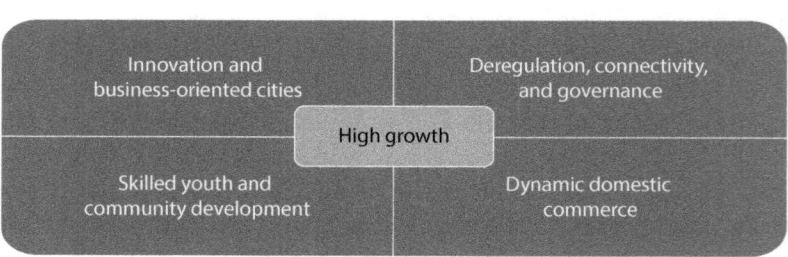

Source: GoP 2011b.

Notes

1. For a detailed analysis of the Pakistan transport sector, see World Bank 2011.
2. Pakistan Economic Survey 2010–11 (GoP 2011a, 13). In many developed countries, transport contributes between 6 and 12 percent of national GDP (Rodrigue et al. 2009). In India, the transport sector contributed between 5.7 and 6.4 percent of GDP between 1999 and 2005 (Singru 2007).
3. See GoP 2011a. Other national highways and motorways include N-55 (Indus Highway), N-25, N-65, N-40 (RCD Highway) N-45, N-50, N-70, N-35 (Karakoram Highway), M-1 (Islamabad-Peshawar Motorway), M-2 (Islamabad-Lahore Motorway), and M-3 (Pindi Bhattian-Faisalabad Motorway).
4. Pakistan International Airlines, 2011.
5. For a detailed analysis of the ports and shipping sector, see World Bank 2011.
6. Primary information on port tariffs is from websites of both the Karachi Port Trust and the Port Qasim Authority.
7. The weighted average of applied tariffs is currently 16 percent, compared to 56 percent in 1994.

References

Aly, Javed H., Abdus Sami Khan, Sheherbano Burki, and Faiza Ghaffar Khan. 2009. *Structural Analysis of Pakistan Railways. Study Conducted for Pakistan Railways Advisory and Consultancy Services (PRACS). Final Report*. Lahore, Pakistan.

Arvis, Jean-François, Monica Alina Mustra, Ben Shepherd, and Daniel Saslavsky. 2010. *Connecting to Compete 2010. Trade Logistics in the Global Economy: The Logistics Performance Index and Its Indicators*. Washington, DC: World Bank. http://siteresources.worldbank.org/INTTLF/Resources/LPI2010_for_web.pdf.

GoP (Government of Pakistan). 2007. National Trucking Policy. National Trade Corridor Improvement Programme. Islamabad. http://www.ntcip.gov.pk/.

———. 2009. *Pakistan Economic Survey 2008–2009*. Ministry of Finance. Islamabad. http://finance.gov.pk/survey_0809.html. Accessed March 28, 2010.

———. 2010. *Pakistan Economic Survey 2009–10*. Ministry of Finance. Islamabad. http://www.finance.gov.pk/survey_0910.html.

———. 2011a. *Pakistan Economic Survey 2010–11*. Ministry of Finance. Islamabad. http://www.finance.gov.pk/survey_1011.html. Accessed November 15, 2011.

———. 2011b. *Pakistan: Framework for Economic Growth*. Planning Commission. Islamabad.

IDS (Innovative Development Strategies). 2011. *SEPSA: Poverty and Social Impact Assessment*. Consultant report prepared for the World Bank. Islamabad.

JICA (Japan International Cooperation Agency). 2006. *Pakistan Transport Plan Study in the Islamic Republic of Pakistan*. Final Report. http://www.ntrc.gov.pk/PTPS-reportSDJR06013FinalReport01.pdf.

Logistics Consulting Group. 2006. *Pakistan: Logistics Cost Study. Final Report*. Kastrup, Denmark: Logistics Consulting Group.

LUMS (Lahore University of Management Sciences). 2011. Abid A. Burki, Kamal A. Munir, Mushtaq A. Khan, M. Usman Khan, Adeel Faheem, Ayesha Khalid, and Syed Turab Hussain. *Industrial Policy, Its Spatial Aspects and Cluster Development in Pakistan*.

Consultant report by the Lahore University of Management Sciences for the World Bank. Lahore, Pakistan.

Pirzada, Ahmed Jamal. 2011. *Role of Connectivity in Growth Strategy of Pakistan*. Islamabad: Planning Commission, Government of Pakistan. http://www.planningcommission.gov.pk/nda/PDFs/role%20of%20connectivity%20in%20growth%20strategy%20of%20pakistan.pdf. Accessed March 20, 2011.

Rodrigue, Jean Paul, Claude Comtois, and Brian Slack. 2009. *The Geography of Transport Systems*. 2nd ed. New York: Routledge. http://books.google.com/books?id=afRodkxRoCsC&printsec=frontcover#v=onepage&q&f=false.

Salai-i-Martin, Xavier, Beñat Bilbao-Osorio, Jennifer Blanke, Margareta Drzeniek Hanouz, and Thierry Geiger. 2012. "The Global Competitiveness Index 2011–2012: Setting the Foundations for Strong Productivity." In *Global Competitiveness Report 2011–2012*, ed. Klaus Schwab, 3–50. Geneva: World Economic Forum.

Singru, Narendra. 2007. *Profile of the Indian Transport Sector*. Manila: Asian Development Bank. http://www.iptu.co.uk/content/trade_cluster_info/india/indian-transport-profile.pdf.

World Bank. 2006. *Transport Competitiveness in Pakistan: Analytical Underpinnings for the National Trade Corridor Improvement Program*. Report 36523-PK. Washington, DC: World Bank.

———. 2011. *Pakistan Transport Sector*. Washington, DC: World Bank. http://go.worldbank.org/A0D9IJ5SH0.

World Economic Forum. 2009. *Global Competitiveness Report 2009–2010*. Geneva: World Economic Forum.

CHAPTER 3

Priority Issues Associated with Freight Transport Reform

This chapter examines the correlation between transport, poverty, and spatial transformation in Pakistan. The chapter discusses the impact of increases in total factor productivity (TFP) on poverty, household income, sectoral value added, industry agglomeration, exports, imports, and gross domestic product (GDP). This chapter is broken down as follows: the "Spatial Transformation" section discusses the correlation between spatial transformation and transport infrastructure in Pakistan, and their linkages to industrialization. The "Effects of Productivity Enhancements of the Transport Sector" section analyzes the intersectoral and welfare impacts of increases in productivity in the transport sector and its subsectors on the economy. Following an analysis of the impact of a 10 percent increase in the productivity of all transport sectors, three further simulation scenarios were undertaken: (i) impact of a 10 percent increase in the productivity of road transport, (ii) impact of a 10 percent increase in the productivity of rail transport, and (iii) a simultaneous increase in the productivity of road and rail transport by 10 percent.

Spatial Transformation

A pronounced feature of industrial economic activity in Pakistan is the high geographic concentration (clustering) of firms around the metropolitan cities of Lahore and Karachi (map 3.1). Even medium-concentrated districts are clustered in proximity to these two big cities. Statistical results show that 35 percent of the industries in Pakistan are highly agglomerated, 38 percent are moderately agglomerated, and 27 percent are not agglomerated.[1] The most highly concentrated industry is ship demolition, followed by sports and athletic goods. The other highly concentrated industries are those sectors for which it is critical to be in proximity to consumers and suppliers.[2] Evidence suggests that firms will

---

This chapter was prepared by Ernesto Sánchez-Triana, Paula Posas, and Sohail Malik. This chapter draws from the IDS (2011) and LUMS (2011) consultant reports prepared for the World Bank.

Map 3.1 District-Level Employment Shares in Pakistan's Manufacturing Sector, 2005–06

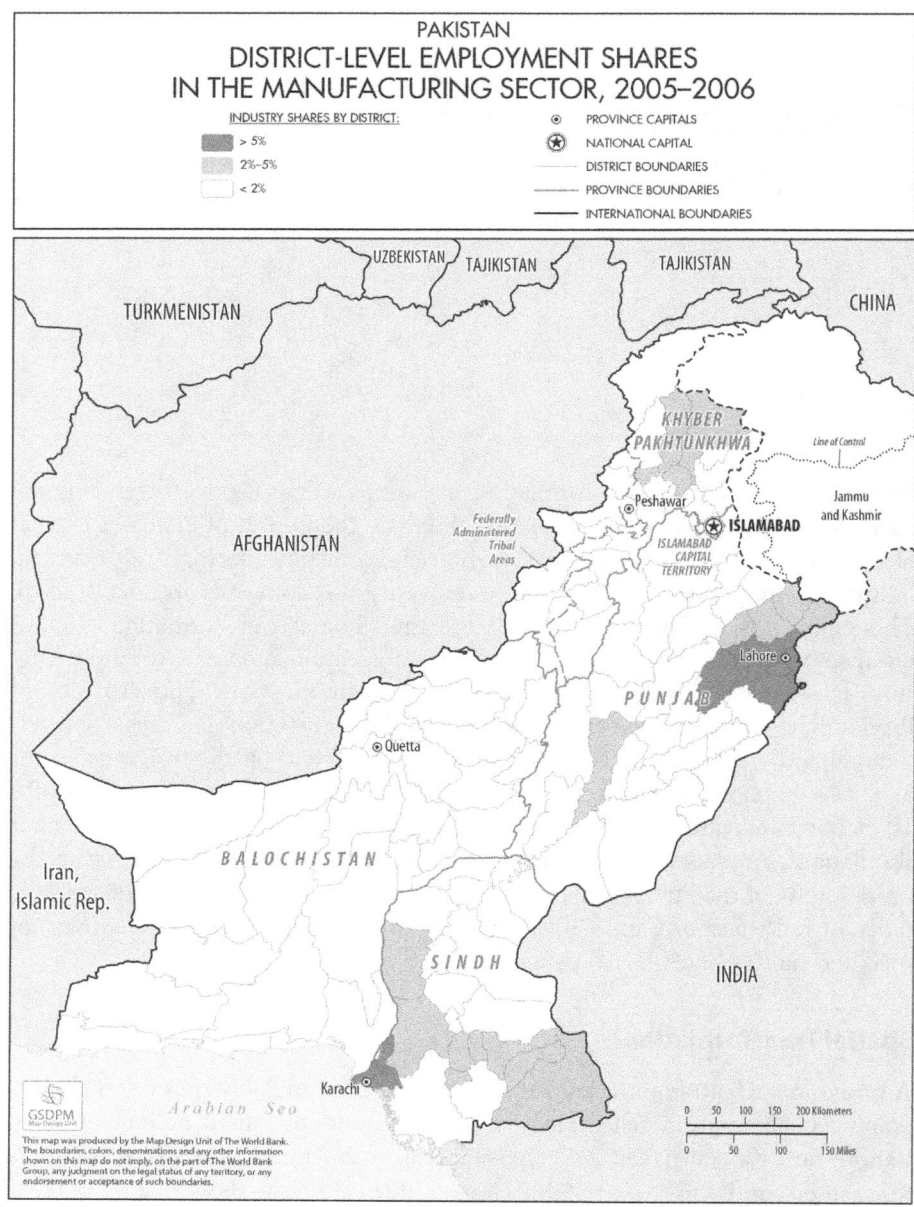

Source: The methodology used to map district-level employment shares in Pakistan's manufacturing sector can be found in the strategic environmental, poverty, and social assessment consultant report prepared by LUMS (2011) for the World Bank.

locate in areas where there are "location economies"—that is, areas that minimize procurement costs (transport costs associated with the transportation of raw materials to the firm) and distribution costs (transport costs associated with distributing the products to customers). These areas have available specialized labor, inter-industry spillovers, local transfers of knowledge, and access to export markets. However, from 2000–01 to 2005–06, industry concentration decreased dramatically by about 33 percent.[3]

Market access is determined by the ease of connectivity to the market, which in turn depends upon the availability of an adequate transport system. Spatial disparities in road infrastructure limit market access, distort factor prices, and reduce the supply of goods and services available. Low-density districts (less agglomeration) are characterized by high levels of poverty, high transport costs, and an overall poor standing in most economic and infrastructure indicators (such as poor road density). Data from the Punjab Highway Department present a sense of spatial disparities in road infrastructure and its links to agglomeration. Road density varies greatly across districts (maps 3.2 and 3.3). The districts in Southern Punjab have less road density than the districts in Northern Punjab. The Sialkot district in north Punjab (which houses major export-oriented firms, such as sporting and surgical instruments, and is the third largest economic center after Lahore and Faisalabad in Punjab) has relatively better road density than south Punjab.[4]

In addition, road density has fluctuated over time in Pakistan: some Southern districts, such as Rajanpur, Bhakkar, Layyah, D.G. Khan, and Rahim Yar Khan, which had relative road density of less than 40 percent of Lahore district's in 1992–03, maintained their relative road density in 2005–06. In contrast, districts such as Faisalabad, Rawalpindi, and Ragodha improved their relative shares of road density from around 70 percent of Lahore to more than 80 percent, primarily due to the construction of a 400 kilometer motorway and other ancillary roads (figure 3.1).[5] Relative road density in the districts of Jhang, Chakwal, Muzaffargarh, and Mianwali substantially increased during this 13-year period. Sialkot, Gujranwala, Sahiwal, Multan, and Gujarat districts are examples of districts that have experienced a large decline in their relative road density. Sialkot had the second highest road density after Lahore in 1992–93, with road density equal to 90 percent of Lahore's. However, by 2005–06, Sialkot's road density had decreased to below 50 percent of Lahore's.

An econometric analysis completed by Lahore University of Management Sciences (LUMS) (2011) finds that there is a strong negative correlation between road density across districts and poverty incidence. Apart from physical infrastructure, the analysis found that access to social infrastructure is highly concentrated in the metropolitan areas. Moreover, the gaps between leading and lagging districts are increasing over time. Empirical results of the LUMS (2011) analysis suggest that an increase of one standard deviation (that is, 0.125) in road density of a district is correlated to roughly a 4.4 percent reduction in poverty. These findings suggest that infrastructure investments that support increasing road density and improvements in transport infrastructure connecting industrial clusters to markets might be associated with greater gains in poverty reduction.[6] Deficient urban transport and congestion are key bottlenecks that significantly reduce connectivity between industrial clusters, and domestic and international markets.

Facilitating the spatial transformation of Pakistan hinges on the availability of road density that can connect industrial clusters to domestic and international

Map 3.2 Spatial Disparities in Road Density in Punjab, 2005–06

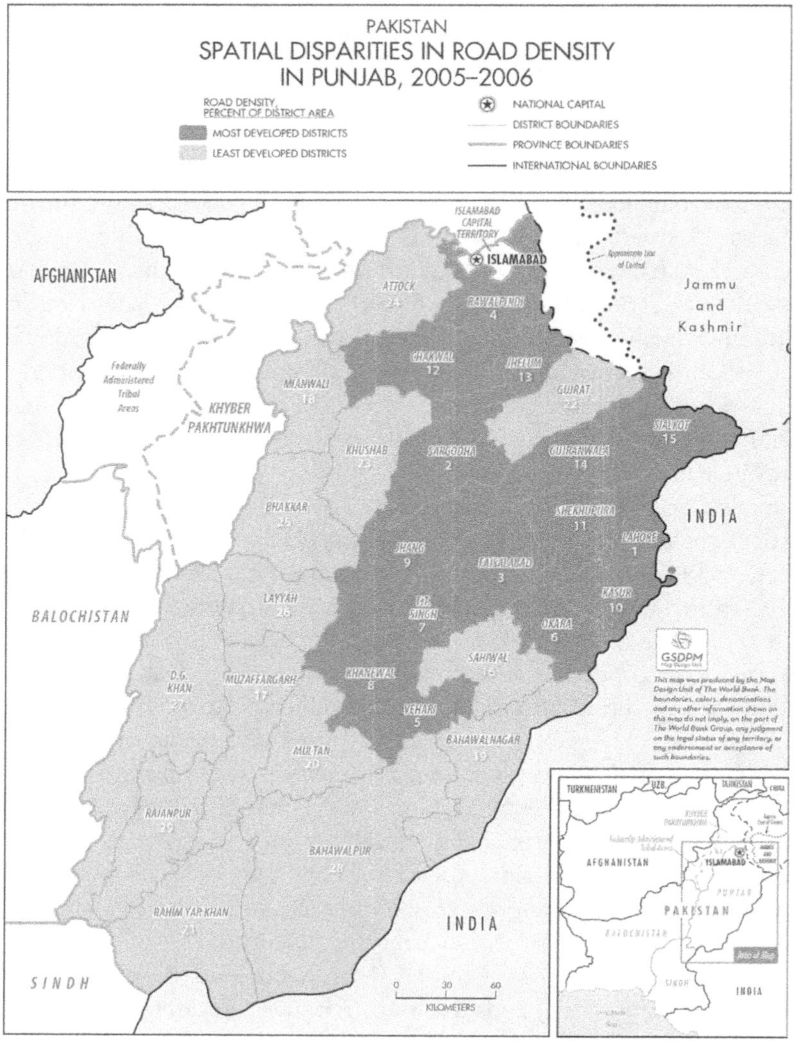

Source: The methodology used to map district-level employment shares in Pakistan's manufacturing sector can be found in the strategic environmental, poverty, and social assessment consultant report prepared by LUMS (2011) for the World Bank.

markets. Sixty-seven percent of the population living in rural areas is landless, and agriculture development generally has a marginal impact on their well-being and living standards. The poorest 40 percent of rural households derive roughly 30 percent of their total income from agriculture due to unequal distribution of land and access to water. Poverty rates are higher in rural areas than in urban areas; about two-thirds of the population and roughly 80 percent of the country's poor people live in rural areas. Average per capita expenditures of rural households in 2004–05 were 31 percent lower than those in urban households (Rs 1,259 per month and Rs 1,818 per month, respectively). The poverty rate in

Map 3.3 Spatial Disparities in Road Density in Khyber Pakhtunkhwa, 2005–06

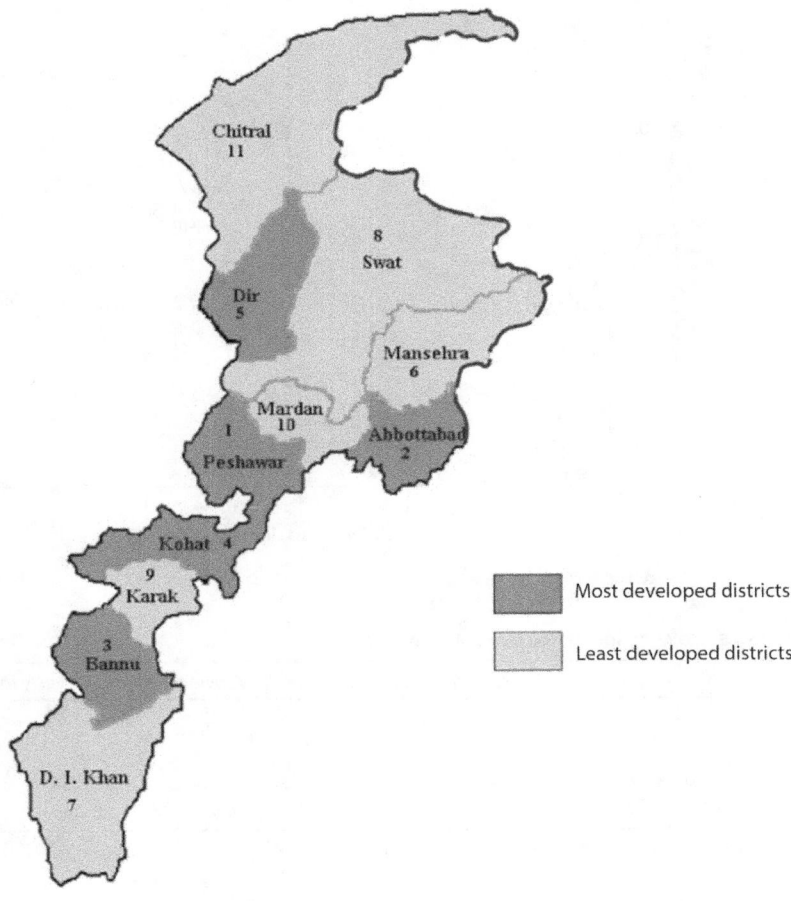

Source: The methodology used to map district-level employment shares in Pakistan's manufacturing sector can be found in the strategic environmental, poverty, and social assessment consultant report prepared by LUMS (2011) for the World Bank.

rural areas is roughly 35 percent, about 17.5 percentage points higher than the 17.5 percent poverty rate in urban areas[7] (table 3.1).

Transport infrastructure is likely to yield high payoffs in promoting localization economies (within-industry externalities) and agglomeration. The benefits of agglomeration of industries are often associated with reduction of three types of transport costs: "moving goods," "moving people," and "moving ideas" (knowledge spillovers and sharing). Agglomeration is fundamental to industrial competitiveness, because it promotes (i) knowledge and information spillovers and innovative ideas among firms, (ii) labor-market pooling, and (iii) input-output linkages (Marshall 1890). Spatial proximity of firms attracts suppliers and consumers to the region. Proximity also promotes the exchange of ideas between firms in the clusters (Breschi and Lissoni 2003). A high concentration of firms can also attract and sustain a large labor force with the skills demanded by that

Figure 3.1 Relative Road Density in Punjab, 1992–93 versus 2005–06

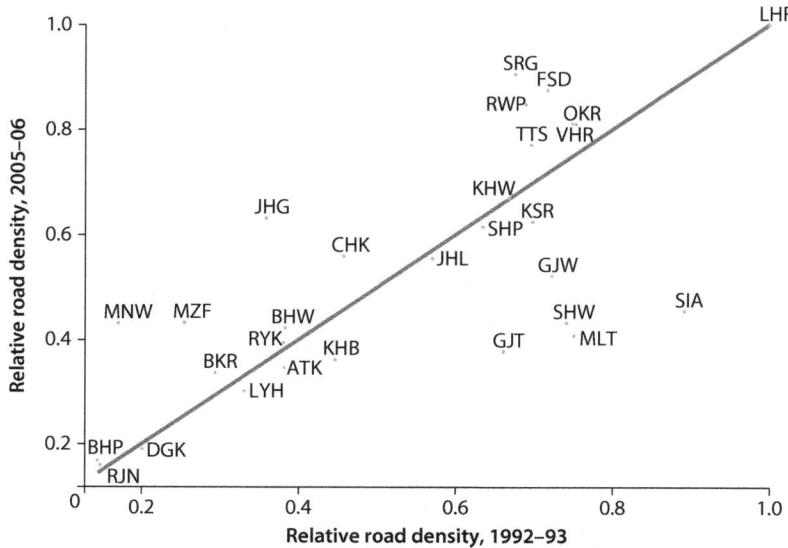

Source: Lums 2011.

Table 3.1 Poverty Incidence by Province

Province	Rural poverty incidence (%)	Provincial capital poverty incidence (%)
Punjab	24	18
Sindh	38	10
Khyber Pakhtunkhwa	27	28
Balochistan	51	14

Source: SPDC 2004, 59.

industry. Hence, location economies help create competitive advantage by improving a firm's access to important resources. The empirical results of the analytical work carried out under strategic environmental, poverty, and social assessment suggest that agglomeration increases with market access, lower transportation costs, and a supply of skilled labor (LUMS 2011). This implies that infrastructure investments in the delivery of infrastructure services are likely to yield relatively higher payoffs.

Effects of Productivity Enhancements of the Transport Sector

This section of the report analyzes the effects of increasing upgradation and construction of the road network, and total factor productivity of the transport sector on micro- and macro-level indicators of poverty. TFP is a variable that accounts for the effect on total output not caused by inputs (labor and capital). In other words, TFP accounts for the effect on output that is contributed by other variables such as technology, institutional changes, and competitive factor markets. These factors are of interest in the context of freight transport reforms, as they are related to enhancing private-sector participation and institutional changes to increase the sector's efficiency. Appendix C contains an overview of the methodology used to inform this section, and appendix D provides technical notes regarding the methodology.

Household-Level Poverty

As with many infrastructure investments, upgrading of freight transport infrastructure, particularly along the main trade corridor—the National Trade Corridor (NTC)[8]—is expected to yield significant dividends in the long run, by boosting trade and export growth, and hence increasing gross domestic product. The upgrading of the main trade corridors includes road construction, road upgradation along the existing North-South Expressway, new rail links, and rehabilitation of some existing rail tracks.

Road construction and upgradation works associated with the main trade corridor start at Karachi, and for the first 800 kilometers, pass through areas of extreme poverty (Dadu, Larkana, and Shikarpur in Sindh province, and Rahim Yar Khan and Bahawalpur in Punjab). Afterward, the path of the road works goes for another 400 kilometers, through areas where poverty incidence is less than 30 percent. The bulk of the last 400–500 kilometers of the proposed road works will then run through the relatively prosperous Barani Punjab region. The figures below show poverty incidence in districts where road construction will take place, or where road upgradation is planned or currently being undertaken.

The areas where road upgradation is planned or currently being executed (areas where the North-South Expressway currently runs) have significantly lower levels of poverty than areas that constitute the non-NTC districts (figure 3.2). In 2005–06, when the poverty incidence was estimated to be high

Figure 3.2 Poverty Incidence in Districts where Road Upgradation Is Planned or Currently Undertaken
Percent

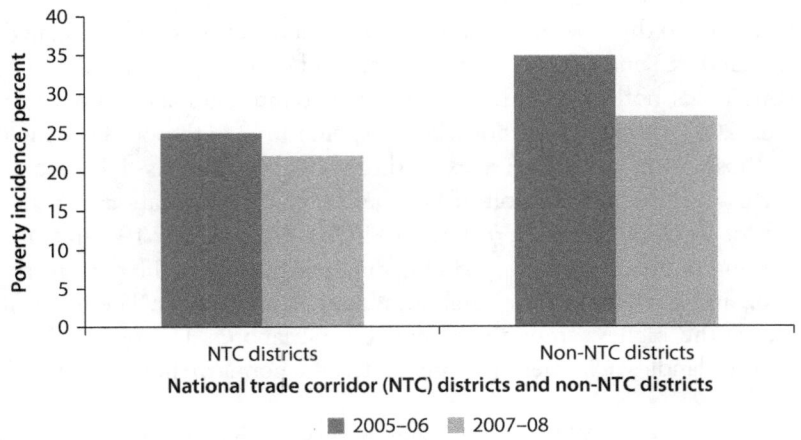

Source: IDS 2011.

Figure 3.3 Poverty Incidence in Districts where Road Construction Is Expected
Percent

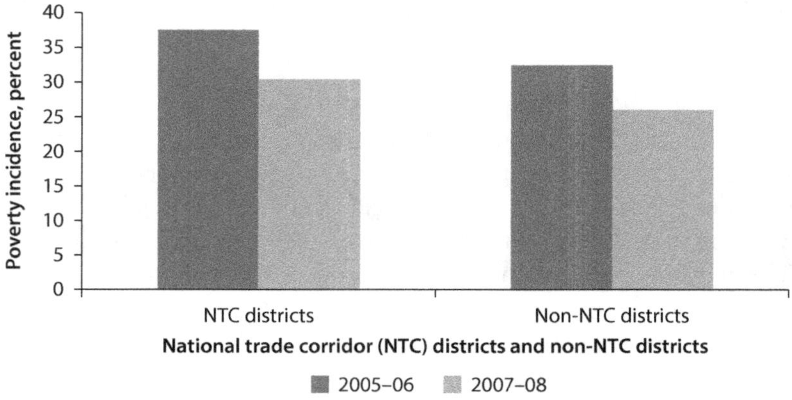

[Bar chart showing poverty incidence percentages for NTC districts (approximately 37% in 2005-06 and 30% in 2007-08) and Non-NTC districts (approximately 32% in 2005-06 and 26% in 2007-08).]

Source: IDS 2011.

overall, the difference in the incidence of poverty between NTC and non-NTC districts was 10 percentage points. In 2007–08, when significant changes occurred in Northern Punjab and Sindh, the difference was reduced to 6 percentage points.[9] These findings suggest that areas near the NTC have relatively lower levels of poverty than non-NTC districts. In contrast to road upgradation, much of the new road construction is expected to take place in districts where the poverty incidence is higher than the average for the country as a whole (figure 3.3).

Household Income

This section analyzes the impact of a 10 percent increase in TFP in all transport subsectors on household income of the 19 household groups identified, based on a simulation analysis undertaken using a 2007–08 social accounting matrix (SAM).[10] Out of these 19 groups, 15 are rural agricultural households, split according to the amount of land cultivated (large farm, small farm, medium farm, and landless) and region (Sindh, Punjab, and other regions in Pakistan). Nonfarm households, both rural and urban, are divided into poor and nonpoor according to their 2007–08 per capita household expenditures, with poor households defined as those with a per capita expenditure of less than Rs 1,140.05 per month per capita. The distribution of farm and nonfarm population in rural areas was almost equal (about 34 percent each) in 2007–08. Nearly 19 percent of the total farming population belongs to the small-farm category, 11 percent are nonfarm poor, and 5 percent of the total population is urban poor. The incidence of poverty is the highest among rural agricultural laborers (57 percent), followed by tenant (landless) farmers (45 percent) and nonfarm households (32 percent) (table 3.2).

The income of all households can increase with a 10 percent improvement in TFP of all subsectors of transport (table 3.3). In rural Pakistan, the gains for farm

Table 3.2 **Distribution of Population and Incidence of Poverty by Household Groups, 2007–08**

Household groups	Population (in thousands)		Concentration of poor (%)		Population below poverty line (%)
	Poor	Total	Poor	Total	
Large farmers	23	453	0.1	0.3	5.1
Sindh	0	71	0	0	0
Punjab	12	318	0	0.2	3.9
Other Pakistan	11	63	0	0	17.2
Medium farmers	834	4,192	1.8	2.6	19.9
Sindh	198	878	0.4	0.5	22.5
Punjab	340	2,678	0.8	1.6	12.7
Other Pakistan	298	635	0.7	0.4	46.9
Small farmers	9,094	30,724	20.1	18.9	29.6
Sindh	1,928	3,911	4.3	2.4	49.3
Punjab	5,162	19,854	11.4	12.2	26.0
Other Pakistan	1,997	6,960	4.4	4.3	28.7
Landless farmers	4,389	9,710	9.7	6	45.2
Sindh	1,857	3,142	4.1	1.9	59.1
Punjab	1,495	4,423	3.3	2.7	33.8
Other Pakistan	1,038	2,145	2.3	1.3	48.4
Rural agricultural laborers	5,322	9,353	11.8	5.8	56.9
Sindh	1,921	3,929	4.2	2.4	48.9
Punjab	3,077	4,771	6.8	2.9	64.5
Other Pakistan	328	653	0.7	0.4	50.2
Rural nonfarm	17,643	54,624	39	33.6	32.3
Nonpoor	0	36,974	0	22.8	0
Poor	17,651	17,651	39	10.9	100
Urban households	7,944	53,318	17.5	32.8	14.9
Nonpoor	0	45,392	0	28	0
Poor	7,926	7,926	17.5	4.9	100
All households	45,302	162,374	100	100	27.9

Source: SAM Simulation 2007–08 completed by IDS 2011.

households are larger (1 percent) than the gains for nonfarm households (0.3 percent). Rural agricultural laborers and the urban nonpoor can realize the largest benefits of an increase in the productivity of the transport sector, with their incomes increasing by 1.4 and 1.2 percent, respectively.

However, an increase in TFP in rail or road reveals that nonfarm households and the urban poor can potentially be made worse off. A 10 percent improvement in TFP of the road sector alone leads to a 0.3 percent overall reduction in the income of the rural nonfarm sector (0.4 percent for the rural nonfarm nonpoor and 0.1 percent for the rural nonfarm poor). The findings also suggest that the income of urban poor households declines by 0.9 percent. The highlighted cells in table 3.3 show the potential negative income effect.

Overall, the computable general equilibrium estimates adverse impacts at the household level on account of TFP improvements in transport. Under the given

Table 3.3 Impact of a 10 Percent Increase in TFP of All Transport Subsectors on Household Income by Household Groups

	Percent change in baseline value if TFP increases by 10 percent					
	Road	Rail	Air	Water	Rail and road	All sectors
Large farmers	1.4	0.04	−0.2	−0.1	1.4	1.0
Sindh	1.5	0.03	−0.3	−0.2	1.5	1.0
Punjab	1.3	0.02	−0.2	−0.1	1.3	1.0
Other Pakistan	1.4	0.03	−0.2	−0.1	1.4	1.1
Medium farmers	1.1	0.03	−0.1	0.0	1.1	1.0
Sindh	1.4	0.03	−0.2	−0.1	1.4	1.0
Punjab	1.0	0.02	−0.1	0.0	1.0	0.9
Other Pakistan	1.3	0.03	−0.2	−0.1	1.3	1.0
Small farmers	0.9	0.02	0.0	0.0	0.9	1.0
Sindh	1.2	0.02	0.0	0.0	1.2	1.1
Punjab	0.9	0.02	0.0	0.0	0.9	1.0
Other Pakistan	0.8	0.02	0.1	0.1	0.8	1.0
Landless farmers	1.0	0.02	0.0	0.0	1.0	1.0
Sindh	1.3	0.03	−0.1	0.0	1.3	1.2
Punjab	0.8	0.01	0.1	0.0	0.8	0.9
Other Pakistan	0.9	0.02	0.1	0.0	1.0	1.0
Rural agricultural laborers	0.7	0.01	0.2	0.1	0.7	0.9
Sindh	0.7	0.01	0.2	0.1	0.7	1.0
Punjab	0.6	0.01	0.2	0.1	0.6	0.9
Other Pakistan	1.1	0.02	0.2	0.1	1.2	1.4
Rural nonfarm	−0.3	−0.02	0.4	0.2	−0.3	0.3
Nonpoor	−0.4	−0.01	0.5	0.2	−0.4	0.3
Poor	−0.1	−0.01	0.4	0.2	−0.1	0.5
Urban households	0.5	0.00	0.3	0.1	0.6	1.0
Nonpoor	0.7	0.01	0.3	0.1	0.7	1.2
Poor	−0.9	−0.02	0.5	0.2	−0.9	−0.1

Source: SAM Simulation 2007–08 completed by IDS 2011.

Table 3.4 Households and Associated Population Being Adversely Affected by Simulated Improvement in TFP of Transport Subsectors

Household group	Effect on income	Households impacted	Population impacted
Rural nonfarm nonpoor	0.4% decline in income	41,824	316,390
Rural nonfarm poor	0.1% decline in income	12,575	97,070
Urban poor	0.9% decline in income	41,755	379,893

Source: SAM Simulation 2007–08 completed by IDS 2011.

model inputs and assumptions, approximately 42,000 households in the rural nonfarm nonpoor sector, 12,600 households in the rural nonfarm poor category, and 42,000 households in the urban poor category could be adversely affected by improvements in TFP in transport (table 3.4). As a result, mitigation strategies would need to be developed to safeguard the welfare of persons within these groups, as elaborated in chapter 4.

Sectoral Value Added

A 10 percent increase in TFP in roads increases manufacturing, mining, energy, and services sectoral value added by 0.3, 0.4, 0.1, and 0.5 percent, respectively (table 3.5). Improvements in the rail sector can increase the value added of all sectors examined, except agriculture. This appears to be because gains in the agricultural sector and in rural households rely much more on capital income. A simultaneous 10 percent increase in the rail and road sector increases manufacturing and mining value added each by 0.4 percent. A further investigation suggests that an improvement in the TFP of rail and road sectors can increase the value added of cotton-textile products, leather products, and petroleum refining at a greater rate than other sectors.

A simultaneous 10 percent increase in TFP of rail, road, water, and air transport increases the value added of water transport by 14 percent, road by 5.3 percent, air transport by 12.9 percent, and rail by 1 percent (table 3.6). A 10 percent increase in TFP of only water transport increases the value added of the water transport subsector by 13.9 percent. As a result, the value of the transport sector increases by 7.4 percent and GDP increases by 0.9 percent.

The analysis also reveals a decrease in the output price of the respective transport mode subsector as a result of an increase in TFP. For example, an improvement in the road transport sector decreases the price of road transport by 7.7 percent. Similarly, the price of air transport decreases by 2.7 percent with a 10 percent increase in TFP of air transport. The fall in the price of the transport sector may be the result of a reduction in the production cost. Price reductions greatly benefit consumers (that is, households), as explained in the previous section's discussion on the effects of improvements in the transport sector on household income.

Economic Indicators

A key finding from the analysis is that efficient rail and road sectors can increase both imports and exports, thus playing a critical role in increasing revenue from indirect taxes. A 10 percent increase in TFP of road and rail transport has

Table 3.5 Impact of a 10 Percent Increase in TFP of Rail and Road Sectors on Sectoral Value Added

Sector	Baseline value (Rs billion)	Road	Rail	Both rail and road
Agriculture	2,088	0	0	0
Mining	62	0.4	0.03	0.4
Manufacturing	1,481	0.3	0.01	0.4
Energy	324	0.1	0.01	0.1
Construction	352	0.1	0.02	0.1
Wholesale and retail trade	1,409	0.3	0.01	0.3
Transport	901	3.9	0.02	3.9
Services	2,699	0.5	0.01	0.5
GDP at factor cost	9,316	0.6	0.01	0.6

Source: SAM Simulation 2007–08 completed by IDS 2011.

Table 3.6 Impact of a 10 Percent Increase in TFP of All Transport Subsectors on the Value Added and Price of these Subsectors

	Road	Rail	Air	Water	Rail and road	All sectors
Impact on value added						
Road	5.3	0	0	0	5.3	5.3
Rail	0	0.9	0.1	0	0.8	1
Air	0.6	0	12.4	−0.2	0.7	12.9
Water	0.7	0	−0.6	13.9	0.7	14
Other	0.4	0	−0.2	−0.1	0.4	0.2
All transport	3.9	0.02	2.4	1.1	3.9	7.4
GDP	0.6	0	0.2	0.1	0.6	0.9
Impact on output price						
Road	−7.7	0	0.3	0.1	−7.7	−7.3
Rail	0.8	−1.4	0	0	−0.6	−0.6
Air	0.8	0	−2.7	−0.2	0.8	−2.1
Water	0.8	0	−0.4	−1.8	0.8	−1.4
Other	0	0	0.2	0.1	0	0.3
All transport	−1.1	−0.3	−0.5	−0.4	−1.3	−2.2

Source: SAM Simulation 2007–08 completed by IDS 2011.

Table 3.7 Impact of a 10 Percent Increase in TFP of Rail and Road Sectors on Macroeconomic Indicators

	Baseline value (Rs billion)	Percentage change in baseline value if TFP increases by 10 percent		
		Road	Rail	Both rail and road
Total domestic absorption	11,211	0.6	0.01	0.6
Fixed investment	2,095	0.1	0.00	0.1
Government consumption	1,279	1.2	0.01	1.2
Private consumption	7,837	0.6	0.01	0.6
Exports	1,315	0.8	0.02	0.9
Imports	2,444	0.4	0.01	0.5
GDP at market prices	10,081	0.6	0.01	0.7
Indirect taxes	765	0.9	0.01	0.9
GDP at factor cost	9,316	0.6	0.01	0.6

Source: SAM Simulation 2007–08 completed by IDS 2011.

a positive impact on economic indicators. The results indicate that a TFP increase in the road sector has a much greater impact than one in the rail sector. As a result, the impact from simultaneously increasing the productivity of both rail and road is mostly driven by the road sector. This may be because the road sector carries a larger share of freight in total freight transport than rails. As a result, GDP at factor cost will increase by 0.06 percent.

Although 10 percent increases in TFP of road and rail have a positive impact on both exports and imports, there is a larger increase in exports relative to imports (table 3.7). This suggests that such an increase can help Pakistan reduce its trade deficit. Results indicate that a 10 percent increase in TFP of the road sector has a larger positive impact in the export of textiles, rice, and leather products, increasing by 1, 1.9, and 2.5 percent, respectively. Imports of wheat and sugar were found to decrease by 1.4 and 1 percent, respectively.[11]

Summary

The analysis finds that infrastructure investments, such as roads, are likely to yield high payoffs in promoting localization economies (within-industry externalities) and agglomeration. Industrial agglomerations form in districts with good market access, low transportation costs, and a skilled labor force. Low-density districts (less agglomeration) are characterized by high levels of poverty, high transport costs, and an overall poor standing on most economic and infrastructure indicators (such as poor road density). Agglomeration is fundamental to industrial competitiveness because it promotes (i) knowledge and information spillovers and innovative ideas among firms; (ii) labor-market pooling; and (iii) input-output linkages. The largest agglomerations are located around the metropolitan cities of Karachi and Lahore. The spatial geography shows that domestic and international markets are not able to connect with these industrial clusters in urban areas because of high transport costs.

Facilitating the spatial transformation of Pakistan hinges on the availability of road density that can connect industrial clusters to domestic and international markets. Sixty-seven percent of the population living in rural areas is landless, and agricultural development generally has a marginal impact on their well-being and living standards. The poorest 40 percent of rural households derive roughly 30 percent of their total income from agriculture due to unequal distribution of land and access to water. Poverty rates are higher in rural areas than in urban areas; about two-thirds of the population and roughly 80 percent of the country's poor people live in rural areas. Average per capita expenditures of rural households in 2004–05 were 31 percent lower than those of urban households (Rs 1,259 per month and Rs 1,818 per month, respectively). The poverty rate in rural areas is roughly 34 percent, about 15 percentage points higher than the 19.1 percent poverty rate in urban areas (World Bank 2006).

Econometric results reveal that there is a strong negative association between road density across districts and poverty incidence. Empirical results of the LUMS (2011) analysis suggest that an increase of one standard deviation (that is, 0.125) in a district's road density is correlated to roughly a 4.4 percent reduction in poverty. These findings might indicate that infrastructure investments that support increasing road density and improvements of transport infrastructure connecting industrial clusters to domestic and international markets might be associated to greater gains in poverty reduction (LUMS 2011).

Simulations using the SAM model reveal that improvements in TFP of the transport sector and its respective subsectors (rail, road, air, and water) have positive impacts on sectoral value added and household income. There is a positive impact of increasing TFP of the transport sector on both exports and imports; however, there is a larger increase in exports relative to imports, which suggests that this can help Pakistan reduce its trade deficit. Improvements in the rail sector can increase the value added of all sectors examined, except agriculture. A simultaneous 10 percent increase in TFP of rail, road, water, and air transport increases the value added of water transport by 14 percent, road by 5.3 percent, air transport by 12.4 percent, and rail by 1 percent. As a result, the value of the transport sector increases by 7.4 percent and GDP increases by 0.9 percent. Rural agricultural laborers and the urban nonpoor can realize the largest benefits of an increase in the productivity of the transport sector, with the income of the former increasing by 1.4 percent and the income of the latter group increasing by 1.2 percent. However, an increase in TFP in rail or road reveals that nonfarm households and the urban poor can potentially be made worse off. Consequently, as explained in the next chapter, mitigation strategies would need to be developed to safeguard the welfare of persons within these two groups.

Notes

1. A detailed description of the clustering of Pakistan's industry can be found in the consultant report prepared by LUMS (2011) for the World Bank.
2. Ibid.
3. Ibid.
4. The methodology used to map district-level employment shares in Pakistan's manufacturing sector can be found in the strategic environmental, poverty, and social assessment consultant report prepared by LUMS (2011) for the World Bank.
5. Figure 3.1 plots the road density of 35 districts relative to the road density of Lahore in 1992–93 and in 2005–06. Here, the road density of each district is divided by the road density of Lahore. The Lahore district was chosen because it had the highest road density in 1992–93 and in 2005–06. Changes in road density in districts are depicted by departures from the 45-degree line in the figure. The share of Lahore in road density relative to Lahore is 100 percent. Districts above the 45-degree line experienced improvements in road density over time, whereas those below the line experienced declines in their relative shares. A detailed description of the spatial disparities analysis can be found in the consultant report prepared by LUMS (2011) for the World Bank.
6. Ibid.
7. World Bank data from 2006 quoted in IFAD (2011, 69).
8. The National Trade Corridor (NTC) refers to the ports, roads, and railways along the corridor that stretches from the southern city of Karachi to the northern Punjabi cities of Lahore and Peshawar. The NTC handles approximately 95 percent of the country's external trade and 65 percent of total land freight.
9. Ibid.
10. A social accounting matrix represents the flow of all economic transactions and transfers between different production activities, factors of production (land, capital, and labor), and institutions (government, enterprises, and households) within the economy and with respect to the rest of the world. For further information and technical notes regarding the methodology, see appendixes C and D.
11. SAM Simulation 2007–08 completed by IDS 2011.

References

Breschi, Stefano, and Francesco Lissoni. 2003. *Mobility and Social Networks: Localised Knowledge Spillovers Revisited*. Working Paper 142. Milan: Centre for Knowledge, Internationalization and Technology Studies, Università Bocconi. http://www.nber.org/CRIW/papers/breschi.pdf.

IDS (Innovative Development Strategies). 2011. *SEPSA: Poverty and Social Impact Assessment*. Consultant report prepared for the World Bank. Islamabad.

IFAD (International Fund for Agricultural Development). 2011. *Islamic Republic of Pakistan. Gwadar-Lasbela Livelihoods Support Project*. Design completion report. http://www.ifad.org/operations/projects/design/102/pakistan.pdf. Accessed April 10, 2011.

LUMS (Lahore University of Management Sciences). 2011. Abid A. Burki, Kamal A. Munir, Mushtaq A. Khan, M. Usman Khan, Adeel Faheem, Ayesha Khalid, and Syed Turab Hussain. *Industrial Policy, Its Spatial Aspects and Cluster Development in Pakistan*. Consultant report by the Lahore University of Management Sciences for the World Bank. Lahore, Pakistan.

Marshall, Alfred. 1890. *Principles of Economics*. London: Macmillan.

SPDC (Social Policy and Development Centre). 2004. *Social Development in Pakistan: Combating Poverty. Is Growth Sufficient? Annual Review No. 4*. Karachi, Pakistan: SPDC.

World Bank. 2006. *Pakistan Strategic Country Environmental Assessment*. Washington, DC: World Bank. http://web.worldbank.org/WBSITE/EXTERNAL/COUNTRIES/SOUTHASIAEXT/0,,contentMDK:21459418~pagePK:146736~piPK:146830~theSitePK:223547,00.html.

CHAPTER 4

Priority Social Issues Associated with Freight Transport

One of the most striking features of economic activity in Pakistan is the geographic clustering of the factors of production in a few cities; this includes unequal spatial distribution of income, poverty, education, health, and physical infrastructure. Spatial transformation, trade, and city growth are each both vectors and outcomes of economic growth. Spatial transformation is an integral part of a country's development; indeed, the size and scope of the freight reforms envisioned in the trade and transport sector can be expected to have a long-term impact on Pakistan's development and translate into social changes. While the benefits to be expected from the increased transport productivity are undeniable, some groups may nevertheless find themselves adversely affected by a number of the direct and indirect consequences of freight transport reforms. As explained before, an increase in total factor productivity in rail or road reveals that nonfarm households and urban poor can potentially be made worse off.

This chapter describes the potential social effects associated with reforms in the freight transport sector. The issues to be discussed were selected, in stakeholder consultations, due to their socioeconomic salience for Pakistan and their mutually reinforcing impacts. The "Freight Transportation and Social Conflicts" section examines how reforms in the freight transport sector in the complex socio-political context of Pakistan may affect social conflicts. The "Connectivity and Migration" section addresses the impacts on migration, which also are both a vector and an outcome of economic growth. The "Spatial Transformation and Urban Sprawl" section addresses the impact on urbanization, while the "Impact on HIV/AIDS" section looks into the issue of HIV/AIDS transmission by truck drivers. The "Resettlement and Displacement" section highlights social issues associated with resettlement and displacement in the context of investments in freight transport infrastructure.

This chapter draws on consultant reports prepared by IDS 2011 and LUMS 2011.

Freight Transportation and Social Conflicts

Overview of Social Conflict in Pakistan

Social conflicts in Pakistan might manifest as sectarian or ethnic strife. Given Pakistan's high sensitivity to ethnic tensions, such issues should be expected to arise in the context of any major reform such as those envisioned for the freight transport sector. Freight transport reforms may affect Pakistan's ethnic equilibrium, notably through the likely increase in migration, as well as through the reforms of the trucking, ports, and shipping sectors.

This complexity needs to be understood in the larger context of the long-standing security situation in Afghanistan, close ties of Pakistan with its troubled neighbor, and the implications of the country's geography on its governance. In the past 10 years, the conflict in Afghanistan has contributed to the growth of various groups that have been implicated in the running feuds between sectarian organizations, as well as with drug traffic groups operating in Afghanistan and Pakistan (see "Connectivity and Migration" section) (World Bank 2011). Furthermore, Pakistan's geography also contributes to the challenge, rendering the governing of part of the country extremely difficult. This combination of challenges can trigger protracted instability if left unaddressed or when the precarious social status quo is disrupted. Indeed, when regional and spatial divisions align with political and ethnic pressures, they give rise to political and social instability in the country (map 4.1).

In 2010, Pakistan witnessed an 11 percent decrease in the number of incidents of violence and terrorism compared to the previous year. However, over the same period, violent incidents increased in the provinces of Sindh, Punjab, and in Gilgit Baltistan (formerly known as Northern Areas), while they substantially decreased in Khyber Pakhtunkhwa's settled areas. The data illustrate the rise of social conflict in Pakistan and thus the sensitive context in which freight transport reform will take place (figure 4.1).

Potential Impacts in the Ports, Shipping, and Trucking Sectors

The scale and the sectors concerned with envisioned reforms in the freight transport sector can be expected to have an impact particularly on social tensions in the case of ports and shipping, as well as in the case of the trucking sector. The majority of low-skilled workers employed at both Karachi Port and Port Qasim are part of a specific ethnic group, which also dominates the trucking and road transport sectors. This group is particularly concerned with the reforms planned for the freight transport sector.

In the case of ports and shipping, ethnic tensions have already arisen from the perception that recent recruitments favored one specific ethnic group from communities in and around Karachi at the detriment of other groups. Indeed, many dockworkers are migrant laborers from the northern part of Pakistan, notably Khyber Pakhtunkhwa, who settled in Karachi slums. Dockers working on a daily wage basis are particularly vulnerable, as they would not be eligible for severance packages and redeployment services.[1] Since those workers tend to be

Map 4.1 Map of Pakistan's Security Landscape in 2010

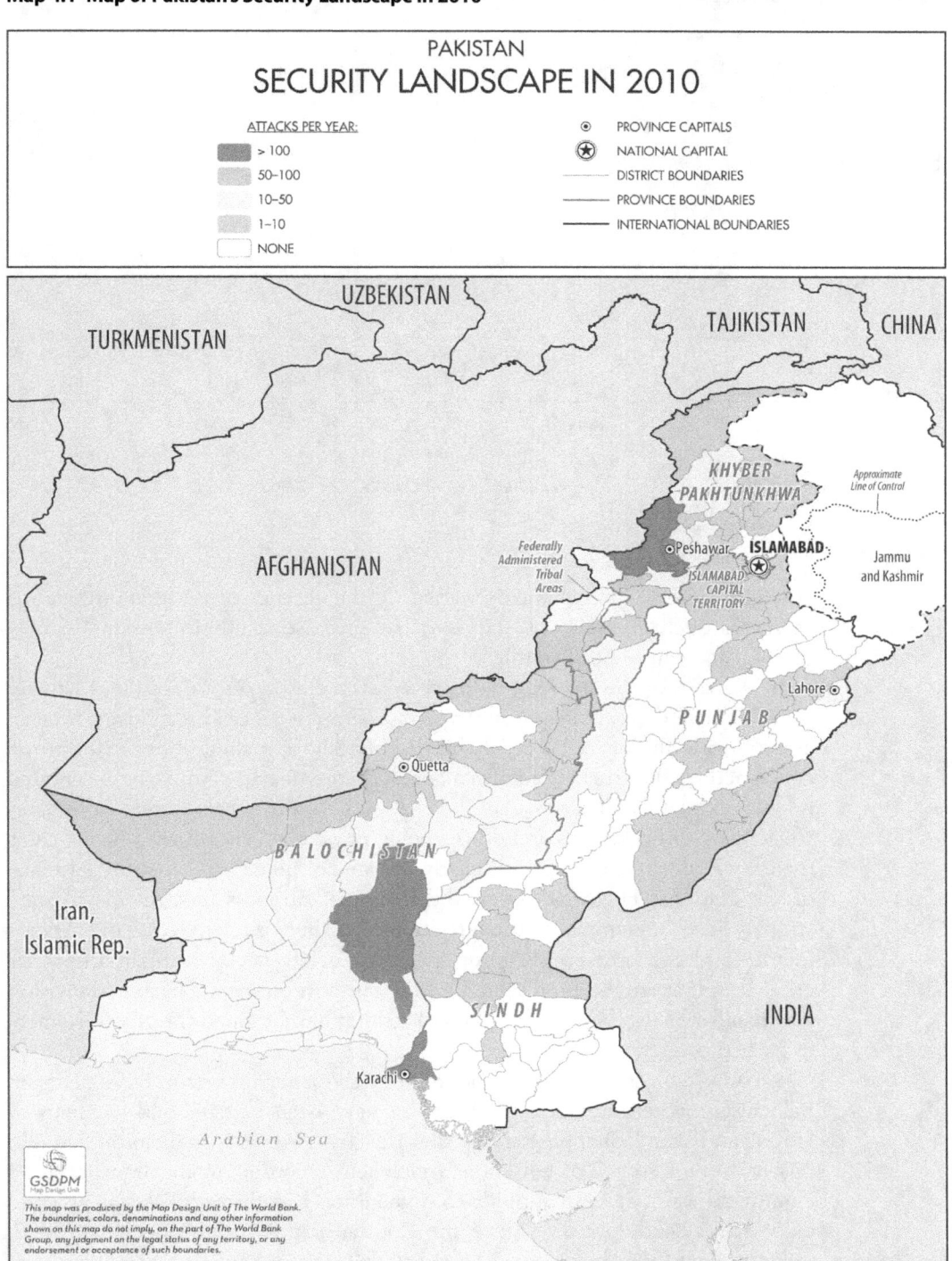

Source: Mezzera and Aftab 2009.

Figure 4.1 Social Conflict Events in Pakistan, 1989–2010

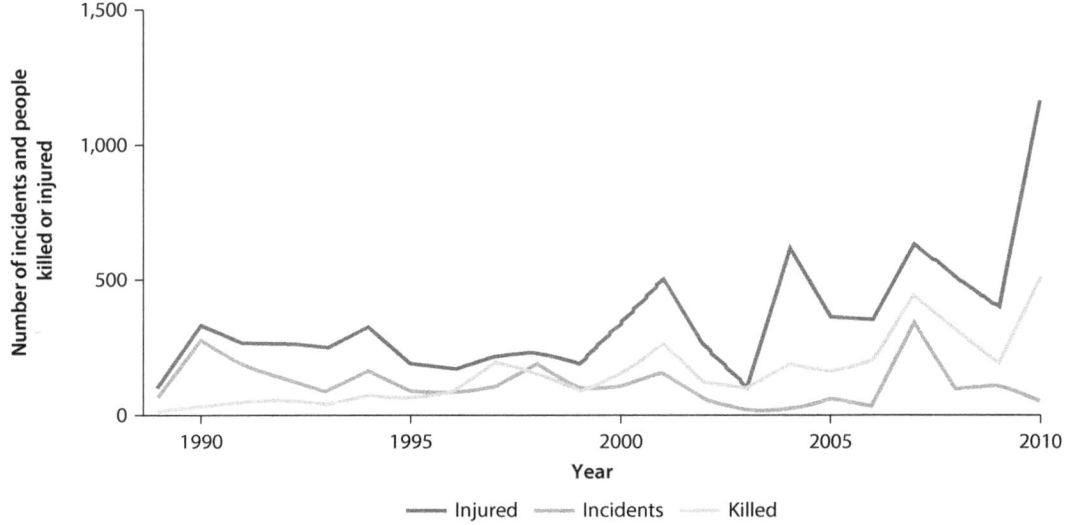

Source: SATP (South Asia Terrorism Portal). http://www.satp.org/.

younger, there is a heightened risk that, in the absence of adequate mitigating measures, such groups could tap into the preexisting ethnic tensions to rally support and cause social conflicts.

In the case of the trucking industry, an ethnic group from Southern Khyber Pakhtunkhwa owns, manages, and works as employees of this industry even in areas outside the province of Khyber Pakhtunkhwa, making it the main group concerned by the trucking reforms. The bulk of trucking companies is centered in the port city of Karachi, but here also the same ethnic group dominates trucking, with brokerages and offices being physically concentrated in the city's majority Pakhtun enclaves, particularly the area of Sohrab Goth at the entrance of the National Highway. Given the nature of business linkages in Pakistan, strongly based on familial or tribal relationships, there is relative ease of entry for members of the same ethnic group into the trucking sector compared to other ethnicities that are less represented in the transport business. This broad division has manifested itself in the ethnic conflicts that have gripped the city of Karachi in particular.

Security concerns have also mounted in the trucking sector, particularly in Balochistan, where nonlocal truck drivers have been targeted and incidents of looting and even kidnapping are on the rise.[2] Trucking with Afghanistan has also proven to be a source of tension and violence. According to the Transportation Command, half of all war supplies to Afghanistan pass through Pakistan at a rate of 580 truckloads per day. Since the Pakistan supply route opened in 2002, militants have killed between 120 and 150 truckers for hauling U.S. military supplies. To avoid attacks, many drivers now detour hundreds of kilometers, driving northeast through Punjab province instead. However, militants have also started to target this route (Shakir 2010). Incidents of *dacoity* (banditry) and looting are also common in interior Sindh, although here the issue is not rooted in ethnic or political conflict.

In the case of communities living along the main freight transport corridors, the opening up of new transportation links offers much potential for the poorest and most deprived, notably in underserved provinces like Balochistan, which is particularly strategic in that respect. For one, it is the only province in Pakistan that shares boundaries with Afghanistan and the Islamic Republic of Iran. Second, besides Punjab, it is also the only province that has direct inland connections with the four provinces of Pakistan. Third, while it only represents 5 percent of the total population, Balochistan constitutes 42 percent of the total land area of Pakistan. Therefore, given the sensitivities in this province, and the political and ethnic tensions that continue to fuel conflict in the province, opportunities that would accrue from trade facilitation carry both potential and risk.

Youth and Social Conflicts

Pakistan is expected to double its already very young labor force by 2025.[3] It is estimated that the economy must grow by 7 percent a year on a sustained basis to absorb the coming increases in the labor force. Reforms in the freight transport sector can contribute to new job creation in the manufacturing sector and others made possible by increased connectivity. In 2011, youth engagement and the transformation of cities into engines of economic growth were identified as key development themes for the country's new *Framework for Economic Growth* that aims to promote sustained high economic growth (GoP 2011). Linking those priorities with freight transport reforms offers much potential.

Youth, particularly from nonfarm households and urban poor households, are also at higher risk of being negatively affected by reforms for the freight transport sector, since these youth, as the last entrants into the labor market, tend to have jobs that are more precarious. The male youth unemployment rate is almost triple the male adult unemployment rate (GoP 2006). Using the 2006–07 labor force survey (LFS), Ahmad and Azim (2010) show that a significant number of youth start their career early, which can be costly for productivity and earnings later in life. Young people also face a higher unemployment rate at the start of their career, which gradually decreases as age increases. In general, the unemployment rate among female youth is much higher than that of male youth in all regions of the country. An important finding of the study with strong implication for reforms in the freight transport sector is that the youth in Balochistan appear to be more willing to work, but least likely to get employment, as compared to youth in other provinces.[4] Furthermore, youth should be regarded as a diverse social group with different characteristics and attitudes about work in different regions of Pakistan. The heterogeneity of jobless people must be taken into account in labor employment policies. In the context of freight transport reforms, this translates into the need to account for youth (particularly from nonfarm households and urban poor households) and region-specific impacts to mitigate potential adverse effects and ensure that they are able to benefit from the positive impacts of trade and transport sector reforms, including those related to new employment opportunities.

In the case of reforms in the port, shipping, and trucking sectors, there is a risk that youth (particularly from nonfarm households and urban poor households) could be directly affected either through direct retrenchment or indirect loss of jobs, as well as through the loss of job prospects they had envisioned and invested in through the *Ustad Shagird* arrangement (Master Apprenticeship). The importance of starting off right is particularly important for young people, since it is the initial transition to the labor force that is a significant determinant of the future economic (and social) well-being of the individual and, if taken collectively, in determining the level of development in Pakistan. Without the proper foothold to start out in the labor market, young people are less able to make choices that will improve their own job prospects and those of their future dependents, thus perpetuating the cycle of insufficient education, low-productivity employment, and poverty from one generation to the next. Finding a new job and source of income will be more difficult for youth who entered the labor market young and have limited education and skills, making the attainment of a stable job all the more difficult. Furthermore, youth who are not in education, employment, or training (NEET), comprised around 36 percent of the total youth population in 2005–06. They could also be particularly affected by other members of their family and community losing their job and source of income, increasing the chances of these young people being locked into this social limbo and more exposed to discouragement.[5] Such circumstances may result in poor choices by these youth and increased social conflict.

Poverty, Social Exclusion, and Violence in Urban Settings

The relationship between poverty, social exclusion, and crime/violence is particularly complex in Pakistan, with crime and lack of safety impeding the capabilities and capital of the poor. Reforms in the freight transport sector will interact with this fragile equilibrium. This equation is particularly complex in Karachi (see "The Case of Karachi" section). Violence, crime, and social exclusion are interrelated in numerous ways. Particularly problematic is the way in which the lack of safety affects the ability of weaker members of society (for example, women, children, youth, and minority groups) to participate in economic activities and subsequently reinforces their marginality. Those who make their living in the informal sector are particularly vulnerable to crime. Plus the poor also have less means to protect themselves from crime and increased insecurity.

The Case of Karachi

Home to up to 18 million people, Karachi is one of the largest cities in the world. Its two commercial ports on the Arabian Sea, banks, and stock market constitute the lifeline of the Pakistani economy. Providing nearly 70 percent of the government's revenue, Karachi accounts for a quarter of Pakistan's gross domestic product (GDP). Social turmoil in Karachi during the 1980s, 1990s, and 2000s has been undermining Pakistan's economic prosperity and political stability.

Karachi is home to all of the ethnic groups in Pakistan and has large migrant communities from Afghanistan, Bangladesh, and Myanmar. The city's politics are also colored by its diversity. One of Karachi's defining characteristics is its "ethnic mix," initiated by the influx of migrants after the country gained independence between 1947 and 1950, at a time when the city had about 425,000 inhabitants. Compounding this ethnic mix was the influx in the 1960s of Pakhtuns looking for work, with a second wave initiated in the early 1980s following the Soviet invasion of Afghanistan. Today, Karachi hosts an estimated 3.5 million ethnic Pakhtuns, the largest urban concentration of this ethnic group outside its homeland in western Pakistan and neighboring Afghanistan. In recent years, tens of thousands of Pakhtuns have joined their extended families in Karachi as insecurity pushed them out of their home regions.

What happens in Karachi has ripple effects across Pakistan. Given Karachi's centrality in Pakistan's economy, trade, and transport, reforms in the freight transport sector will find in this city a concentration and test of the potential social challenges, as well as a priority for Pakistan's future. The compounded effects of reforms in the freight transport sector are likely to crystallize in Karachi, where their potential social impacts are also among the greatest. Establishing adequate dialogue and engagement mechanisms to give a voice to groups that may be affected by reforms in the trade and transport sector should be a priority.

Connectivity and Migration

Reforms in the freight transport sector are expected to lead to greater connectivity, migration, and spatial transformation, amplifying historical trends in such increases and associated impacts. To avoid the compounding of existing problems, positive and negative influences of these trends need to be understood in advance and proactively managed or mitigated. The discussions below illustrate the trends, challenges, and need for planning and readiness for changes that the reforms are likely to bring about.

Overview of Migration in Pakistan

Migration will be another important vector of social impact for reforms in the freight transport sector. These reforms can be expected to influence migration flux, patterns, and composition at the national, regional, and international levels by facilitating connectivity. Robust evidence indicates that migration can help to integrate leading and lagging regions within a country. In fact, migration constitutes one of three main market forces (along with agglomeration and specialization) that can facilitate economic integration, leading to both the geographic concentration of economic activity and a convergence in living standards. The potential contributions of migration can be further taken advantage of if they are complemented with progressive urbanization policies, as well as improved education and health services that can help potential migrants become more productive and thus, take advantage of employment opportunities in urban centers (World Bank 2009). While migration is a market force that can be harnessed to support economic growth, it also has the potential to drive other social impacts discussed in this chapter, such as social conflict, HIV, or urban sprawl. The following section looks into the different levels of impact that reforms in the freight transport sector can be expected to influence.

Migration is ingrained in Pakistan's history, notably with the massive "partition migration" following the emergence of independent states in South Asia. It remains a defining feature of the country's socioeconomic dynamics, both internally and internationally. For one, Pakistan hosts the largest number of refugees in the world, with 1.8 million refugees at the end of 2008, almost all of whom are Afghans.[6] Furthermore, at the end of 2010, there were around 2 million internally displaced people, 1.4 million of them registered by the government. Second, migration is a key factor defining Pakistan's society and labor markets. Migration operates at three levels: internationally, regionally, and internally, all of which have strong socioeconomic implications for Pakistan. These migrations are both vectors and outcomes of Pakistan's present and future spatial transformation.

The UN projected that, by 2010, internationally, migrants from Pakistan would represent 2.3 percent of the country's population (UN ESA 2011, 247). An increased interregional connectivity through improved freight transportation can also be expected to yield an increase in bi-directional interregional migration. Pakistani migrants are estimated to send back about US$8.6 billion in remittances (Ratha and Mohapatra 2009). At the regional level, Pakistan hosts 2.8 million intraregional migrants. In facilitating connectivity, reforms for the freight transport sector could also contribute to the international migration of workers from Pakistan, an option that may particularly appeal to younger migrants. It will also likely increase the attractiveness of Pakistan's major cities, and notably Karachi, to migrants from the region (table 4.1).

At the national level, internal migration is particularly strong. In Pakistan the share of rural-to-urban migration increased over time (1996–2006), while urban-to-urban migration declined, yet remaining highest in internal migration. Reforms in the freight transport sector are likely to facilitate such migrations and have strong socio-political implications for Pakistan. Indeed, the regional distribution of population also has key significance for provinces due to its repercussions on their political representation and rights in the federation, distribution

Table 4.1 International Migration

Year	Estimated number of international migrants at mid-year	International migrants as a percentage of the population
1990	6,555,782	5.7
1995	4,076,599	3.1
2000	4,242,689	2.9
2005	3,554,009	2.1
2010	4,233,592	2.3

Sources: UN ESA 2011, 247; United Nations 2009.

Table 4.2 Inter- and Intramigration in Pakistan, by Province, 2009

Province	Total			Interprovincial			Intraprovincial		
	Total	Male	Female	Total	Male	Female	Total	Male	Female
Punjab	63.7	56.4	69.0	34.6	31.1	39.3	71.7	66.7	74.8
Sindh	25.1	28.3	22.7	41.5	37.9	46.0	20.6	24.4	18.2
Khyber Pakhtunkhwa	10.7	14.7	7.8	23.2	30.4	13.8	7.2	8.3	6.6
Balochistan	0.5	0.6	0.5	0.7	0.6	0.9	0.5	0.6	0.4
Total	100	100	100	100	100	100	100	100	100

Source: GoP 2009.

of resources, and employment quotas as provisioned in the Constitution. About 30 percent of total migration as of 2008–09 (or up to 3 million people), has been from rural to urban areas. Gains in agricultural productivity are also promoting migration from rural settings to industrial clusters in urban centers. Punjab accounted for the bulk of migrant labor, both inter- and intraprovincial, while the proportion of migrant labor in other provinces tapered down roughly in consonance with their total population (GoP 2009). Intraprovincial migration has been particularly strong in Punjab, with 71.7 percent of all those who reported intraprovincial migration being based in Punjab (table 4.2). The direction of interprovincial migration seemed more toward Sindh, particularly Karachi, Pakistan's largest city and commercial center, where 41.5 percent of all workers who had migrated across provinces were found to be working. About 15 percent of the total workforce consists of internal migrants, and the proportion goes up to almost 20 percent for wage employment. Given that the total civilian labor force in the country consists of 53.72 million people (GoP 2009), this would mean that from 7 to 10 million people have migrated to join the labor force outside their place of origin as of 2008–09. These migrants generally moved toward wage employment (in larger cities) or self-employment in services (in smaller towns).[7] This trend is accentuated by the structure of labor markets in Pakistan, where almost a third of firms in Pakistan tend to rely on seasonal or temporary labor, thus being able to add to, or shed from, the labor force as per trends in market demand (GoP 2009).

Gender and Migration

Reforms in the freight transport sector are likely to affect the composition of migration, with the share of women continuing to increase, particularly in the case of long distance and interregional migration. Female migrants constituted the larger share of internal migration (aged 10 and above), with marriage playing a major role.[8] Furthermore, the trend of intra- and interprovincial migration indicates that in all provinces, long-distance movement of females rose. Not only did the share of female rural-to-urban migration increase, but family migration to cities also increased over that period. This seems to be due to changes in the agrarian structure and rural economy, particularly in landless households, decline in sharecropping, and rise in small land holding.[9] Such longer term and long-distance family migrations have strong implications for infrastructure and service delivery in urban settings and are likely to remain a defining feature of internal migration.

Female migration excluding that related to marriage reasons also presents stark differences within provinces. In the context of the freight transport sector reforms, which can be expected to foster both migration and urbanization, this type of migration also has strong policy implications for labor markets and service delivery. Over a period of 10 years, the LFS data indicate that women from Sindh represent a much larger share of interprovince rural-to-urban migration, while the share of women from Punjab and Khyber Pakhtunkhwa is overall more important in intraprovince migration. While women's unemployment has decreased in recent years, it remains much higher than that of men, particularly in the case of female youth (Ahmad and Azim 2010). However, while migration increases the likelihood of unemployment for both male youth and male adults, it decreases the likelihood of unemployment for female adults. One possible explanation may be that individuals tend to move from rural areas to urban areas, where there are more opportunities for women to work. Yet women who manage to find employment in nonagricultural sectors mainly work in the informal economy (71.7 percent in 2008). Further, the majority of employed women are classified as at "risk of lacking decent work," since they are working as contributing family or own account workers. Insecure employment arrangements, low earnings, and low productivity are likely to characterize both status groups (UN 2009). Incidentally, change brought by reforms in the freight transport sector may offer some opportunities to increase female participation in labor markets. However, this requires taking into account regional differences, the specific situation of female youth, and the risks associated with their work in the informal sector.

Cross-border Movement between Pakistan and Afghanistan

Trade and transport reforms and the cross-border movement between Pakistan and Afghanistan will influence migration. More than with any of its other neighbors, Pakistan's spatial transformation is also connected to Afghanistan, for both socioeconomic and security reasons. Regarding migration, fluxes have been observed both from and to Pakistan. While Afghanistan hosts migrants from Pakistan—most of them semi-skilled, given the country's needs for skilled labor—the flux has been dominated by Afghans migrating to Pakistan. Indeed, Afghans have a long tradition of economic migration to neighboring countries. Conflict-related involuntary migration has further contributed to the development and reinforcing of social, economic, and cultural ties between those refugees and the host country. However, while at the end of 2002 Pakistan hosted 2.2 million Afghan refugees, one of the largest refugee populations in the world, today the majority of Afghans traveling to and from Pakistan are temporary migrants.[10]

Economic motivations represent the main decision-making factor, with 64.4 percent of labor migrants citing the lack of work in Afghanistan as the factor leading them to migrate temporarily to Pakistan. Indeed, wages in Pakistan are not favorable enough to justify permanent resettlement. Instead, the objective of the migration is for the head of household and main wage earners to meet the needs and expenses of their families, rather than accumulate wealth or savings with a medium or long-term perspective (UN HABITAT 2011). While the cost of migration is low, so is its long-term benefit. Thus, casual labor has become a livelihood solution for Afghans who benefit from their network and past experiences in Pakistan and have more readily available economic opportunities.[11] In the context of trade and transport reforms, improved connectivity could be expected to increase the attractiveness of temporary economic migration from Afghanistan, which would in turn have socio-political implications (as discussed in the "Freight Transportation and Social Conflicts" section).

Spatial Transformation and Urban Sprawl

Urbanization in Pakistan

Urbanization facilitates intra-industry spillovers and is therefore an important factor in agglomeration economies, as discussed above. While the benefits of urbanization are significant, a number of externalities, such as congestion and pollution, can offset them. As in the case of Pakistan, urbanization tends to occur during a country's development stage characterized by low income and nascent institutions (World Bank 2009). Pakistan's urbanization, largely fueled by migration, has accelerated over the last decades, during which the urban growth rate has been twice that of population growth. While recognizing that urbanization is desirable in general terms for Pakistan, this report focuses on the potentially mutually reinforcing social implications of urbanization and other social priorities associated with trade and transport sector reforms, particularly those concerning the most vulnerable groups (day laborers, youth, and women). Indeed, the share of Pakistan's urban population has continued to increase since 1996 and it is now estimated that 35.9 percent of the country's population lives in urban settings (UN HABITAT 2011). Pakistan already has eight cities over one million. By 2020, Pakistan is expected to have one mega-city (over 10 million), Karachi, and nine additional cities over one million (table 4.3) (UN HABITAT 2011).

Table 4.3 City Population of Urban Agglomerations 2000–20
Thousands

	2000	2010	2020
Failsalabad	2,140	2,849	3,704
Gujranwala	1,224	1,652	2,165
Hyderabad	1,222	1,590	2,084
Islamabad	595	856	1,132
Karachi	10,021	13,125	16,693
Lahore	5,449	7,132	9,150
Multan	1,263	1,659	2,174
Peshawar	1,066	1,422	1,868
Quetta	614	841	1,113
Rawalpindi	1,520	2,026	2,646

Source: UN HABITAT 2011.

With economic motivations dominating rural-to-urban migration, it is not surprising to find Lahore and Karachi, the two most highly concentrated districts in large-scale manufacturing employment, among those facing the most challenges in relation to urban sprawl.

In Pakistan's rapidly expanding cities, authorities have faced significant challenges to increase the provision of basic infrastructure in a manner that is commensurate with population growth. While the growth rate of urban agglomeration is expected to slow down progressively (UN HABITAT 2011), the infrastructure deficit remains a key challenge for urbanization in Pakistan and bears strong social implications. This challenge has notably translated into one of the highest rates of slum prevalence in South Asia, with 71 percent of the total urban population living in slums (UN HABITAT 2011). The gap between housing demand and supply in major urban areas is rapidly increasing and people, particularly those falling in low- and middle-income classes, are forced to live in substandard housing. Twenty-five percent of the gap between housing demand and supply is met through informal settlements (*katchi abadis*), 60 percent through informal subdivisions of land, and 15 percent through densification of inner cities. Most of the people are unable to afford decent housing in urban areas because of limited income, and escalating prices of land and building materials. As a result, a major trend in Pakistan's urbanization has been the growth of slums and irregular settlements.

Furthermore, the high geographic concentration of manufacturing industries in Pakistan reinforces spatial disparities, with investments being prioritized toward leading districts at the cost of lagging ones. Such dynamics further spur migration toward urban agglomerations. Indeed, 35 percent of the industries are found to be highly agglomerated (Ellison and Glaeser concentration index > 0.05) and 38 percent of the industries are moderately concentrated (Ellison and Glaeser concentration index between 0.02 and 0.05).[12] While migration presents undeniable benefits for agglomerated industries (for instance, through expanded labor markets located near demand centers and input suppliers), without the corresponding infrastructure investments and public service delivery, those migrants, particularly in the case of daily wage workers, may continue to live in poverty.

Urban Sprawl in Pakistan

Recent estimates suggest that there was a deficit of 6 million housing units in Pakistan in 2005; the sustained flux of rural-to-urban migration is likely to accentuate this situation. In urban areas, the deficit is met largely by informal housing units (that is, not sanctioned by city administrations), which increased from 1.9 million in 1981 to 2.7 million in 1995. The same study quoted estimates that are more recent indicating that there are about 3.5 million housing units in informal settlements, housing 24.5 million people (Hasan and Raza 2009).

While both contribute to Pakistan's urban sprawl, a distinction should be made between *katchi abadis* and slums. *Katchi abadis* are informal settlements created through squatting or informal subdivisions of state or private land.[13]

In Karachi, the largest city in the country, an estimated 60 percent of the population lives in *katchi abadis*.[14] Informal settlements do not fall under the realm of responsibility of city administrations and as such tend to be unserviced or critically underserviced (Hasan and Raza 2009). The government of Pakistan (GoP) initiated the Katchi Abadi Improvement and Regularization Programme (KAIRP) in 1978 to start the provision of basic amenities to residents.[15] The process has been painfully slow, with the pace estimated at 1 percent of *abadis* regularized per year in the 1990s. Data that are more recent (2007) suggest it has not speeded up, and net progress is particularly slow as new settlements keep coming up. Poor record keeping of land records, which typically leads to prolonged legal arbitration, has hampered KAIRP (Hasan and Raza 2009). According to varying estimates, land disputes constitute 60–80 percent of court caseloads in Pakistan (UN HABITAT 2011). Policies that require determination of land ownership are therefore liable to be delayed. Another issue with KAIRP is the alleged "… failure of government agencies to identify and accept existing infrastructure…" (Hasan 2000, 2).

Slums, on the other hand, are settlements of villages absorbed in the urban sprawl or the informal subdivisions created on community and agricultural land.[16] While tenure security may be greater in slums than in *katchi abadi*, they are not usually concerned with programs to improve living conditions. More than 55 million people, or 71.7 percent of the country's urban population, lived in slums in 2005. It is estimated that more children now live in slums in Pakistan than in nonslums. While other countries in South Asia have a larger share of their population living in slum areas, Pakistan has comparatively experienced a particularly slow decline in this ratio.

Pakistan's slums have common characteristics, such as high poverty concentrations and lack of access to basic services and infrastructure. An analysis completed by UN HABITAT shows that the estimated number of people living in slums will continue to grow rapidly over the coming decade (UN HABITAT 2011). While the proportion of slum dwellers over total urban population in Pakistan is expected to gradually decrease from the 71.7 percent observed in 2005 to 61 percent in 2020, systems for solid waste management, sewerage and sanitation, and water supply are either nonexistent, rudimentary, or overall inadequate to respond to the current and future needs of the country's urban population. In a country where existing city administrations recover barely 50 percent of the solid waste generated even in main metropolitan areas, the scale of service extension needed to cover nonregularized settlements is considerable (Haider 2006).

Water is of notable concern for Pakistan's areas of urban sprawl. Most people living in *katchi abadis* and slums do not have an access to clean water. Apart from the obvious health problems, lack of potable water is leading to social, economic, and political difficulties.[17] Karachi is facing particularly acute water shortages, in part due to a dilapidated water supply and sewerage infrastructure,[18] but also due to the population pressure faced by the mega-city.[19] Capitalizing on the current shortage, a tanker/water "mafia" has mushroomed. Apart from five official hydrants allowed by the Karachi Water and Sewerage

Board, dozens of illegal hydrants alongside the Lyari River, which passes through the city, have emerged. These hydrants are supplying contaminated subsoil water from the river into which the city's sewage is pumped. Such tensions over water can be expected to increase as population growth adds to the pressures on Pakistan's water supply. The United Nations Economic and Social Commission for Asia and the Pacific estimates that water is likely to emerge as one of the most pressing problems in Pakistan in coming years due to the high demand for irrigation.[20]

Urban Sprawl and Road Infrastructure

Urban sprawl in Pakistan is partially correlated with road transportation. The observed expansion of slums along the main roads and highways is the result of the concentration of informal economic activity associated with road transportation, used for both freight and passenger transportation. Not surprisingly, the increase in the total number of people living in slums has run parallel to the exponential growth of the freight road transport sector during the last two decades (figure 4.2). In most cases, local authorities lack the ability to anticipate population growth, which in turn may constrain their ability to provide land for the urbanizing poor. Another contributing factor is the issue of land rights and tenure security, which tend to be denied to the urban poor, driving people to the periphery of towns and further contributing to urban sprawl in Pakistan.

Figure 4.2 Urban Sprawl and Road Freight Transport Development in Pakistan, 1990–2005

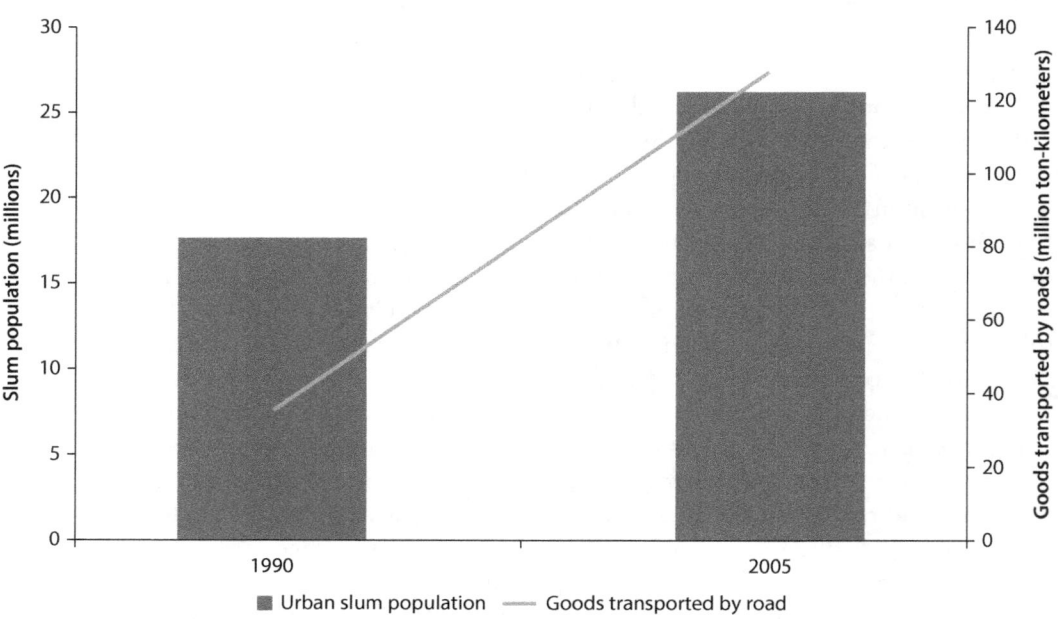

Source: UN HABITAT 2008.

The expected improvements in road infrastructure and freight transport policy reforms and investments are likely to increase job creation mainly in the manufacturing and service sectors. Since most firms in these sectors are located in or near urban areas, the availability of new and better-paid jobs in the formal economy will result in greater incentives for low-income people to migrate from poor rural areas to urban centers. Although these poor migrants are typically not qualified for the better-paid jobs in the manufacturing and service sectors, the creation of formal and higher paying jobs in urban centers results in an increased demand for low-paying jobs for which many of them are qualified. Poor people living in rural areas who will be lured by these types of low-paying jobs in the informal economy will likely populate new or expanded shantytowns located on the outskirts of large urban areas, or slums in the downtown areas where they would likely find friends and relatives.

Available evidence indicates that Pakistani cities tend to grow along transport infrastructure, particularly informal settlements. Therefore, a major potential effect of the planned reforms is that they may further increase the rate of urban sprawl in a country that suffers from an already high slum population. In Karachi, *katchi abadis* initially developed along railways. Currently, they are expanding to the city's north and west, partly because that is where road infrastructure is available (Hasan and Mohib 2003). In both Lahore and Faisalabad, each city's expansions that are more recent have taken place in areas that are close to main roads and highways (LUMS 2011).

Example of Urban Sprawl: The Case of Karachi

Karachi illustrates how unplanned urbanization as a result of improvements in freight infrastructure contributes to slum development, and hence has negative impacts on living standards. Karachi is the commercial hub and gateway of Pakistan. The city handles 95 percent of Pakistan's foreign trade, contributes 30 percent of Pakistan's manufacturing sector, and retains 40 percent of the total national employment in this sector. Unsurprisingly, the city also attracts a large number of economic migrants. In Karachi, densification and spatial expansion have occurred with little or no developmental planning. Since 1949, five development plans were prepared for Karachi, but never implemented. Due to the absence of development plans and the subsequent influx of migrants from within and outside the country, the city has suffered from a chronic shortage of dwelling units, water supply, electricity, and public transport, among other basic services (see map 4.2).

The shortage of dwelling units has been largely responsible for the emergence of a large number of squatter settlements in the city. About 50 percent of the total population resides in squatter settlements, in which the socioeconomic and the environmental conditions are dismal. Residents who live in the inner city slums are exposed to air, noise, and water pollution. Those living in peripheral slums lack accessibility to jobs and have trouble satisfying their basic socioeconomic needs. Furthermore, they are captive riders of limited and low-level public transport service, which also limits their opportunities.

Map 4.2 Karachi Urban Sprawl

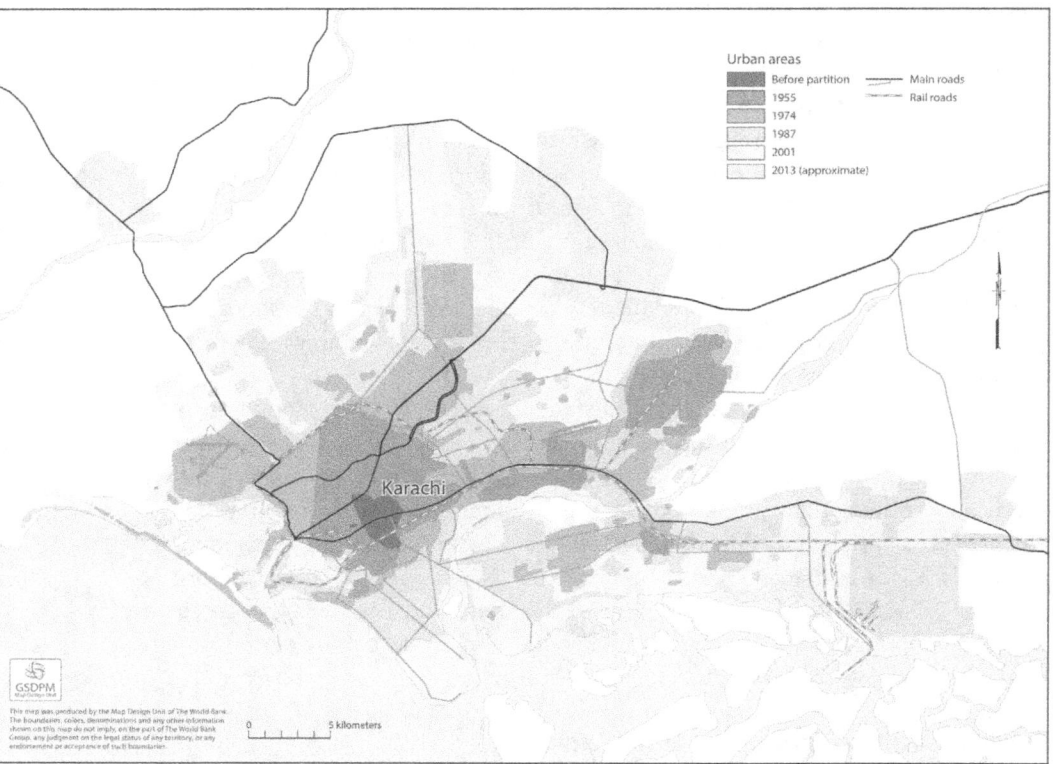

Source: City District Government of Karachi 2007.

The creation and expansion of *katchi abadis* is now taking place almost exclusively to the west and north of Karachi. According to Hasan and Mohib (2003), the reasons for this are the following:

- Government land and road infrastructure are available.
- These areas are closer and better connected with employment-generating areas.
- They are closer to the larger *katchi abadis*, where informal industrial activities and large populations provide jobs and a demand for services.
- In other locations, land is privately owned or is controlled by cantonments.

The urban transportation system of Karachi is mainly road-based. The development of the city's infrastructure in also highly inequitable, and additional demographic pressure from migration can be expected to reinforce this in the absence of policy aimed at addressing this divide. Though Karachi has a railway system known as Karachi Circular Railway System, its share in mode split is almost negligible. During recent years, Karachi has undertaken important urban transportation projects.[21] However, transportation infrastructure has so far

Map 4.3 Social Groups in Influence Area of Urban Transportation Infrastructure in Karachi

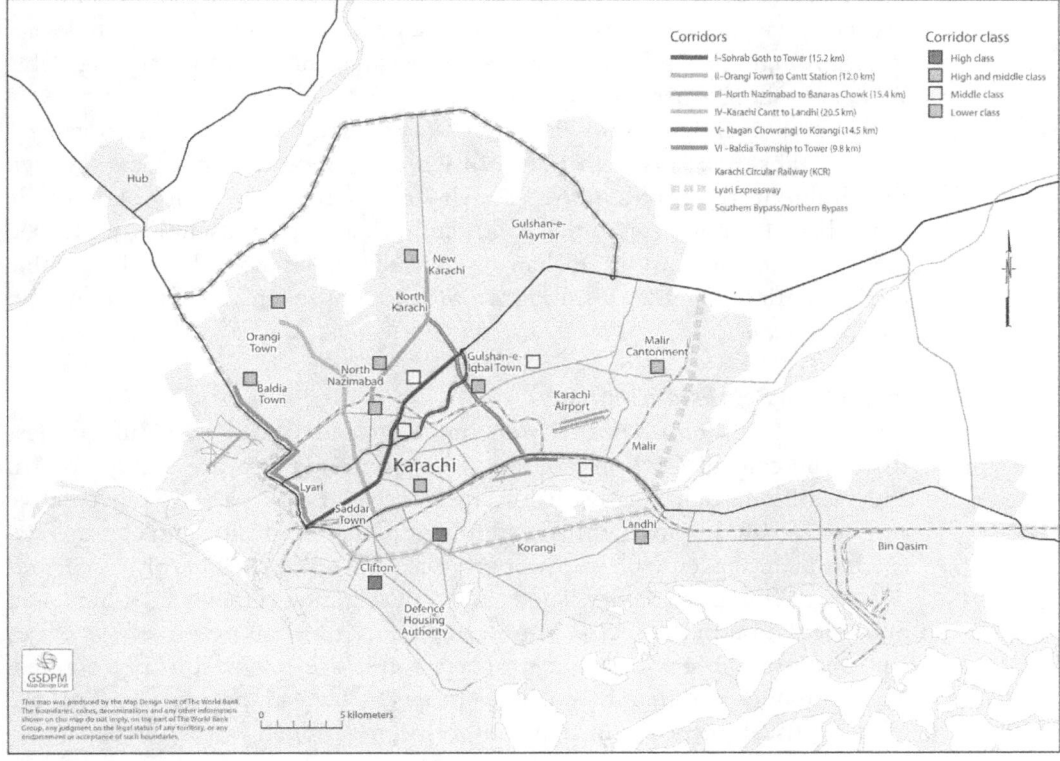

Source: City District Government of Karachi 2007.

mainly benefited the high to middle classes while bringing little benefit to the city's poor[22] (see map 4.3).

Access to Markets and Facilities

Reforms in the freight transport sector—whether through increased connectivity, changes in the trucking sector, or the extension of urban sprawl—may also modify access to markets. In large cities like Karachi and across the Punjab province, the provincial Agriculture Departments, through market committees set up at the district level, control wholesale markets for fruits and vegetables. Outside of those markets, the local *mandi* (market) for fruits and vegetables acts as the central link between producers and consumers. Despite variance in the size of such markets, there is a relatively standardized model of transactions with precisely defined roles for key players in the supply chain and a largely uniform set of rules. In Pakistan, most fruit and vegetable markets are privately owned in the smaller towns and many cities. *Mandi* owners can be characterized as commission agents who charge a fixed sum from the growers for usage of their facility and services. Wholesalers buy in lots through an auction conducted under the supervision of the *mandi* owner or his designated lieutenant (sometimes called a *munshi*). Having auctioned the goods, the *mandi* owner (also known as the *aarti*) pays off the growers after deducting his commission. The wholesaler (*beopaari/tajir*) then sells to individual retailers ranging from fruit and vegetable vendors to shopkeepers in retail markets.

Changes in freight through reforms may bring changes to the organizations of those markets with the diffusion of socioeconomic effects through the different stakeholders. Actors who are more vulnerable, particularly individuals from nonfarm households and urban poor households, may need more time to adjust to those changes and thus experience a lag in harnessing the potential benefits resulting from the improvement of freight and connectivity.

Impacts on Real Estate Markets

The real estate sector is not fully documented, and officially accounts for less than 2 percent of GDP in Pakistan. Real estate markets are highly cyclical and volatile.[23] Traditionally, real estate has lent itself to a lot of speculative activity. Urban development and supply of plots for housing and commercial use has been inadequate, and property prices tend to rise sharply in periods of strong economic activity. The cost of construction remains very high, and poor regulation in the sector, as well as the lack of a computerized system of land registration, ensures that property rights are not adequately defined. The state does not guarantee title to property. Instead, property records are used for fiscal purposes, in that the person mentioned as the owner is presumed to be responsible for payment of taxes on the property. The problem is particularly acute in urban areas, where there is no unified system of registration and no single public office responsible for keeping a conclusive record of rights. Instead, each urban development authority and housing society has its own system of record keeping, including keeping records of transfers.

A poorly regulated and volatile market offers many opportunities of malpractice in the real estate market in Pakistan.[24] Speculation could further arise from the increased demand for land and housing resulting from the growth dynamic triggered by the reformed freight transport sector. Prices of both land and built property in urban areas are likely to increase in tandem with growth in manufacturing and services and in response to trade and transport growth. Avoiding malpractice and speculative activity in the real estate market will be as much of a necessity as it will be a challenge.

Impact on HIV/AIDS

Status of the Epidemic in Pakistan

The greater degree of connectivity, migration, and urbanization, fostered by trade and transport sector reforms, can also be expected to affect the status of HIV/AIDS in Pakistan. For now, Pakistan remains a country with "a concentrated epidemic with prevalence levels consistently reported to be greater than 5 percent amongst injecting drug users (IDUs) and cross-dressed sex workers" (Brecorder 2010). Pakistan had an estimated 97,400 people living with HIV at the end of 2009, with 2,917 patients registered in 13 treatment and 7 Prevention of Parent-to-Child Transmission centers across the country, of which 1,320 are on antiretroviral drug therapy (HIV and AIDS Data Hub for Asia-Pacific 2010). IDUs constitute the core group driving the epidemic and exhibit the highest prevalence of 20.8 percent followed by 6.1 percent among cross-dressed sex workers and 0.9 percent among male sex workers (MSWs) (HIV/AIDS 2009). In Pakistan, although HIV infection rates among female sex workers (FSWs) (HIV/AIDS 2009) remain low at 0.91 percent, there is evidence of sexual networking between FSWs and IDUs (table 4.4). Considering the overlap between IDUs and at-risk sexual networks, the rising HIV prevalence among IDUs increases the risk of spillover into networks of commercial sex workers and their clients, particularly along trade routes (HIV/AIDS 2009).

However, the geographic trend of the epidemic is expanding from major urban cities and provincial capitals to smaller cities and towns. Although national adult HIV prevalence in the general population remains under 0.1 percent, exceptions were observed in Gujarat, where 88 HIV-positive cases were found out of a sample of 246 from the general population that included a large number of exmigrant workers. Among many factors, one important factor contributing to this development is unsafe injecting practices in formal and informal healthcare settings. The feminization issue of HIV infections among women is also emerging within marriages (through transmissions by partners), and mother-to-child transmission is increasingly probable. Pakistan is considered to be transforming from a low-prevalence, high-risk category of nations, to a concentrated epidemic one. In such a situation, monitoring sexual behavior among long-distance transporters is imperative, as is designing mitigation programs.

Table 4.4 HIV Prevalence by City and High-Risk Group
percent

City/province	IDU	MSW	Cross-Dressed	FSW
Karachi—provincial capital Sindh	23	3.1	3.5	2
Hyderabad—Sindh	30	0	0	0
Larkana—Sindh	28	0.5	27	0.61
Lahore—provincial capital Punjab	15	0.1	2.5	0.98
Faisalabad—Punjab	12	—	2.5	0.75
Sargodha—Punjab	23	—	—	1.2
Peshawar—provincial capital NWFP	13	—	1.2	—
D.G. Khan—Punjab	19	—	—	—
Overall study results	20.8	0.9	6.1	0.91
	N = 2971	N = 1205	N = 1186	N = 2197

Source: HIV/AIDS Surveillance Program 2009.
Note: HIV/AIDS Surveillance Project Integrated Biological and Behavioral Surveillance (IBBS) round III, and IBBS female sex workers round. NWFP = North West-Frontier Province. — = not available.

HIV and Freight

Long-distance truckers, assistants, and sex workers constitute a major vector of HIV/AIDS in Pakistan. The time that truckers spend on the road away from homes and families, and thus free from the social pressures that constrain sexual behavior within their home communities, explains the spread of HIV/AIDS through truckers. The sexual interactions between these high-risk groups have the potential of spreading HIV/AIDS among a wider population. Truck drivers, cleaners, and assistants remain engaged on long trade routes for several weeks.[25] When they make stopovers and take breaks during such periods, a high prevalence of sex providers, both male and female, frequent their stops. Such services mushroom and grow in tandem with the expansion of trade. The drivers may also sexually exploit the young cleaners who take care of and clean the trucks.

The National AIDS Control Program (NACP) has developed programs to address the issue of HIV/AIDS prevention in at-risk groups. NACP, in collaboration with the nongovernmental organization (NGO) Family Health International, implemented a project to reduce behavioral and biological risks of HIV transmission among Pakistan's long-distance truckers, cleaners, attendants, and associated population from 2006 to 2009.[26]

Reforms in the freight transport sector have the potential to reduce significantly the risk of HIV transmission. Improved connectivity and the transport sector's modernization increased by the participation of railways in moving freight over long distances would decrease the risk of transmission. In addition, information campaigns would be an important tool to mitigate the risk of HIV transmission. Information campaigns to prevent HIV spread among truck drivers have been used in India (Cornman et al. 2007) and South Africa (Ramjee and Gouws 2002). In these cases, the intention was to collect background information and implement a program designed to prevent the spread of HIV/AIDS. Campaigns to increase risk awareness should emphasize the importance of condom use as a sexually transmitted infection (STI)/HIV prevention method, rather than simply as contraception. Interpersonal communication is likely to be important in convincing truckers that STIs can be prevented (see box 4.1).

Resettlement and Displacement

Resettlement and the concomitant issues emerge as major social development concerns whenever there is large-scale involuntary land acquisition.[27] This may be a priority issue in the construction of new roads or railways for transportation.[28] The Land Acquisition Act 1894 (with amendments) is the instrument used to acquire land for public purposes but does not encompass issues of resettlement, relocation, and income livelihood restoration in cases of losses, nor does it protect persons without land titles, or with usufruct rights. There is also no national policy to cover these issues. Resettlement action plans are made and implemented for projects that international financing organizations or donor agencies support, because those organizations normally require such plans and

Box 4.1 NACP Mapping of HIV Risk Behavior among Truck Drivers in Pakistan

Awareness about HIV/AIDS is 81.2 percent, that of STIs is 55.5 percent, and knowledge about two correct ways of HIV transmission is 40 percent.

- 65 percent have heard of condoms mainly for use in contraception, of which 44 percent believe in their efficacy in the prevention against HIV/STIs. Most believe they are priced at low or very low levels.
- 19 percent express the view that condom users are at high risk of HIV/AIDS.
- 72.4 percent of drivers and cleaners indulge in extramarital/premarital sex; while of those ever having had sex, 42.3 percent had done so before the age of 21.
- Only 5.2 percent of those having heard about HIV/AIDS had heard of someone living with HIV/AIDS or having died from it.
- Personal risk perception of STIs and HIV/AIDS is 20 percent and 12.6 percent, respectively.
- Approximately 65.8 percent and 64.5 percent report ever having substance abuse and current abuse, respectively.
- Substance most commonly used is marijuana or cannabis, followed by alcohol.

Recommendations:

- Interventions aimed at providing information about HIV/AIDS should be more specific and less ambiguous regarding the modes of transmission and the methods of protection. The messages aired on electronic media are the most widely heard and should be more open.
- The risk of truckers acquiring HIV infection must be emphasized to improve the risk perception.
- The program should emphasize the dual benefit of the use of condoms, which would be best done through generic rather than branded advertising.
- Program interventions may also include components regarding substance abuse, which could, in the long run, lead to intravenous drug use.

Source: NACP 2005.
Note: The NACP study consisted of a literature review, mapping of truckers and health facilities, and a qualitative and quantitative survey conducted in three cities in Pakistan (Gujranwala, Karachi, and Khanewal). The qualitative component included 146 in-depth interviews with truckers and gatekeepers (truck agencies, en-route restaurant/hotel owners/staff, mechanics, truck association staff, and so on). The quantitative component included a representative sample of the total population at the time of the intercity truck drivers and cleaners in the three cities. Truck drivers aged 21 or more, and cleaners aged 15 or more, were interviewed. The total sample was 821, comprising 683 drivers and 138 cleaners. Greenstar Social Marketing was contracted by the NACP to conduct the study. Mean age was 33 years and the majority of drivers were married; 44 percent of the sample lives at the truck stop alone or with someone else. Monthly income of most averaged between Rs 2,500 and Rs 5,000.

their implementation. The National Highways Authority, for example, designs and implements involuntary resettlement plans for works financed by the Asian Development Bank and the World Bank.

In the absence of donor-supported projects in this sector, there are usually no mitigation plans; hence, the issues tend to remain unaddressed. This particularly affects the poor and voiceless who are unable to obtain redress in the absence of a national law/policy ensuring the guarantee of this right. In the transport sector (and in most infrastructure programs) the usual practice is to invoke the urgency clause of the Land Acquisition Act, thereby obviating the right to appeal, and where land can be taken over immediately, circumventing the process and procedures laid out in the Act.

Safeguarding the rights of landowners who do not have the power or voice, as well as the landless and those without land titles, becomes necessary to protect the vulnerable and prevent further deterioration of the poverty levels of some groups, particularly where there may be large-scale taking of land for new roads or for significant widening. Two other interrelated issues involve design and construction activities that may split communities or restrict access to means of income or livelihood, businesses, amenities, sources of water, and even divide agricultural lands.

Resettlement tends to be viewed without adequate consideration of gender and the rights of those who lack formal land titles. Since women are less visible, the social impact of road construction is not recognized or acknowledged. The rectification of this view becomes necessary for a society (such as Pakistan's) where women lack voice, access, and are constrained due to lack of mobility and purdah (segregation) that constrains them from accessing compensation for land lost. They are also most likely to lack titles or proof of the title to the land. In the absence of deliberate efforts to meet their needs, they will remain marginalized. The Land Acquisition Act (1894) also provides for compensation for assets on the land acquired for those with title. However, for those without title to the land, the Act does not guarantee the right to assets and infrastructure on the land.

Displacement of communities is of particular concern for fishing communities whom the proposed expansion programs of the two seaports, particularly in the case of the Karachi Port, are likely to affect. There have been instances of tensions between port authorities and the community of fishers in the past. Karachi Port Trust's (KPT) major expansion program centers on the Keamari area, which also houses a large fishing community. In 2005, KPT had allowed the fishers of Keamari to berth their boats at an inlet called China Creek, and had allowed fishing in adjoining channels. This agreement followed earlier tensions, when fishing had been banned near Oil Platform 3, which falls in Keamari town. In June 2008, the KPT issued a new order barring fishers from berthing at China Creek. The issue was finally resolved in favor of the fishing communities, but this was only after a sustained media campaign by some NGOs, and the intervention of the province's Chief Minister. This had an impact on their livelihood and income.

Summary

The proposed reforms for the trade and transport sector will take place in a complex and evolving socio-political context, characterized by ethnic tensions, demographic growth, and spatial transformation, among other salient features. While the proposed reforms will have overall positive effects for Pakistan's population, they may affect directly or indirectly some social groups. If the effects are in fact, or are perceived to be, particularly severe for vulnerable groups such as ethnic minorities, women, youth, or nonfarm rural and urban poor households, they may exacerbate existing tensions. Addressing this risk will require the development of participatory mechanisms, adequate safeguards, and redress mechanisms that are available particularly for potentially affected groups.

The social effects of the envisioned reforms are anticipated to be felt particularly in geographic areas along the main trade corridors and in urban areas. While Pakistan is already experiencing a spatial transformation, the proposed reforms are likely to accelerate the process by facilitating agglomeration economies in urban areas, thereby increasing job opportunities in those places, while also increasing mobility. Urbanization is associated with a country's economic development; however, in the case of Pakistan, the transformation is anticipated to take place within a short time frame, thereby increasing already severe negative externalities, including urban sprawl, congestion, and pollution. Key social problems associated with geographic areas along the main trade corridors also include a potential expansion of HIV/AIDS and resettlement and displacement of communities.

Notes

1. This vulnerability would be compounded by the loss of medical and insurance benefits, likely to have a strong impact on women.
2. See the case of the Karakoram Highway, "Highway Robbery: From Gesham to Gilgit, Truckers Protesting," *Tribune Express* (Karachi, Pakistan), May 3, 2011.
3. The window of opportunity will close around 2045, by which time the society is expected to begin aging rapidly. Therefore, during this period, protection and promotion of the next generation will have a huge impact on Pakistan's long-term prospects (DFID 2009).
4. Balochistan is the province where the unemployment rate is highest both in urban and rural areas and remains highest for youth aged 15–24 when compared with other provinces. Results suggest that in that province, youth are 43.7 percentage points less likely to find employment. Results also showed that, contrary to common belief, the unemployment rate in Sindh is less than that in Punjab. See Ahmad and Azim 2010.
5. Although on a declining trend since 1999–2000, the NEET rate in Pakistan is very high in comparison with other regions, both at the low end of the income per capita range, such as sub-Saharan Africa (27 percent), and at higher levels of income per capita, such as Central and South America (21 percent). It should be noted that the female NEET rate in Pakistan would be reduced, because more women would be counted as employed, if the list of probing questions aiming "to net-in marginal economic activities" in the labor force survey were taken into account. It is important to keep in mind that this measure contains both unemployed, nonstudent youth and youth who are inactive for reasons other than educational enrollment, including discouragement (that is, inactive nonstudents).
6. At the end of 2008, Pakistan also hosted the largest number of refugees in relation to its economic capacity. The country hosted 733 refugees per US$1 GDP (purchasing power parity) (UNHCR 2009).
7. Although about 40 percent of Pakistan's population is now thought to reside in urban areas, these estimated 65 million persons are concentrated in a few centers. The 1998 census showed about 200 towns and cities with more than 25,000 people,

but also revealed that 8 cities with populations of over 1 million accounted for almost 60 percent of the total urban population in Pakistan, while almost a quarter of the urban population was housed in cities ranging in size from 100,000 to 1 million. This distribution is unlikely to have changed.

8. More than 50 percent of female migrants change their place of residence due to marriage (Hamid 2010).
9. "The major factor in the family migration decision is the nonavailability of opportunities in rural areas to earn a sufficient livelihood. These opportunities for a segment of population, particularly landless households, have increasingly shrunk in rural Pakistan. Changes in both agrarian structure and rural economy have contributed in limiting these opportunities" (Arif and Hamid 2007a, 2007b).

    It should be noted that land is not only a factor of production and a source of livelihood, its ownership also reflects the socioeconomic status within society. Therefore, being landless has a compounding socioeconomic effect likely to make migration all the more attractive.
10. Since 2002, the United Nations High Commissioner for Refugees (UNHCR) assisted the repatriation of 3.6 million Afghans from Pakistan (UNHCR 2009). The GoP has instituted a new comprehensive Management and Repatriation Strategy for Afghan Refugees (UNHCR 2010).
11. Most Afghans refugees who have lived in Pakistan have acquired expectations of what is the necessary level of social services they need. In its survey, UNHCR (2009) found that 46.7 percent of all respondents have spent 10 years or more in Pakistan and 82 percent are established and live in Pakistan. This is a population that has therefore benefited over a sustained period of time of better infrastructure (access to water, gas, electricity, and so on) and notably of better social services (health and primary education) (UNHCR 2009).
12. A description of the methodology used to estimate the Ellison and Glaeser concentration index can be found in the consultant report completed for SEPSA by LUMS (2011).
13. The *katchi abadis* are of two types:
    - Settlements established through unorganized invasion of state lands at the time of partition; most of them were removed and relocated during the 1960s or have been regularized;
    - Informal subdivisions of state land, further divided into notified *katchi abadis*, settlements earmarked for regularization through a 99-year lease and local government infrastructure development; and nonnotified *katchi abadis*, which are settlements not to be regularized because they are on valuable land required for development, or on unsafe lands.
14. This 60 percent estimate is from the Orangi Pilot Project, an urban development NGO active in the city. The estimate is on their website http://www.oppinstitutions.org/. Accessed May 10, 2011.
15. Other nongovernment-led initiatives to integrate the urban poor such as the Orangi Pilot Project are also worthy of notice.
16. The slums can also be divided into two types:
    - Inner-city, traditional pre-independence working-class areas now densified and with inadequate infrastructure;
    - Goths or old villages now part of the urban sprawl; those within or near the city center have become formal—others have developed informally into inadequately serviced high-density working-class areas.

17. A 2011 report by the Pakistan Council of Research in Water Resources found that 82 percent of water sources tested in 24 (of the country's more than 100) districts across all four provinces provided water that is unsafe to drink. The report estimated that as many as 250,000 children a year die as a result of unsafe water (IRIN 2011).

18. Water losses due to poor infrastructure may be in the order of 30–35 percent (Winarni 2009).

19. "[In Karachi] two ethno-political parties staged a rally against water shortages last June [that is, 2001], which turned violent after police fired at the protestors killing two and leaving six injured. The protestors set vehicles on fire and ransacked property. The tension eased when additional water supplies were brought in from the river Indus, the key source of water for Karachi and the rest of the province. Karachi, with an unofficial population figure of 15 million, needs about 600 million gallons of water per day, but the city currently receives only about 435 million" (IRIN 2002).

20. Anatol Lieven (2011, 30) argues that Pakistan "can be described as a 'gamble on the Indus.'" In the context of climate change this gamble becomes increasingly perilous. Lieven notes that, with an average of 240 mm of rainfall per year, Pakistan is one of the most naturally arid of the world's most heavily populated states. Without the Indus River system and the canals flowing from it, most of the country, including Punjab, would be semi-desert and scrub-forest as it was before irrigation projects were implemented.

21. Construction of Lyari Expressway and Northern Bypass cost US$88 million, whereas the elevated expressway and rail-based transit system will cost US$225 and US$69 million, respectively. Moreover, for fiscal year 2005/06, the city government approved US$100 million for construction of roads, bridges, flyovers, underpasses, and other infrastructure projects.

22. The City Government of Karachi provides a map that illustrates the social groups in the influence area of urban transportation infrastructure in Karachi in greater detail.

23. Real estate here refers to valuations on land and buildings, including structures of houses, apartments, commercial property, open space for multiple uses, and so on.

24. While reference to "land mafias" exists across Pakistan, Karachi appears to be particularly associated with this land grabbing, likely due to the high value of land resulting from its development and unmet demand.

25. S. Agha (2002) finds that, in the case of truckers, being away from home for more than a month is associated with a higher likelihood of having had sex with an FSW (45 percent). The percentage of truckers who had sex with an MSW was higher for truckers who had been away from home for longer than 1 month on the present trip. Nineteen percent of men who had been away from home for more than a month have had sex with an MSW, compared to 9 percent of men who had been away from home for less than a month.

26. The key components of the project included the following: (i) implementation of appropriate strategic behavioral communication strategies; (ii) provision of condom education and distribution; (iii) provision of education on sexual health and STIs along with acceptable, accessible, and appropriate STI services; (iv) provision of access to HIV voluntary counseling and testing services; (v) promotion of enabling environment in the project area; and (vi) monitoring the organization and location of the sex work. The project wrapped up in early 2009 after registering over 72,000 truckers as its beneficiaries, ensuring availability of condoms at key sites, and overseeing the delivery of primary health care, STI and HIV counseling services.

27. Work on the Faisalabad Khanewal section of the E-4 motorway is currently ongoing with support from the Asian Development Bank, but the bulk of the investment component has yet to be undertaken.
28. The legal framework governing land acquisition and compensation issues in Pakistan currently is the Land Acquisition Act of 1894, which delineates a process for acquiring land for public purposes, a method for determining the cost of land (based on location, type, and quality of land, and so on). It is a provincial law, and each province has its own version, interpretation, and procedure.

References

Agha, S. 2002. "Sexual Behavior among Truck Drivers in Pakistan." *Culture, Health & Sexuality* 4 (2): 191–206.

Ahmad, Rizwan, and Parvez Azim. 2010. "Youth Population and the Labour Market of Pakistan: A Micro Level Study." *Pakistan Economic and Social Review* 48 (2): 183–208. http://pu.edu.pk/images/journal/pesr/PDF-FILES/2%20AHMAD%20and%20 AZIM%20Youth%20Population%20and%20the%20Labour%20Market_V48_ No_2%20(Winter%202010).pdf.

Arif, G. M., and Shahnaz Hamid. 2007a. "Gender Dimensions in Rural-Urban Migration in Pakistan." Paper presented at the 8th Population Association of Pakistan Conference, Islamabad, November 18–19.

———. 2007b. *Life in the City: Pakistan in Focus*. Islamabad: UNFPA (United Nations Population Fund).

Brecorder. 2010. "BR-epaper: Ministry Fully Aware of Growing Threat of HIV." www.brecorder.com/epaper/2010/04/13/13-page/167794-news.html, posted April 13, 2010.

City District Government of Karachi. 2007. http://www.karachicity.gov.pk/.

Cornman, D. H., S. J. Schmiege, A. Bryan, T. J. Benziger, and J. D. Fisher. 2007. "An Information-Motivation-Behavioral Skills (IMB) Model-based HIV Prevention Intervention for Truck Drivers in India." *Social Science & Medicine* 64 (8): 1572–84.

DFID (Department for International Development). 2009. *Eliminating World Poverty: Building Our Common Future*. London: Department for International Development. http://www.infodev.org/en/Publication.671.html.

GoP (Government of Pakistan). 2006. "Labor Force Survey 2005–06." Federal Bureau of Statistics. Islamabad.

———. 2009. "Labor Force Survey 2008–09." Federal Bureau of Statistics, Islamabad.

———. 2011. *Pakistan: Framework for Economic Growth*. Planning Commission, Islamabad.

Haider, Murtaza. 2006. "Urbanization Challenges in Pakistan. Developing Vision 2030." Peshawar, Pakistan: National Institute of Urban Infrastructure Planning. http://www.regionomics.com/INDUS/Vision%202030%20urbanization%20Pakistan.pdf.

Hamid, Shahnaz. 2010. *Rural to Urban Migration in Pakistan: The Gender Perspective*. Islamabad: Pakistan Institute of Development Economics. http://www.eastasiaforum.org/testing/eaber/sites/default/files/documents/PIDE_Hamid_2010.pdf.

Hasan, Arif. 2000. "Scaling Up of the Orangi Pilot Project Programmes: Successes, Failures and Potential." Paper presented at the Asian Mayors' Forum on "Fighting Urban Poverty," Shanghai, May 5, 2000.

Hasan, A., and Masooma Mohib. 2003. "Urban Slums Reports: The Case of Karachi, Pakistan." In UN HABITAT, *Global Report on Human Settlements 2003: The Challenge of Slums.* Part IV: Summary of City Case Studies, 195–228. Oxford, U.K.: Earthscan.

Hasan, A., and Mansoor Raza. 2009. "Migration and Small Towns in Pakistan." Working Paper Series on Rural-Urban Interactions and Livelihood Strategies, No. 15. London: IIED (International Institute for Environment and Development). http://books.google.com.pk/books?id=U7imPH4KVJUC&printsec=frontcover#v=onepage&q&f=false.

HIV and AIDS Data Hub for Asia-Pacific. 2010. *Pakistan: Sex Work and HIV/AIDS.* Bangkok, Thailand: HIV/ADS Data Hub. http://www.aidsdatahub.org/dmdocuments/sex_work_hiv_pakistan.pdf.

HIV/AIDS Surveillance Program. 2009. NACP, IBBS Round III report 2008–09. See UNGASS Pakistan Report. *Progress Report on the Declaration of Commitment on HIV/AIDS for the United Nations General Assembly Special Session on HIV/AIDS.* Islamabad: National AIDS Control Program, Ministry of Health. https://docs.google.com/viewer?a=v&q=cache:s-9K0NRByUgJ:www.unaids.org/en/dataanalysis/knowyourresponse/countryprogressreports/2010countries/pakistan_2010_country_progress_report_en.pdf+HIV/AIDS+Surveillance+Program.+2009.+NACP,+%22IBBS+Round+III%22+report+2008%E2%80%9309.&hl=en&gl=us&pid=bl&srcid=ADGEESgZQ-s_I1Y_kpOkavZ45LJDCmIFGQKnoSwh_xHPaa7hTdz4JaFsh7UqbJ9hfjcsIrdT_zg8bcFE9tCeQ8XPRM8XTjjAbCOUvC9Ugs7lf1XkBWR5iZEFMcdP94xnX1XVBwDYOPUi&sig=AHIEtbRPOd1e2EwoKQnUmShYecRoibUvYA.

IDS (Innovative Development Strategies). 2011. *SEPSA: Poverty and Social Impact Assessment.* Consultant report prepared for the World Bank. Islamabad.

IRIN (UN Office for the Coordination of Humanitarian Affairs). 2002. "Pakistan: Karachi Water Shortage." Press Release by IRIN on January 16, 2002. http://www.irinnews.org/fr/Report/17826/PAKISTAN-Karachi-water-shortage.

———. 2011. "Pakistan: Unsafe Water Kills 250,000 Children a Year—Government." Press Release by IRIN on April 19, 2011. http://www.irinnews.org/Report/92518/PAKISTAN-Unsafe-water-kills-250-000-children-a-year-government.

Lieven, Anatol. 2011. *Pakistan. A Hard Country.* New York, NY: Public Affairs.

LUMS (Lahore University of Management Sciences). 2011. Abid A. Burki, Kamal A. Munir, Mushtaq A. Khan, M. Usman Khan, Adeel Faheem, Ayesha Khalid, and Syed Turab Hussain. *Industrial Policy, Its Spatial Aspects and Cluster Development in Pakistan.* Consultant report by the Lahore University of Management Sciences for the World Bank. Lahore, Pakistan.

Mezzera, M. and S. Aftab. 2009. "Pakistan State-Society Analysis." Initiative for Peacebuilding, Brussels, and the Netherlands Institute of International Relations. The Netherlands: Clingendael.

NACP (National AIDS Control Program, Ministry of Health). 2005. *National Study of Reproductive Tract and Sexually Transmitted Infections.* Islamabad. http://www.aidsdatahub.org/dmdocuments/BSS_Pakistan_2005_National_Study_of_Reproductive_Tract_and_Sexually_Transmitted_Infections.pdf.pdf.

Ramjee, Gita, and Eleanor Gouws. 2002. "Prevalence of HIV among Truck Drivers Visiting Sex Workers in KwaZulu-Natal, South Africa." *Sexually Transmitted Diseases* 29 (1): 44–49.

Ratha, Dilip, and Sanket Mohapatra. 2009. "Forecasting Migrant Remittances during the Global Financial Crisis." *Migration Letters* 7 (2): 203–13.

Shakir, Anwar. 2010. "Pakistan Pays Price for Trucking in Afghan War Cargo." *Businessweek*, July 7.

UN ESA (United Nations, Department of Economic and Social Affairs, Population Division). 2011. *International Migration Report 2009: A Global Assessment* (United Nations, ST/ESA/SER.A/316). New York: United Nations. http://www.un.org/esa/population/publications/migration/WorldMigrationReport2009.pdf.

UN HABITAT. 2008. *State of the World's Cities 2008/2009: Harmonious Cities*. London, U.K.: Earthscan.

———. 2011. *Global Report on Human Settlements 2011: Cities and Climate Change*. Oxford, U.K.: Earthscan.

UNHCR (Office of the United Nations High Commissioner for Refugees). 2009. *UNHCR Statistical Yearbook 2009*. Geneva: UNHCR. http://www.unhcr.org/4ce532ff9.html.

———. 2010. *Global Report 2010*. Geneva: UNHCR. http://www.unhcr.org/gr10/index.html#/home.

United Nations. 2009. *Trends in International Migrant Stock: The 2008 Revision*. United Nations Department of Economic and Social Affairs, Population Division. (United Nations database, POP/DB/MIG/Stock/Rev.2008).

Winarni, W. 2009. "Infrastructure Leakage Index (ILI) as Water Losses Indicator." *Civil Engineering Dimension* 11 (2): 126–34. https://docs.google.com/viewer?a=v&q=cache:1Ejt2gpz5gwJ:puslit2.petra.ac.id/ejournal/index.php/civ/article/viewFile/17230/17771+pakistan+water+losses+due+to+poor+infrastructure&hl=en&gl=us&pid=bl&srcid=ADGEESiZuOC4yOscZTv11MjTUDhfeWcOJnyPVY42JsHKI5feC3Om12UcMumLfqeJ_ah9B34wgz7tAUxA87l54kYqPDxZHyj7okt4Dj99Hgxc4uaFnNvsvUHI0ai_eCJq3N-TbjcXYbix&sig=AHIEtbRsEzoeDedtfd1gi6fAeat4a3MTIA.

World Bank. 2009. *World Development Report 2009: Reshaping Economic Geography*. Washington, DC: World Bank. http://web.worldbank.org/WBSITE/EXTERNAL/EXTDEC/EXTRESEARCH/EXTWDRS/0,,contentMDK:23080183~pagePK:478093~piPK:477627~theSitePK:477624,00.html.

———. 2011. *Pakistan Transport Sector*. Washington, DC: World Bank. http://go.worldbank.org/A0D9IJ5SH0.

CHAPTER 5

Priority Environmental Issues Associated with Freight Transport

Discussion with stakeholders, and structured and semi-structured interviews, conducted under strategic environmental, poverty, and social assessment (SEPSA), identified the following priority environmental problem areas associated with transport in Pakistan: air and noise pollution, road safety, transport of hazardous materials, climate change, and habitat fragmentation and natural resource degradation. This chapter examines these priority environmental problems associated with transport in Pakistan.

Air Pollution

Transport contributes to ambient air pollution, one of the most serious public health problems in Pakistan (World Bank 2006a, 2011). The main source of ambient air pollution is the combustion of fossil fuels by both stationary and mobile sources. The transportation sector is in general responsible for a significant share of the ambient air pollution in urban areas. A 2006 World Bank report found that more than 22,600 deaths per year are directly or indirectly attributable to ambient air pollution at the national level (World Bank 2006a, 2011). A 2011 World Bank analysis concluded that outdoor air pollution was responsible for more than 10,000 premature deaths in 2009 in the province of Sindh alone, with roughly 80 percent of them happening in Karachi.

Ambient air quality problems tend to be most severe in urban areas where both population and pollution sources, particularly automobiles and industry, are most concentrated. By 2006, the effects of urban air pollution on human health (excluding pain and suffering) in Pakistan had an annual cost of Rs 62 billion–Rs 65 billion, or around 1 percent of gross domestic product (GDP) (World Bank

---

This chapter draws from the work of World Bank consultant Elena Strukova (see, for example, Strukova 2004, 2007, 2010); the consultant report prepared by Bjorn Larsen and John Magne Skjelvik (2012); and from the work of World Bank consultant Rahi Abdula.

2006a, 2011). These costs are likely to be even higher, because studies that are more recent have concluded that lung infections as a result of air pollution exacerbate the risks and effects of malnutrition in children and consequently hinder their human development. By 2009, in the province of Sindh, the World Bank estimated that the cost of urban air pollution was equivalent to 0.9–2.2 percent of the province's GDP, particularly due to the health effects of high concentrations of damaging pollutants in urban agglomerations such as Karachi. Particulate matter (PM) released into the air, particularly PM with a diameter of less than 2.5 microns ($PM_{2.5}$), is one of the primary causes of poor health outcomes in Pakistan.[1]

Estimates based on limited available information suggest that mobile sources (including 2 and 3 wheelers, cars, trucks, and buses) contribute a significant percentage of emissions of fine and ultrafine particles (World Bank 2011). The number of vehicles in Pakistan has increased rapidly, from less than 2 million in 1991–92, to more than 9.5 million in 2008–09 (GoP 2009b). These vehicles run on fuels that have high sulfur content, a main ingredient in the formation of PM (see figure 5.1). Most fuel in Pakistan has a sulfur level of 5,000–10,000 parts per million, a level much higher than Euro II, Euro III, or Euro IV emission standards, which have already been adopted in some South Asian countries (World Bank 2006c). The Government of Pakistan has adopted a plan to reduce sulfur content in fuels. However, the plan has been delayed because of various reasons.[2]

Although trucks represent a minor fraction of Pakistan's vehicle fleet, they emit pollutants of local and global concern. As the number of registered vehicles

Figure 5.1 Legally Binding Sulfur Content in Diesel in Selected Countries, and Average PM_{10} Concentrations in Urban Centers, 2006

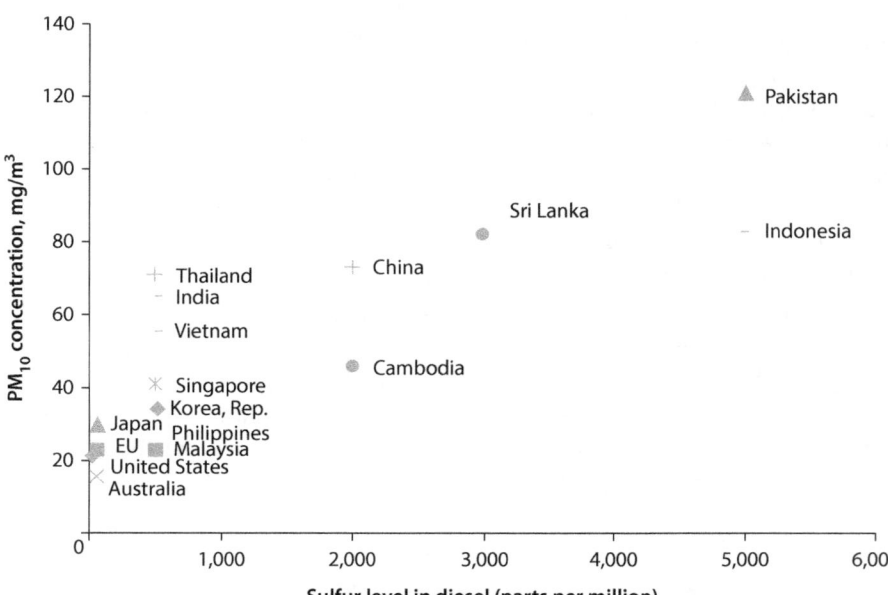

Sources: CONCAWE (2006), Timilsina and Dulal (2008).

increases in Pakistan, so does the level of air pollution in urban areas, particularly in densely populated metropolitan regions such as Karachi, Lahore, Hyderabad, and Islamabad-Rawalpindi. By 2010, registered trucks represented from 3 percent to 3.5 percent of registered vehicles (see figures 5.2–5.5).

The ambient air concentrations for fine PM were found to be quite high relative to the appropriate international standards (table 5.1). Fine particulate matter ($PM_{2.5}$) is well documented to have a robust association with several serious public health effects (for example, significant increase in cardiovascular and pulmonary diseases that may result in death or permanent incapacitation). The limited data that are available indicate that concentrations of $PM_{2.5}$ in Pakistan's main cities exceed by several times the limits recommended by

Figure 5.2 Number of Registered Vehicles in Pakistan, 2000–10

Source: Government of Pakistan.

Figure 5.3 Carbon Monoxide Emissions from Vehicle Fleet ($MtCO_2$), 2000–06

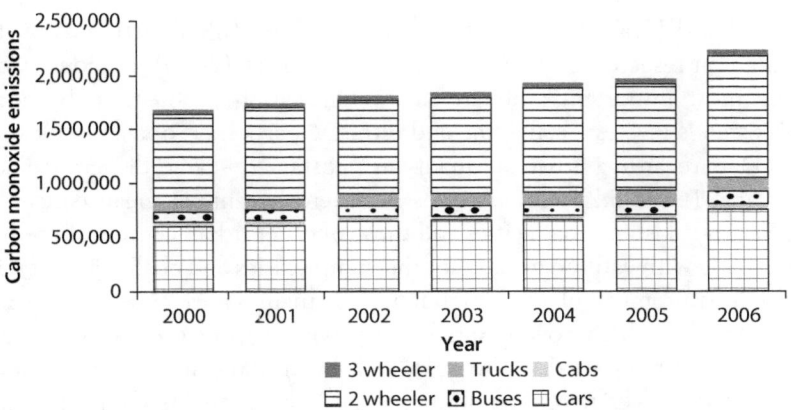

Figure 5.4 NO$_x$ Emissions from Vehicle Fleet

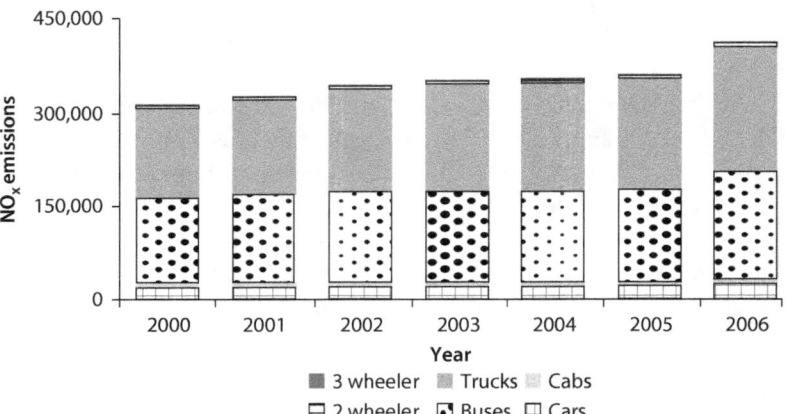

Figure 5.5 Suspended Particulate Matter from Vehicle Fleet

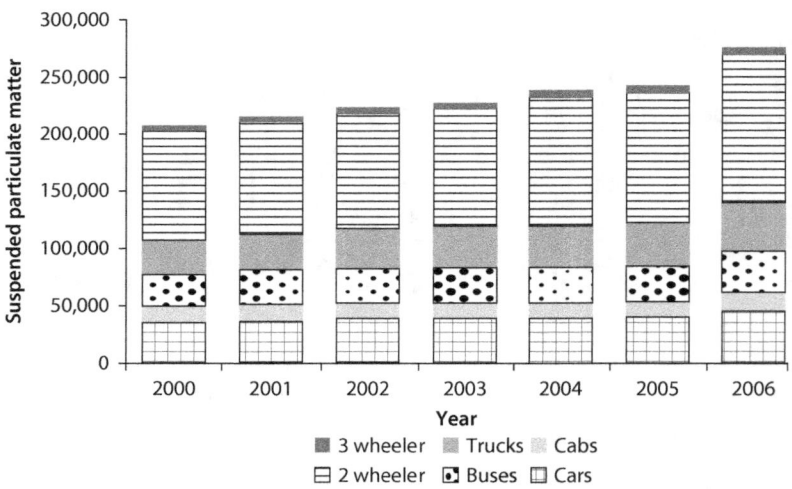

the World Health Organization (WHO) (World Bank 2011). Analytical work based on research findings by Pope and Dockery (2006) provides evidence that the most important ambient air contamination problem to be addressed in Pakistan is PM, especially fine and ultrafine particles (Pope and Dockery 2006).[3]

Data regarding urban air quality in Pakistan are scarce, dispersed, and not fully reliable (table 5.2). Comparisons between the annual mean concentrations of PM$_{10}$ in Pakistan's main cities and those of other urban centers of the world must be made with caution because of the complexities and challenges associated with the measurement of these pollutants. In many cases, cities have a monitoring network in which concentrations vary widely from one station to another or from one time period to the next, and thus the mean value may not accurately reflect the severity of air pollution. The latest available data for Pakistan were

Table 5.1 Comparison of Pakistan's Draft National Air Quality Standards with WHO, EU, and U.S. Air Quality Guidelines

Pollutant	Time-weighted average	Pakistan ambient air quality standards		WHO air quality guidelines[a]	EU ambient air quality standards	U.S. ambient air quality standards
		Effective 2010	Effective 2013			
Suspended particulate matter	Annual average[b]	400 µg/m³	360 µg/m³	—	—	—
	24 hours[c]	550 µg/m³	500 µg/m³	—	—	—
Particulate matter (PM₁₀)	Annual average[b]	200 µg/m³	120 µg/m³	20 µg/m³	40 µg/m³	—
	24 hours[c]	250 µg/m³	150 µg/m³	50 µg/m³	50 µg/m³	150 µg/m³
Particulate matter (PM₂.₅)	Annual average[b]	25 µg/m³	15 µg/m³	10 µg/m³	25 µg/m³	15 µg/m³
	24 hours[c]	40 µg/m³	35 µg/m³	25 µg/m³	—	35 µg/m³
	1 hour	25 µg/m³	15 µg/m³	1 µg/m³	—	—
Lead (Pb)	Annual average[b]	1.5 µg/m³	1 µg/m³	0.5 µg/m³	0.5 µg/m³	—
	24 hours[c]	2 µg/m³	1.5 µg/m³	—	—	—
Sulfur dioxide (SO₂)	Annual average[b]	80 µg/m³	80 µg/m³	—	—	85.8 µg/m³
	24 hours[c]	120 µg/m³	120 µg/m³	20 µg/m³	125 µg/m³	—
Nitrogen dioxide (NO₂)	Annual average[b]	40 µg/m³	40 µg/m³	40 µg/m³	40 µg/m³	100 µg/m³
	24 hours[c]	80 µg/m³	80 µg/m³	—	200 µg/m³	85.8 µg/m³
Nitric oxide (NO)	Annual average[b]	40 µg/m³	40 µg/m³	—	—	—
	24 hours[c]	40 µg/m³	40 µg/m³	—	—	—
Carbon monoxide	8 hours[c]	5 mg/m³	5 mg/m³	—	10 mg/m³	10 mg/m³
	1 hour	10 mg/m³	10 mg/m³	—	—	40 µg/m³

Source: Pakistan Environmental Protection Agency and World Bank 2011.
Note: — = not available. EU = European Union; WHO = World Health Organization.
a. Guidelines only given if the averaging period is identical.
b. Annual arithmetic mean of minimum 104 measurements in a year, taken twice a week every 24 hours at uniform intervals.
c. Twenty-four-hours/8 hours values should be met 98 percent of the year. It may be exceeded 2 percent of the time, but not on consecutive days.

Table 5.2 Estimated Health Impacts of Urban Air Pollution from Particulate Matter in Pakistan

Health categories	New cases	Total annual costs (Rs billion)
Premature mortality	21,791	59–62
Chronic bronchitis	7,825	0.06
Hospital admissions	81,312	0.28
Emergency room visits/outpatient hospital visits	1,595,080	0.80
Restricted activity days	81,541,893	2.06
Lower respiratory illness in children	4,924,148	0.84
Total		62–65

Source: World Bank 2006a.

collected by means of a recently installed Air Quality Monitoring Network provided by Japan's International Cooperation Agency (JICA). Problems, such as the high concentration of desert dust during summer time, contribute to the misinterpretation of collected data and their attribution to different polluting sources. Furthermore, the concentration of $PM_{2.5}$, one of the most harmful pollutants for human health, is currently only being monitored infrequently, and needs to be included in a continuous monitoring regime.

As of 2011, there was no systematic monitoring of exhaust emissions or ambient air quality in large urban centers or in industrial clusters. From 2007 to 2010, the Japanese government supported the government establishing an air quality-monitoring network in the main cities (JICA 2010). However, administrative and budget problems have disturbed the functioning of the monitoring network. By early 2010, restricted budget support had been reported for the JICA-funded stations, which affected the availability of trained personnel, maintenance parts, and consumables. There is no quality control or quality assurance or auditing of the monitoring and evaluation program to verify the accuracy of results. Furthermore, the data that are generated have not been used to identify or prioritize interventions.

Environmental regulation in Pakistan is lax compared to most other countries, and regulations tend to be confusing and enforced erratically. In the 2004–05 World Economic Forum rankings, Pakistan was the worst-ranked country with regard to clarity and stability of environmental regulations and the second-to-worst country with regard to stringency of regulations. Lack of business considerations to environmental issues has increased pollution levels in key industries (table 5.3) (Lopez-Claros et al. 2005, 616–17).

By mid-2012, the organizations charged with the implementation of the existing legal and regulatory framework had ambitious mandates but insufficient staff, small budgets, low political prestige, and high staff turnover rates. As a result, the enforcement of mandatory regulations is lax, and stricter penalties that are sometimes available in the laws are almost never imposed. This is due to, among other reasons, a deficient regulatory framework, a poor air quality-monitoring system, and the lack of technical capacity to provide sound evidence of infractions (World Bank 2011).

Table 5.3 Environment and Competitiveness in Pakistan, 2004–08

	2004–05 Out of 104 countries	2005–06 Out of 117 countries	2006–07 Out of 125 countries	2007–08 Out of 131 countries
Stringency of environmental regulations	103	93	77	68
Clarity and stability of regulations	104	94	65	—
Extent of government-mandated environmental reporting	75	95	—	—
Importance of environment in business planning	—	51	—	—
Protection of ecosystems by business	—	104	95	—
Prevalence of corporate environmental reporting	85	74	—	—
Prevalence of environmental management systems	24	—	—	—
Prevalence of environmental marketing	90	—	—	—
Importance of environment management for companies	102	—	—	—
Importance of environment in business planning	84	51	—	—
Prioritization of energy efficiency	94	43	—	—
Compliance with environmental international agreements	97	—	—	—
Prevalence of socially responsible investing	103	—	—	—

Sources: Table prepared by consultant Luis Miglino based on Lopez-Claros et al. 2005 and data from the World Economic Forum (2006, 2007, 2008, and 2009).
Note: — = not available.

The organizational structure of the Ministry of Environment, which was dissolved in 2011, did not respond to the magnitude and complexity of air quality issues in Pakistan. The Pakistan Environmental Protection Agency (Pak-EPA), responsible for implementing the Pakistan Environmental Protection Act in the national territory, does not have the necessary resources to carry out its mandates with regard to air quality management. A broad range of environmental functions, many related to air quality management, was recently delegated to provincial environmental authorities as a result of the 18th Constitutional Amendment. None of the national or provincial authorities has sufficient means with regard to trained staff and budget for air pollution control (World Bank 2011).

Pakistan lags behind other regional countries in the implementation of activities to manage air quality. A review of air quality management interventions in Bangladesh, China, India, and Sri Lanka confirms the gaps and weaknesses in Pakistan's implementation of air pollution control interventions. The lag is especially apparent in the essential air quality measurement pillars—setting, defining, and enforcing standards—that form the basis for so many other targeted interventions, including constituency building. These regional initiatives plus international good practices might become benchmarks for a Pakistan Clean Air Program. International experiences confirm that regional (and global) air quality management solutions exist and have been implemented elsewhere by governments facing challenges and problems similar to those confronting Pakistan (World Bank 2011).

The economic damages caused by PM emissions are higher in Pakistan than in the rest of South Asia. In addition, these costs have increased during the last years, in a period when countries such as India, Sri Lanka, Bhutan, and Nepal have taken steps to improve urban air quality (figure 5.6). The contrast is even starker when Pakistan is compared to other developed and developing countries that have introduced measures to reduce urban air pollution.

Poor environmental regulation has severe consequences for Pakistan. These are, among others, poor ambient quality (especially in urban areas), further destruction of valuable natural resources, and a disproportionate burden of disease on poor and vulnerable communities, especially women and children, and an excessive judicialization of the environmental permitting process (World Bank 2007, 2011).

Modernization of the trucking sector as well as a modal shift from the trucking sector to railways sector (which will be discussed in further detail later on in this report) will help reduce the number of trucks on the road, thereby contributing to reduced air pollution as well as noise pollution. The main objective of modernizing the trucking sector is to replace polluting and underpowered small trucks with a larger more modern fleet that are fuel-efficient. A multimodal freight transport system, in which rail covers distances longer than 500 kilometers and is complemented by trucking at the origin and destination, will reduce the number of long-distance trucks on the road. This reduces emission of air pollutants by trucks in urban and rural areas, and improves ambient air quality with beneficial impacts to public health.

Figure 5.6 Particulate Emission Damage in Selected Asian Countries, 2001 and 2007

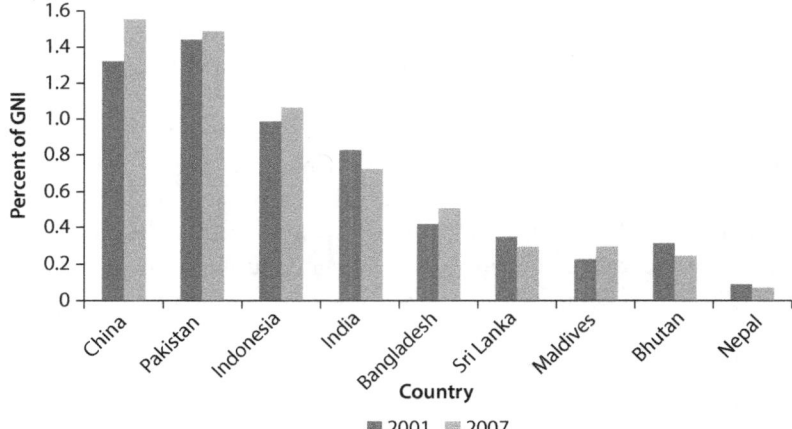

Source: Clean Air Initiative 2010. See, for example, "Clean Air Initiative for Asian Cities (CAI-Asia)." http://www.aecen.org/sites/default/files/forums/2010/CAI%20Asia-%20GOZUN.pdf.
Note: GNI = gross national income.

Noise Pollution[4]

The recognition of noise as a potential serious health hazard as opposed to a nuisance is a recent development. The health effects of excessive and loud noise exposure are now considered an increasingly important public health concern. Besides its harmful effects on the ears, noise can cause sleep disturbances and interfere with speech. Excessive noise levels may permanently or temporarily damage ears, and lead to an increase in aggressive behavior and other psychiatric conditions. Analysis by WHO confirms that persistent noise stress increases the risk of cardiovascular disorders, including high blood pressure and ischemic heart disease. Babisch (2006) provides a meta-analysis that derives a common risk curve for the relationship between road traffic noise and myocardial infarction incidence.

There are no national standards for determining noise limits for residential, industrial, and commercial areas, or silence zones in Pakistan. The National Environmental Quality Standards (NEQS) for Motor Vehicle Exhaust and Noise apply only to noise emanating from motor vehicles, and there are no standards for noise generated from trains, airplanes, airports, or industrial/construction activities. Road traffic noise is a major source of noise pollution in urban areas in Pakistan.

Noise levels in most urban locations are well above the WHO recommended limits.[5] According to Pak-EPA, although some random surveys have been carried out in the last decade, there is no national monitoring system of environmental noise levels in cities. Table 5.4 presents the results of six surveys carried out between 2001 and 2003; the findings of these tests indicate that the noise levels in most urban locations are well above the WHO recommended limits.

Table 5.4 Noise Levels in Major Cities in Pakistan

City	Maximum recorded noise level dB(A)	Minimum recorded noise level dB(A)	Average
Gujranwala (2003)	100.0	41.0	72.5
Faisalabad (2003)	100.0	47.0	72.0
Islamabad (2002)	104.5	47.0	72.5
Rawalpindi (2002)	108.5	48.0	72.5
Karachi (2002)	88.9	62.4	76.5
Peshawar (2001)	78.5	68.2	86.0

Source: Pak-EPA 2005.
Note: Number in parentheses indicates the year of the survey. dB(A) = A-weighted decibels.

By November 2006, in Rawalpindi (five locations) and Islamabad (three locations), the daily maximum and daily equivalents were higher than the maximum allowed limit of 85 decibels (A) of the NEQS for motor vehicle noise at 7.5 meters from the source (Pak-EPA 2006). The highest noise level of 98 decibels (A) was found near the Pirwadhai general bus stand, from which intercity and intracity heavy traffic operates all the time (24 hours). The daily equivalent level for this location was 97.1 decibels (A), well above the NEQS limit. The second highest noise level location, 97 decibels (A), was found near Choare Chowk, at Peshawar Road, in Rawalpindi. Data from Sindh indicate that a significant number of urban locations face continuous noise levels well above the WHO-used threshold of 55 decibels (A) above which noise levels cause cardiovascular disease and cognitive impairment in children, and a threshold of 45 decibels (A) above which noise levels cause sleep disturbance and annoyance (Larsen and Skjelvik 2012).

Analytical work carried out by the World Bank in Punjab found that, in 2008, the mean estimated annual cost of noise pollution in the province was Rs 8 billion (figure 5.7). Health costs were mostly associated with ischemic heart disease. Total disability-adjusted life years loss is broken down into two separate losses: (i) mortality and morbidity losses from ischemic heart disease (80 percent), and (ii) hearing loss (20 percent). Annual new cases of ischemic heart disease and the mortality associated with it and annual hearing loss in DALYs from noise pollution was calculated to be 26,619.[6]

The implementation of the new trucking policy that modernizes the trucking sector and upgrades road infrastructure will reduce noise levels in urban areas. The substitution of the existing old, poorly maintained, and noisy trucks for newer models that are more fuel-efficient would reduce the noise emanating from them. Moreover, the upgrading of road infrastructure and the construction of roads with smooth-surfaced pavement would reduce noises when truck tires come in contact with pavement.

Another study carried out by the World Bank found that road traffic noise had a cost of Rs 25.8 billion in the province of Sindh. Road traffic noise in cities with a population of more than 100,000 in Sindh is the cause of 13–19 percent of ischemic heart disease mortality and 16–21 percent of cerebrovascular mortality in these cities. In addition, 31–43 percent of children (6–15 years of age) have

Figure 5.7 Annual Cost of Environmental Health Effects

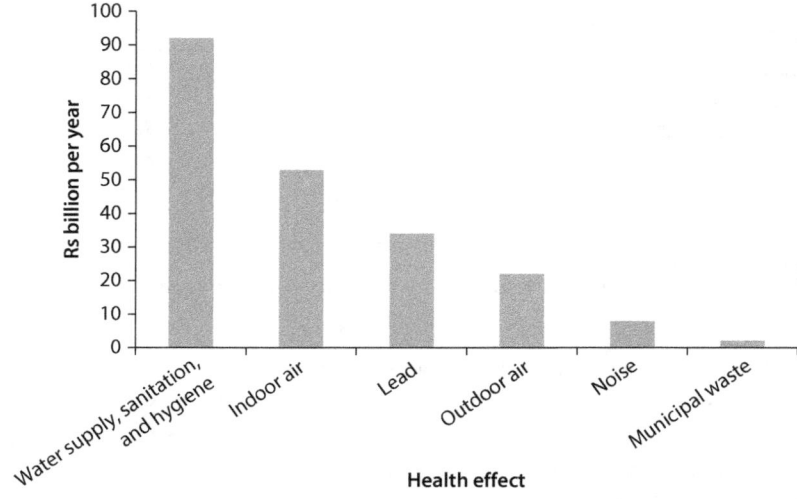

Source: Larsen and Skjelvik 2012.

noise-induced cognitive impairment, and 10–13 percent of the population is highly sleep-disturbed as a result of noise in these cities. About 58 percent of the cost of road traffic noise is associated with morbidity, while the remaining 42 percent is caused by premature mortality.

Road Safety

According to estimates by WHO, in 2007 the total number of road fatalities in Pakistan equaled 41,494. In relative terms, this implies a rate of 25.3 deaths per 100,000 inhabitants. In the rest of South Asia, the observed rates range from 12.6 to 18.3 (table 5.5). In contrast, the observed rates in industrialized countries range between 5 and 10 fatalities per 100,000 inhabitants (figure 5.8). Pakistan's rate is also higher than many other developing and middle-income countries around the world.

Cross-country differences in road traffic fatality rates can be associated with a series of explanatory factors such as traffic density, the quality of roads, and road density (figure 5.9). A first look at the relationship between traffic density and fatality rates shows that industrialized countries manage to keep low levels of mortality despite the high number of vehicles on the road. In contrast, in developing countries like Pakistan, relatively low levels of vehicle density do not necessarily bring the number of road fatalities down. A plausible explanation for that might be found in the quality of roads. The share of paved roads shows a quite significant negative correlation with the level of road fatalities. However, Pakistan suffers from very high road mortality rates despite ranking among the mid-upper countries in the share of paved roads. The level of road density, measured as the

Priority Environmental Issues Associated with Freight Transport

Table 5.5 Road Traffic Deaths, Population, and Road Traffic Death Rate in the South Asia Region

	Road traffic deaths	Population (2007)	Road traffic death rate per 100,000 population
Bangladesh	20,038	158,664,959	12.6
Bhutan	95	658,479	14.4
India	196,445	1,169,015,509	16.8
Maldives	56	305,556	18.3
Nepal	4,245	28,195,994	15.1
Pakistan	41,494	163,902,405	25.3
Sri Lanka	2,603	19,299,190	13.5

Source: WHO 2009.

Figure 5.8 Estimated Number of Road Traffic Deaths per 100,000 Inhabitants, 2007

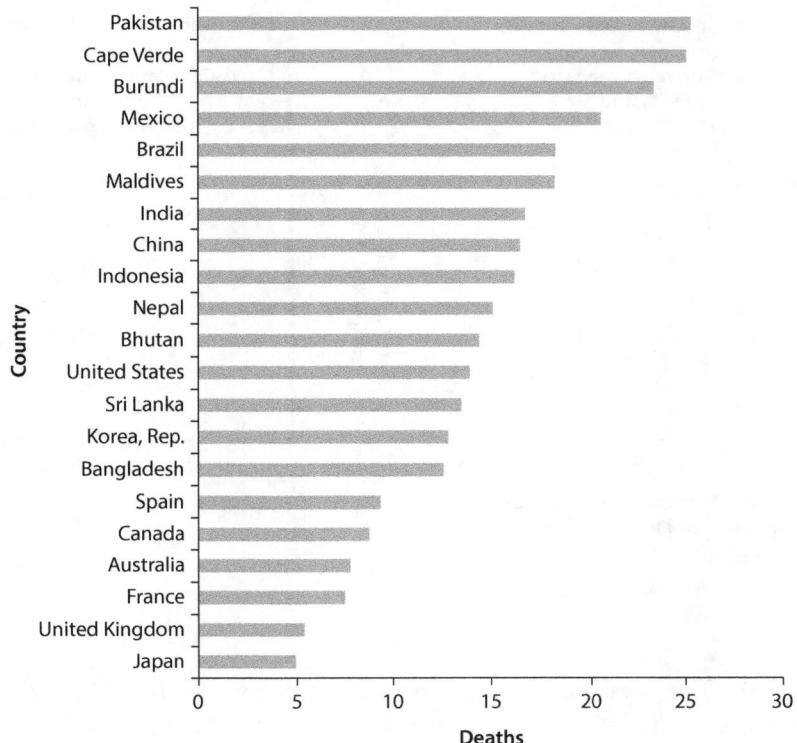

Source: WHO 2009.

rate between total road length and the overall national surface is a highly significant explanatory variable of fatality rates. However, when examining only the subset of low- and middle-income countries the simple correlation is almost insignificant.

According to official data, the total number of road accidents, fatalities, persons injured, and severity of accidents seems to have remained steady from 2000 to

Figure 5.9 Correlation between Total Road Traffic Deaths and Several Explanatory Factors

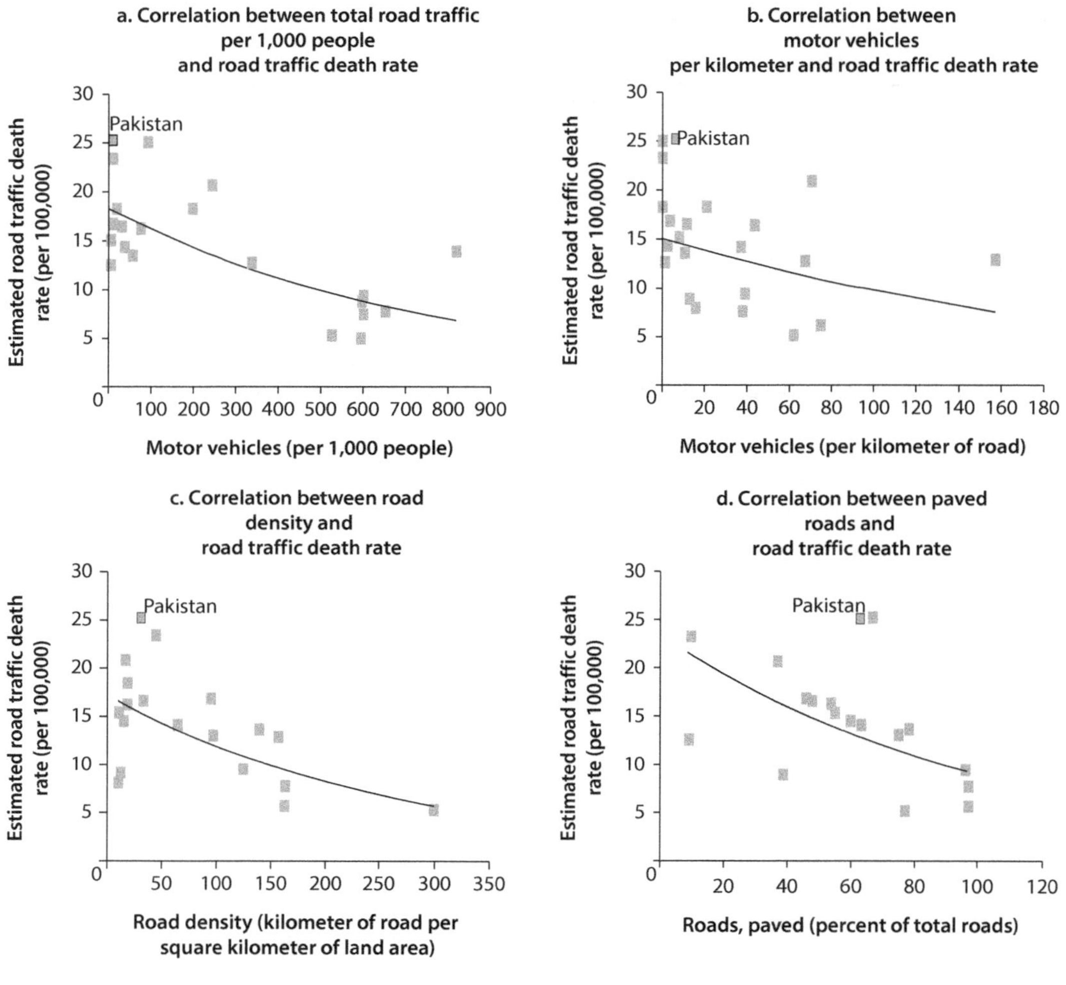

a. Correlation between total road traffic per 1,000 people and road traffic death rate

b. Correlation between motor vehicles per kilometer and road traffic death rate

c. Correlation between road density and road traffic death rate

d. Correlation between paved roads and road traffic death rate

Source: WHO 2009.

2010.[7] The total number of reported accidents was 10,644 in 2008, which implies a cumulative growth rate of 10.2 percent with respect to 1998. However, the general trend over the last decade has been rather stable with around 10,000 accidents occurring a year. The same pattern can be observed for the total number of fatalities, which from 1998–2008 has been fluctuating around an average of 5,200 (5,622 in 2008; figure 5.10). Since the traffic growth rate has been increasing over this period, the accidents per million vehicle-kilometer of travel and per 1,000 vehicles have been decreasing. However, available data are not fully reliable and there is evidence of significant under-reporting.

The traffic density rate has experienced a dramatic increase from 14.8 vehicles per kilometer of road in 1998 to 36.4 vehicles in 2008. This is because the

Figure 5.10 Number of Road Accidents, Fatalities, and Injuries in Pakistan, 1998–2008

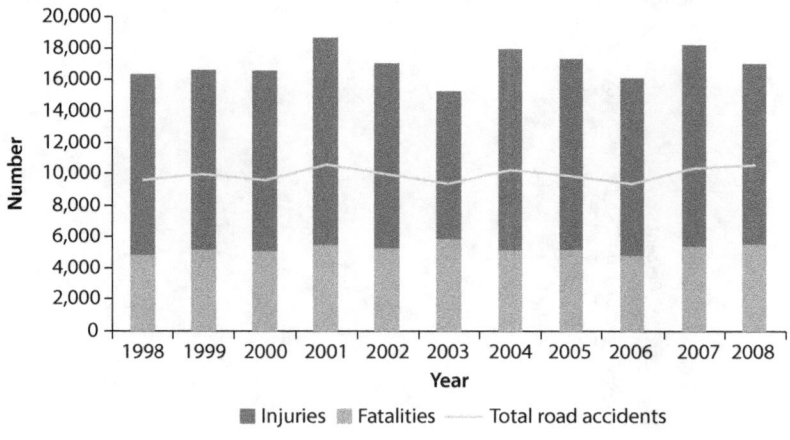

Source: GoP 2009a.

Figure 5.11 Evolution of Total Accidents, Road Length, Vehicles on Road, and Population in Pakistan, 1998–2008

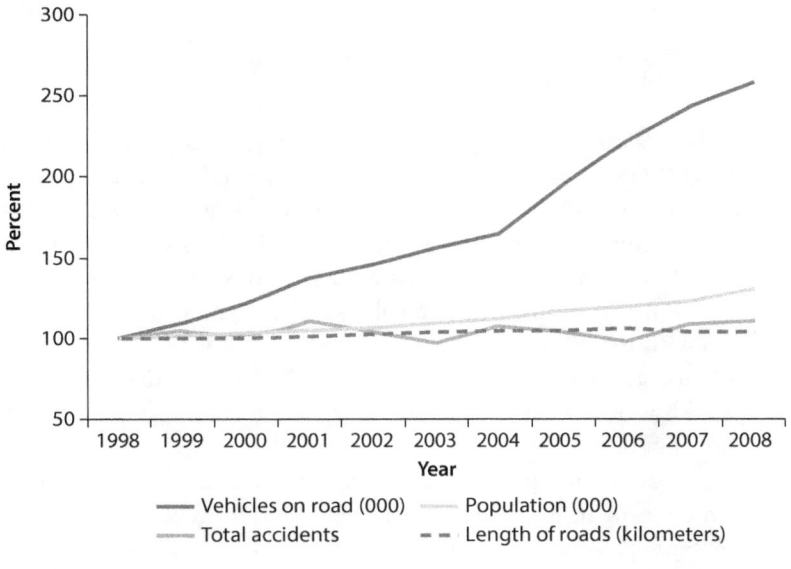

Source: GoP 2009a.
Note: Baseline 100% corresponds to 2008.

number of vehicles circulating has grown during recent years (from 3,651,000 in 1998 to 9,413,800 in 2008) while the overall road length has increased by only 4 percent (figure 5.11). This outcome, together with the high population growth in Pakistan, has led to a significant increase in the number of road passengers (70.8 percent cumulative growth rate for the 1998–2008 period) and accidents (see figure 5.12).

Figure 5.12 Evolution of Accidents per Inhabitant, Rate of Paved Roads, Traffic Density, and Road Passengers in Pakistan, 1998–2008

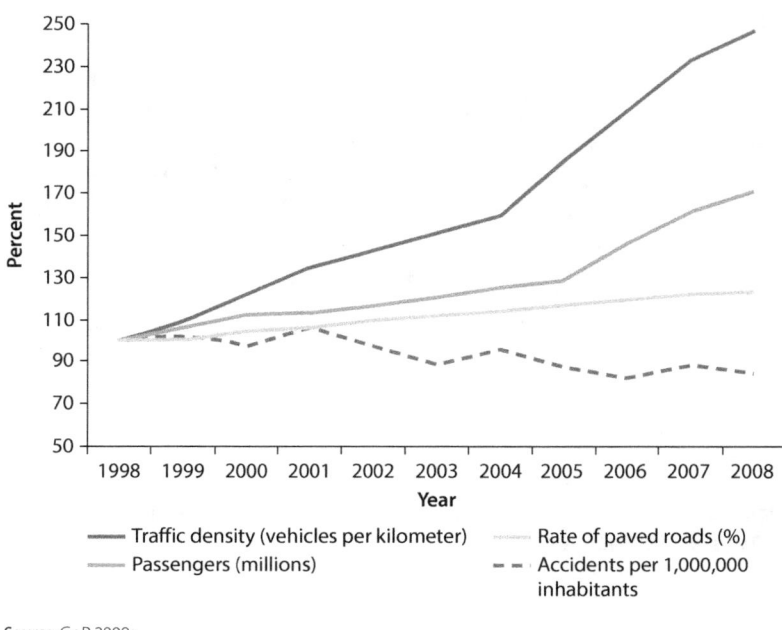

Source: GoP 2009a.
Note: Baseline 100% corresponds to 1998.

Khyber Pakhtunkhwa shows the highest incidence of accidents and fatalities per 100,000 inhabitants (figure 5.13). The regional disparities in the number of accidents per 100,000 inhabitants are quite significant, ranging from 4.7 in Sindh to 13.6 in Khyber Pakhtunkhwa (see figure 5.13). However, the relative number of fatalities is rather homogeneous across regions (4.4 in Khyber Pakhtunkhwa and 3.2 in Sindh as the extreme values). There are also significant regional disparities with regard to severity of accidents. Sindh is the region with the highest rate of fatal accidents, as well as in the number of fatalities per accident. Khyber Pakhtunkhwa is the least hazardous province in Pakistan with regard to accident severity (figure 5.14).

In addition to pain and suffering, road accidents generate significant economic costs. In Karachi, pedestrians and motorcyclists represented 43 and 32 percent of accident fatalities, respectively (Ahmed and Sánchez-Triana 2008). The limited information that is available suggests that a significant share of road accidents and fatalities in Pakistan involved a truck, even though these vehicles comprise only around 3 percent of the vehicle fleet (World Bank 2006b). The record for trucks might be better than buses and cars, but it is still extremely poor. The cost of road accidents in Sindh is estimated to represent around 1.15 percent of the province's GDP (Larsen and Skjelvik 2012; Strukova et al. 2012).

The pain, suffering, and economic costs caused by road accidents may be significantly more severe than official estimates suggest. Several studies carried

Figure 5.13 Number of Accidents and Fatalities per 100,000 Inhabitants in Pakistani Provinces, 2007–08

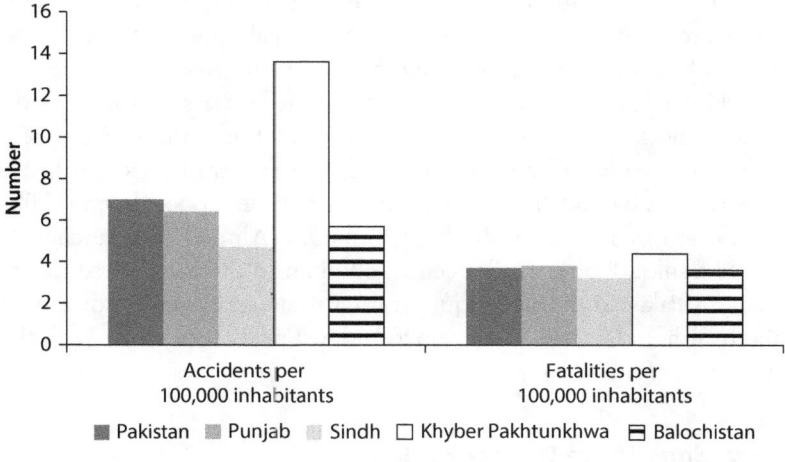

Source: GoP 2009a.

Figure 5.14 Percentage of Fatal Accidents and Number of Deaths per Accident in Pakistani Provinces, 2007–08

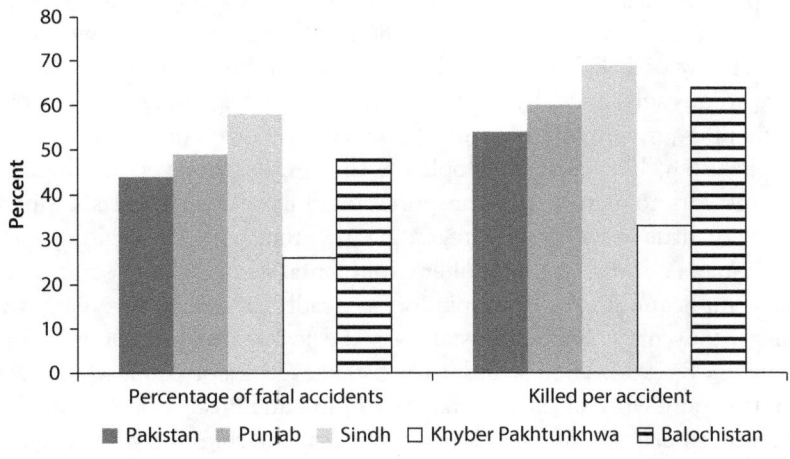

Source: GoP 2009a.

out in Karachi indicate that the actual number of deaths and injury caused by road accidents may be two or more times higher than those reported in police recordings. A study conducted under SEPSA estimated that in 2009, in the province of Sindh, road accidents (associated with all kinds of vehicles) caused 1,800–2,200 deaths, 5,400–6,600 cases of permanent disabilities, 59,000–105,000 other serious injuries, and 423,000–474,000 minor injuries. The cost stemming from these accidents is equal to Rs 42.6 billion per year. The largest costs are those related to permanent disability (Rs 23.4 billion), fatalities (Rs 9 billion), and serious injuries (Rs 7.7 billion) (Larsen and Skjelvik 2012).

Poor road conditions, inadequate driving practices, and poor vehicle maintenance are key variables affecting road safety. Pakistan does not have a solid information base on road safety, including the main causes behind its high accident rate. However, available reports suggest that key risk factors include poor road quality and lack of appropriate signage. In addition, the trucking sector is likely to be involved in a disproportionately high number of accidents because of practices such as overloading, poor condition of trucks, poor driving skills, and driver exhaustion as a result of driving long hours (Ahmed and Sánchez-Triana 2008; World Bank 2006b). Until recently, obtaining a driver's license to drive a freight truck in Pakistan did not require formal training or testing of the driver's skills and health. In fact, the process involved just a few formalities with the provincial authorities (GoP 2007).

Hazardous Waste Transportation

By stimulating trade and economic growth, freight transport reforms will contribute to the acceleration of the industrialization process in Pakistan and also increase the use of many types of chemicals and other hazardous products being transported. Many industrial sectors (such as leather processing, and pulp and paper) are heavily dependent on many chemicals during production, and some of them are very dangerous to public health. According to Oggero et al. (2005) in a study of 1,932 accidents that occurred in the world during the transport of hazardous substances by road and rail from the beginning of the 20th century to July 2004, roughly 63 percent of accidents occurred on roads.

Pakistan, like most developing countries, has not yet developed a national framework to manage the transportation of hazardous materials. Moreover, there is very little reliable data regarding the transport of hazardous materials in Pakistan. Poor management of environmental waste leads to serious environmental implications. An example of a deadly accident involving transport of hazardous materials in Pakistan was the leakage of poisonous chlorine gas on January 8, 1997. The Hazardous Substances Rules of 2003, which were adopted in the framework of the Pakistan Environmental Protection Act of 1997, regulate the transportation of hazardous substances. The rules are very general, and while they do cover aspects such as packing and labeling of hazardous substances, general safety precautions, and notification of major accidents, they do not provide specific details on how they should be implemented. The analysis of the transport of hazardous material found

- Overall lack of regulations pertaining to the transport of hazardous materials;
- Absence of standards for vehicles used to transport hazardous materials;
- Outdated information on new chemicals/substances that are transported on Pakistan's roads and railways; no information on who should be responsible for periodically updating the list of substances;

- Legal responsibilities are unclear, and there is poor institutional capacity to regulate the transport of hazardous materials;
- Lack of maps of the most traveled routes in Pakistan used in the transport of hazardous materials, or identification of the most dangerous products transported on them;
- Lack of resources to enforce regulations pertaining to the transport of hazardous materials; and
- Weak institutional capacity of National Highways & Motorway Police, urban traffic police agencies, or local fire departments, which do not have the knowledge, training, or resources required to enforce the necessary regulations regarding the transportation of hazardous materials.

Climate Change

Pakistan's emissions of greenhouse gases (GHGs) are relatively small, but have been growing and are anticipated to increase at high rates over the coming years. In 2007–08, the transport sector contributed to 21 percent of the energy sector's emissions (GoP 2011).[8] Most of the sector emissions originate from road transportation, which consumed about half of the country's total petroleum products during 1997–98 to 2006–07. GHG emissions from railways were only 0.17 percent of total transport carbon emissions in 2006–07. Such minor contribution is a result of both rail's small percentage in freight and passenger transport, as well the differences in emissions between road and rail. Road transport emits an average 0.17 $TgCO_2eq$ per billion ton-kilometers, compared with railway transport emissions of 0.02 $TgCO_2eq$ per billion ton-kilometers.

Estimates based on GDP future trends suggest that transport demand for freight will increase steadily in the coming years and will hence increase GHG emissions. Table 5.6 summarizes projections of freight transport demand and expected GHG emissions, under the assumption that the road sector remains the main mode of freight transport. The projections are based on emission factors from the United States, and therefore, should be considered as a conservative scenario. The results clearly indicate that in future years, the road sector will generate the lion's share of emissions. For example, in 2030–31, total $TgCO_2eq$ emissions for road transport are anticipated to be 90.17, compared to 3.05 for rail.

Table 5.6 Projections of Freight Transport Demand and GHG Emissions

Year	Freight, million ton-kilometer			$TgCO_2eq$		
	Total	Road	Rail	Total	Road	Rail
2010–11	207,881	197,107	10,774	33.7	33.51	0.22
2015–16	293,268	254,086	39,184	43.98	43.19	0.78
2025–26	530,037	412,976	117,061	72.55	70.21	2.34
2030–31	682,787	530,433	152,354	93.22	90.17	3.05

An assessment of three alternative scenarios on road/rail mode split shows the following:

- If the current split mode in inland freight transport remains (96 percent road and 4 percent freight), annual emissions will amount to 48 TgCO$_2$eq by 2025. Diesel consumption (billions liters per year) would be 5.97 by 2025 (see figures 5.15 and 5.16).
- If the current split mode in inland freight continues to favor road (86.7 percent road and 13.3 percent rail)[9] annual emissions will be reduced to 43.1 TgCO$_2$eq by 2025. Diesel consumption (billions liters per year) would be 5.5 by 2025.
- If the current split mode for inland freight changes to 70 percent road and 30 percent rail, annual emissions will be reduced to 36.8 TgCO$_2$eq by year 2025.

Figure 5.15 Estimated GHG Emissions (TgCO$_2$eq) by 2025 under Different Policy Options

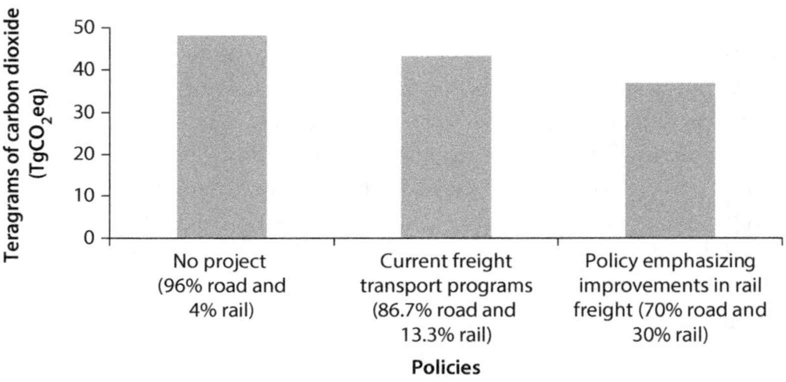

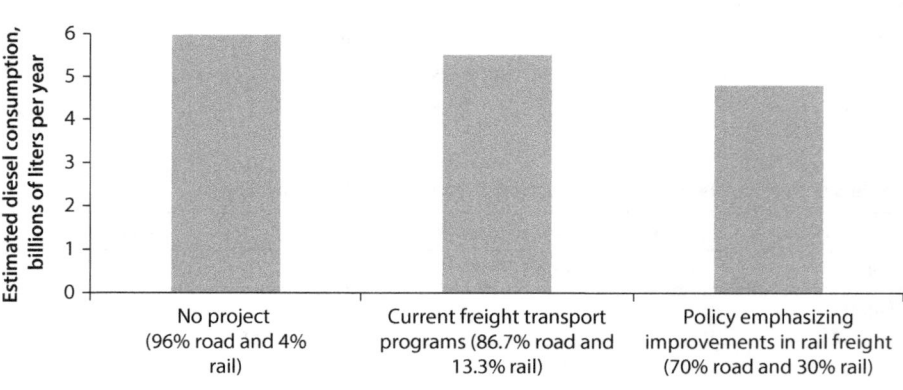

Note: For a detailed description of the methodologies used to estimate emission of GHG and diesel fuel consumption, see Miglino 2011; see also UIC 2011 and Loubinoux 2011.

Figure 5.16 Estimated Diesel Consumption (Billions of Liters per Year) by 2025 under Different Policy Options

Figure 5.17 Average Environmental Costs of Different Transport Modes

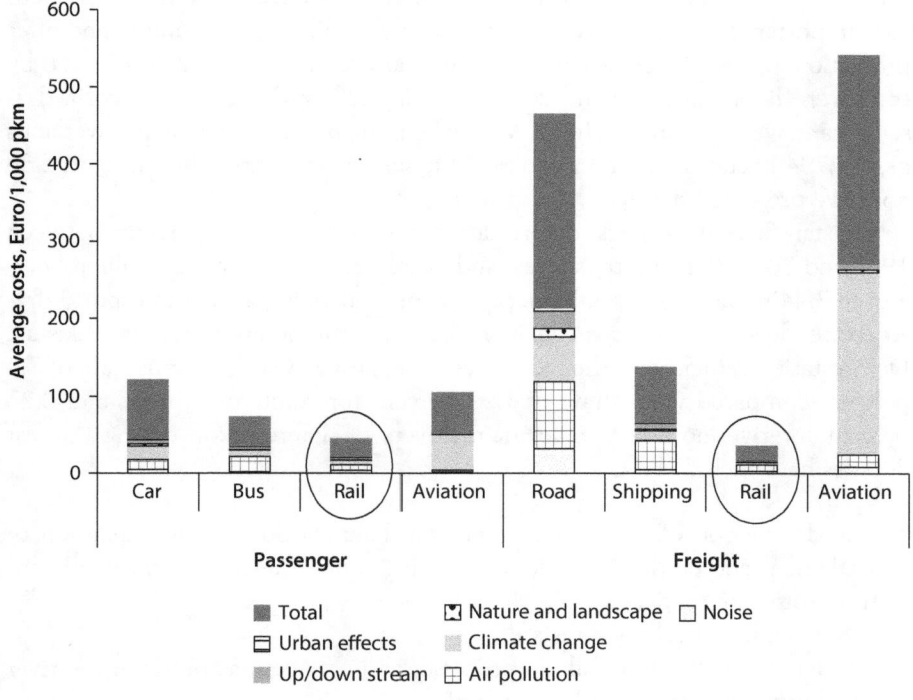

Source: INFRAS 2004.

(23.3 percent reduction or a reduction of about 11.2 million tons of GHG discharged into the atmosphere). Diesel consumption (billions liters per year) would be 4.7 by 2025.

These results indicate that shifting toward investments in rail most greatly reduces GHG emissions and diesel consumption.

The above finding is in line with studies that indicate that rail has the lowest environmental impact with regard to air pollution, CO_2 emissions, safety, capacity, and noise, relative to other modes of transport (figure 5.17). Transport accounts for over 50 percent of world consumption of fossil fuels; within transport, rail accounts for 2 percent of CO_2 emissions, and road accounts for 73 percent. The study finds that relative to road, rail is a lower carbon transport mode and has fewer environmental impacts. Rail is also considered a safer transport mode and a very resource-efficient mass transport system.

Habitat Fragmentation and Natural Resource Degradation

Pakistan's ecosystems already face significant threats and these could be aggravated by direct and indirect induced growth, and cumulative impacts associated with the expansion of transport infrastructure. Forests, wetlands, and other ecosystems are home to an important biodiversity and provide a range of ecosystem services that are crucial for Pakistan's economy. Wetlands are particularly important to Pakistan, as they provide livelihoods to communities and offer protection against floods, which recurrently affect the country, as evidenced by the severe floods of 2010 and 2011. In total, 220 wetlands are categorized as significant wetlands in the Indus Watershed, including 42 protected wetlands (1,479,794 hectares) and four additional Ramsar sites (60,646 hectares) that do not have protected status.

Pakistan faces the highest deforestation rate of Asia, at 2.1 percent. Between 1992 and 2001, the country's forestland decreased from over 4.24 million hectares to 3.44 million hectares. Induced and cumulative impacts of transport infrastructure development have been associated with deforestation in Pakistan. Deforestation is highest in the Indus Delta mangroves, with an annual rate of 2.3 percent, compared with a rate of 1.99 percent for coniferous forests and 0.23 percent for riverine forests. The main drivers of deforestation during the last decades have included

- The destruction of, or encroachment on, habitats due to the expansion of settlement and cultivation fields, decreasing water availability, and flood control protection services;
- Deforestation of gallery forests;
- Interference with natural flood processes and connections between the river and natural lagoons and other wetlands;
- Pollution of rivers and streams from untreated sewage discharges and untreated industrial effluents; and
- Lack of appropriate management plans and skilled personnel.

Currently, there is no clear policy to arrest deforestation, much of which is driven by governmental initiatives.

The potential effects of the expansion of transport infrastructure on ecosystems include habitat fragmentation, wetland destruction, and induced increases in deforestation, as roads facilitate access to these natural resources. Areas that would be particularly susceptible to increased deforestation include the Indus Watershed and its tributaries, as well as its affluents' gallery forests and wetlands. In the past, wetlands have also been drained and destroyed to build dykes.

Degradation and destruction of these ecosystems would have significant implications, including heightening Pakistan's vulnerability to extreme weather events. The floods that affected Pakistan in 2010 alone caused damages estimated at US$8.74–US$10.85 billion (ADB et al. 2010), while those of 2011 also resulted in a significant loss of lives, property, and assets. While a natural phenomenon initiated the floods, anthropogenic interventions exacerbated their impact, particularly as destruction and degradation of natural ecosystems reduced the capacity of natural vegetation to provide flood protection services. In addition, the development of settlements and croplands in flood plains and riverbeds, along with sole reliance on embankments and other types of inadequate flood protection measures, created the conditions for the human tragedy.

The effective and efficient use of environmental impact assessment (EIA) could inform decision making and identify alternatives to reduce or mitigate the negative effects of transport infrastructure development, including those related to habitat fragmentation or deforestation. EIA was first introduced in Pakistan in 1983 and was later strengthened under the Pakistan Environmental Protection Act of 1997 and the EIA regulations of 2000. Despite its use for more than 20 years in Pakistan, EIA still faces a number of shortcomings, including problems in screening and scoping, insufficient public participation, poor quality of environmental assessment reports, and weak capacities of environmental authorities to review environmental reports and monitor compliance with the conditions of the environmental authorization (Nadeem and Hameed 2008). A 2008 review found that "EIA is used presently as a project justification tool rather than as a project planning tool to contribute to achieving sustainable development" (Nadeem and Hameed 2008, 562).

To summarize the analysis presented in this chapter, improvements in Pakistan's freight transport sector are likely to have both positive and negative impacts on environmental indicators (see table 5.7). Although some of the potential effects can be classified as beneficial or adverse, others can be either one, depending on specific project characteristics or operational conditions. As an example, better designed and constructed roads might increase average road speeds, reduce transit time, and decrease the total number of accidents, but increase the fatality rate of accidents due to the increase in the average speed.

Table 5.7 Potential Environmental and Social Effects on Priority Environmental Issues

Priority issue	Potential positive and negative effects of freight transport programs
Air quality and noise	• Reduction in the emission of air pollutants by trucks in urban and rural areas • Improved ambient air quality and noise levels in urban areas with beneficial impacts on public health
Transport of hazardous materials	• Improved response capacity to accidents (prevention and management) • Reduced number of accidents and spills (road and railway) • Reduction in the number of injuries/fatalities and property losses • Improved environmental quality near ports, airports, and along transport corridors
Road and railroad safety	• Better road safety conditions • Reduction in the rates of road accidents • Potential increase in the rate of road accident fatalities due to increase in average speeds • Better railway traffic safety, particularly at critical track-crossing points
Climate change	• Reduction in the emission of air pollutants and greenhouse gases due to the reduction in (i) number of trucks on the roads, (ii) traffic gridlock and accidents, and (iii) use of fossil fuels • Increased country adaptation capacity to climate change
Habitat fragmentation and natural resource degradation	• Potential habitat fragmentation, wetland destruction, and induced deforestation • Increased vulnerability to natural disasters

Notes

1. PM is the term for airborne particles, including dust, dirt, soot, smoke, and liquid droplets. Particles can be suspended in the air for long periods. Some particles are directly emitted into the air. They come from a variety of sources such as vehicle exhaust, factories, construction sites, tilled fields, unpaved roads, stone crushing, and burning of wood. Particles also can be created by atmospheric conversion of SO_2 and NO_x into sulfates and nitrates. Most measurements of PM in Pakistan are of total suspended particles. There is strong scientific evidence that elevated concentrations of fine and ultrafine PM of less than 2.5 microns ($PM_{2.5}$) and 1.0 micron ($PM_{1.0}$) pose an even greater health risk than PM of less than 10 microns (PM_{10}). However, no systematic monitoring information on $PM_{2.5}$ or $PM_{1.0}$ is available at this time in Pakistan.
2. New stricter standards were scheduled to be phased in during mid-2012.
3. The most significant health effects of urban air pollution can be attributed to fine PM. Several urban air pollutants affect human health, including ozone (O_3), nitrogen dioxide (NO_2), and sulfur dioxide (SO_2). However, PM of less than 10 millionths of a meter ($PM_{2.5}$) tends to have the strongest association with health effects, and in Pakistan alone, by 2006, was responsible for approximately 22,000 premature deaths, among many other effects. PM of less than 1.0 millionths of a meter ($PM_{1.0}$) is the most dangerous subset of $PM_{2.5}$.
4. Environmental noise (also called residential noise or domestic noise) is defined as noise emitted from all sources, except noise at the industrial workplace. The main sources of environmental noise include (i) road, rail, and air traffic; (ii) construction and public works; and (iii) the neighborhoods (such as noise from discos, sporting events, car parking lots, and restaurants).
5. The WHO Guidelines for environmental noise in outdoor living areas is as follows: serious annoyance, in daytime and evening: 55 decibels (base time = 16 hours); and moderate annoyance, daytime and evening: 50 decibels (base time = 16 hours).
6. World Bank consultant Elena Strukova has provided detailed descriptions of the methodology used to estimate the annual cost of environmental health damages associated with noise (see, for example, Strukova 2004, 2007, 2010).
7. Data collected by the provincial police departments only capture a small share of the actual number of road crashes that are reported to the authorities. However, for examining long-term trends, the time series are still valid, assuming that the reporting capacity has remained constant over time.
8. Climate change might negatively affect Pakistan, including its main transport and trade corridors. Extreme natural events, such as floods, droughts, and cyclonic activity in coastal areas, are expected to increase in frequency and intensity over time. In the country's main transport arteries (such as Highways N-5 and N-55), increased river flows resulting from glacier melt, coupled with increases in rainfall, are likely to result in flooding of roads in the medium term, particularly in areas along the Indus River, including National Highways N-5 and N-55.
9. This split mode change most closely resembles current freight transport improvement initiatives in Pakistan. For a detailed description of the methodologies used to estimate emissions of GHG and diesel fuel consumption, see Miglino (2011) and Loubinoux (2011).

References

ADB (Asian Development Bank), GoP (Government of Pakistan), and World Bank. 2010. *Pakistan Floods 2010: Preliminary Damage and Needs Assessment.* Islamabad. http://siteresources.worldbank.org/PAKISTANEXTN/Resources/293051-1264873659180/6750579-1291656195263/PakistanFloodsDNA_December2010.pdf.

Ahmed, Kulsum, and Ernesto Sánchez-Triana, eds. 2008. *Strategic Environmental Assessment for Policies: An Instrument for Good Governance.* Washington, DC: World Bank. https://openknowledge.worldbank.org/bitstream/handle/10986/6461/446390PUB0Stra101OFFICIAL0USE0ONLY1.pdf?sequence=1.

Babisch, Wolfgang. 2006. "Transportation Noise and Cardiovascular Risk: Updated Review and Synthesis of Epidemiological Studies Indicate that the Evidence Has Increased." *Noise & Health* 8 (30): 1–29.

CONCAWE. 2006. "Motor Vehicle Emission Regulations and Fuel Specifications—Part 2: Historic Review (1996–2005)." CONCAWE, Boulevard du Souverain 165, B-1160, Brussels, Belgium.

GoP (Government of Pakistan). 2007. "National Trucking Policy." National Trade Corridor Improvement Programme. Islamabad. http://www.ntcip.gov.pk/.

———. 2009a. "Labor Force Survey 2008–09." Federal Bureau of Statistics. Islamabad.

———. 2009b. "Pakistan Economic Survey 2008–2009." Ministry of Finance. Islamabad. http://finance.gov.pk/survey_0809.html. Accessed March 28, 2010.

———. 2011. *Pakistan: Framework for Economic Growth.* Planning Commission. Islamabad.

INFRAS. 2004. *External Costs of Transport: Update Study.* Zurich: University of Karlsruhe. http://habitat.aq.upm.es/boletin/n28/ncost.en.pdf.

JICA (Japan International Cooperation Agency). 2010. *Boosting Growth: Annual Report 2010. Final Report.* http://www.jica.go.jp/english/publications/reports/annual/2010/pdf/all.pdf.

Larsen, Bjorn, and John Magne Skjelvik. 2012. *Environmental Health Priorities in the Province of Sindh, Pakistan.* Consultant report prepared for the World Bank. Washington, DC.

Lopez-Claros, A., M. Porter, and K. Schwab, eds. 2005. *Global Competitiveness Report 2005–2006.* London: Palgrave Macmillan.

Loubinoux, J. P. 2011. "Green Logistics." PowerPoint Presentation, Washington, DC, March 29, 2011.

Miglino, Luis. 2011. *SEPSA: Environmental Management Component.* Consultant report prepared for the World Bank. Washington, DC.

Nadeem, Obaidullah, and Rizwan Hameed. 2008. "Evaluation of Environmental Impact Assessment System in Pakistan." *Environmental Impact Assessment Review* 28: 562–71.

Oggero, A., R. M. Darbra, M. Muñoz, E. Planas, and J. Casal. 2005. "A Survey of Accidents Occurring during the Transport of Hazardous Substances by Road and Rail." *Journal of Hazardous Materials* 133 (1–3): 1–7.

Pak-EPA (Pakistan Environmental Protection Agency). 2005. "Position Paper for Environmental Quality Standards of Noise in Pakistan." Islamabad: Pak-EPA.

———. 2006. "Measurement of Noise Level at Different Locations of Rawalpindi and Islamabad." Islamabad: Pak-EPA. http://www.environment.gov.pk/pub-pdf/noise%20study%20isb-rpindi.pdf.

Pakistan Environmental Protection Agency and World Bank. 2011. "Policy Options for Air Quality Management in Pakistan." Mimeo. Islamabad.

Pope, C. Arden, III, and Douglas W. Dockery. 2006. "Health Effects of Fine Air Pollution: Lines that Connect." *Journal of the Air & Waste Management Association* 56: 709–42. http://www.noaca.org/pmhealtheffects.pdf.

Strukova, Elena. 2004. "Opportunity Cost of Deforestation in the Brazilian Amazon: Aggregated Estimate per ton of Avoided Carbon Emission." Working Paper, World Bank, Washington, DC.

———. 2007. "Health Costs of Environmental Damage." World Bank, Washington, DC. http://siteresources.worldbank.org/INTRANETENVIRONMENT/Resources/Annex4AHealthCostofEnvironmentalDegradation.pdf.

———. 2010. "Cost-Benefit Analysis of Development and Conservation Alternatives in the Sundarbans of India." Prepared for Climate Change Adaptation, Biodiversity Conservation & Socio-Economic Development of the Sundarbans Area of West Bengal World Bank Technical Assistance. World Bank, Washington, DC.

Strukova, Elena, Oleg Guchgeldyiev, Fateh Marri, and Julie Terell. 2012. *Natural Resource Management Priorities in the Province of Sindh, Pakistan.* Consultant report prepared for the World Bank. Washington, DC.

Timilsina, Govinda R. and Hari B. Dulal. 2008. "Fiscal Policy Instruments for Reducing Congestion and Atmospheric Emissions in the Transport Sector: A Review." Policy Research Working Paper Series 4652, The World Bank.

UIC (International Union of Railways). 2011. *High Speed Rail and Sustainability.* International Union of Railways' Report, November 2011. http://www.uic.org/etf/publication/publication-resultat.php?domaine=5.

WHO (World Health Organization). 2009. *Global Status Report on Road Safety: Time for Action.* Geneva: WHO. http://whqlibdoc.who.int/publications/2009/9789241563840_eng.pdf.

World Bank. 2006a. *Pakistan Strategic Country Environmental Assessment.* Washington, DC: World Bank. http://web.worldbank.org/WBSITE/EXTERNAL/COUNTRIES/SOUTHASIAEXT/0,,contentMDK:21459418~pagePK:146736~piPK:146830~theSitePK:223547,00.html.

———. 2006b. *Transport Competitiveness in Pakistan: Analytical Underpinnings for the National Trade Corridor Improvement Program.* Report 36523-PK. Washington, DC: World Bank.

———. 2006c. *World Development Report 2006: Equity and Development.* Washington, DC: World Bank.

———. 2007. *Tools for Institutional, Political, and Social Analysis of Policy Reform: A Sourcebook for Development Practitioners.* Washington, DC: World Bank. https://openknowledge.worldbank.org/handle/10986/6652.

———. 2011. *Pakistan Transport Sector.* Washington, DC: World Bank. http://go.worldbank.org/A0D9IJ5SH0.

CHAPTER 6

Policy Options for Environmentally and Socially Sustainable Trade and Transport

The inefficiencies of the transport sector make up increasing costs to Pakistan's economy. To realize the targeted 7–8 percent annual growth rate, there is a need for developing a sustainable transport system that will allow Pakistan to gain a competitive edge by making supply chains more efficient and reliable for the transport of goods to and from industrial clusters. While within-sector reforms are identified to reduce inefficiencies in individual freight sectors, the overarching approach focuses on promoting integration and complementarities of freight transport modes to improve efficiency, reduce the cost of doing business, and efficiently link other sectors of the economy with each other without sacrificing major shares of gross domestic product (GDP) to environmental externalities. An efficient logistics system serves as a key catalyst for enhancing industrial growth to allow Pakistan to evolve rapidly into a globally competitive economy (Government of Pakistan [GoP] 2009). In an era that demands on-time delivery, these induced costs can even affect countries' potential to diversify from time-intensive commodities. The challenge herein is creating a transport and logistics system that combines the competitive advantages of different modes into one integrated system. In light of rail's more socially and environmentally sustainable characteristics and its competitiveness in long distances over road freight, shifts in policy reforms are likely to be needed for Pakistan to enhance the sustainability of its freight transport system in the long term. Failure to integrate a multimodal transport system would have adverse consequences for Pakistan, including lack of competitiveness and the ensuing difficulties in meeting the country's development objectives, and increased social and environmental costs.

This chapter identifies sectoral opportunities for improving the environmental and social sustainability of the freight transport system. Enhancing positive impacts and reducing negative impacts requires stronger institutional capacity of sectoral and regulatory agencies and measures that safeguard the well-being of groups that may be potentially harmed during transport projects.

Multimodal Transport System

Pakistan's freight transport system could adapt to the "era of co-modality," which is based on the integration and complementarities of transport modes to improve efficiency and decrease social and environmental impacts. The transport supply chain system is not providing the value-added services—such as multimodal systems that combine the strengths of different transport modes into one integrated system—that have become the hallmark of modern logistics in many advanced and even some developing economies. In general, logistic services provided by freight forwarders (business as usual system) do not always utilize the most efficient mode of transport for the movement of a good from origin to destination. Each freight transport mode has characteristics that renders it more efficient, and generally less costly, for particular transport tasks. For example, rail freight generally has a competitive advantage and lower costs over road freight for longer distances and for the transport of bulk commodities. In urban areas, the combination of often-dispersed origins and destinations, relatively shorter distances, and lighter shipment amounts means freight is more effectively carried by road than by rail. Moreover, given that rail is more environmentally sustainable than road, the case for integrating rail into freight logistic itineraries for goods is critical. A multimodal system recognizes that different modes, when integrated together under a single contract, can transport goods more efficiently and effectively to their destinations.

Under a multimodal system, the rail sector would be in charge of heavy lifting for long distances, with trucking complementing it at both ends. An efficiently run rail freight system is generally not competitive with trucking for short distances (below 300 kilometers); however, rail is far more competitive than road freight for long distances (over 500 kilometers) and possibly competitive at medium distances (300–500 kilometers). Moreover, as fossil fuels become scarcer and more expensive in the future, rail's competitive advantage for long distances is likely to become larger. While rail is more efficient for the long-distance segment of the journey, it is reliant on road freight transport for the pick-up and delivery of freight to and from the rail terminal. The benefit of road is that it can provide direct door-to-door services more reliably and faster than rail. An efficient multimodal system minimizes time losses at transshipment points; provides faster delivery of freight goods, which reduces the disadvantage of distance between markets; and helps reduce the cost of exports, decreases the burden of documentation and formalities, and improves their competitive position in the international market.[1]

Table 6.1 **Approximate Road Distances in Pakistan**

From	To	Distance (km)
Karachi	Lahore	1,260
Karachi	Rawalpindi	1,540
Karachi	Peshawar	1,700
Karachi	Khyber Pass (Afghan border)	1,756
Karachi	Khungerab Pass (Chinese border)	2,400
Gwadar Port	Lahore[a]	1,771
Gwadar Port	Rawalpindi[a]	2,051
Gwadar Port	Peshawar[a]	2,211
Gwadar Port	Khungerab Pass—Chinese border[a]	2,900
Gwadar Port	Karachi	460

Source: National Highways Authority website http://www.nha.gov.pk/Info/RDistances.asp.
Note: a. The Gwadar-Sukkur segment is going to be built as part of the National Trade and Corridor Improvement Program's Road Investment Program.

The actual modal distribution will be determined by a number of factors, including cost, reliablity, and quality of service. Road freight rates in Pakistan are among the lowest in the world, with an average cost of US$0.015–US$0.021 per ton kilometer (World Bank 2006). Still, railway costs and tariffs are lower than for trucks over longer distances, particularly above 500 kilometers, while the costs of trucks are lower for shorter distances. It should be noted that distances between Pakistan's ports in the south and most of country's main cities in the north, as well as border crossings, are above 500 kilometers (table 6.1).

Such modal shifts to railways could begin by focusing on freight that is currently transported for long distances, in which railways tend to have lower costs (as seen in Figures 6.1 and 6.2), and in areas where most of the necessary railway infrastructure is already in place. It is proposed to increase the share of national railway in national freight from the current 4 percent to 22 percent by 2030. National Highway N-5 extends over 1,700 kilometers and connects Karachi with Peshawar, while N-55 connects Hyderabad with Peshawar, over a distance of 1,265 kilometers. About 60 percent of the total road freight is transported through these highways. Shifting freight from roads to railways in the areas covered by these roads would result in a significant reduction of greenhouse gas (GHG) emissions.

The adoption of the multimodal transport freight system will reduce the number of trucks traveling long distances, thereby decreasing the amount of GHG emissions generated by the trucking sector. As the road freight sector is a contributor to air pollution, a shift toward railway freight will help significantly reduce the inland freight sector's emissions. As discussed in chapter 5, policy shifts favoring rail most reduce environmental impacts. As an example, if the split mode is changed for inland freight transportation to 30 percent rail and 70 percent road (currently it is 4 percent rail and 96 percent road), the annual GHG emissions would be reduced to 36.8 $TgCO_2eq$ by 2025 (23.3 percent reduction or a reduction of about 11.2 million tons of GHG discharged into

Figure 6.1 Comparison of Economic Cost between Trucks and Railways

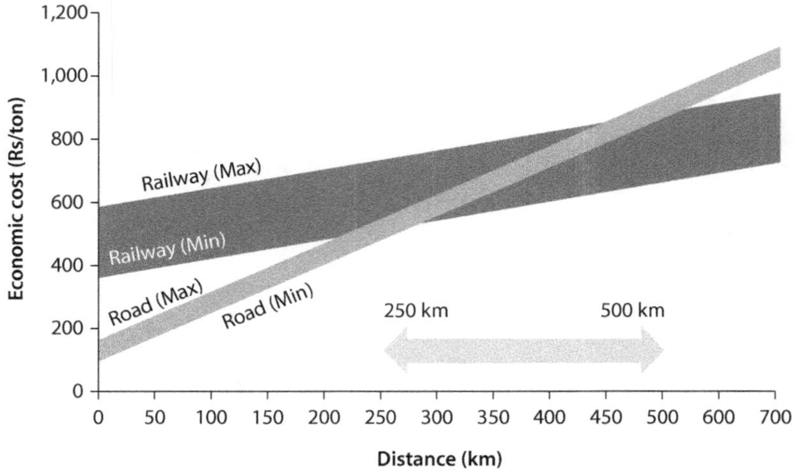

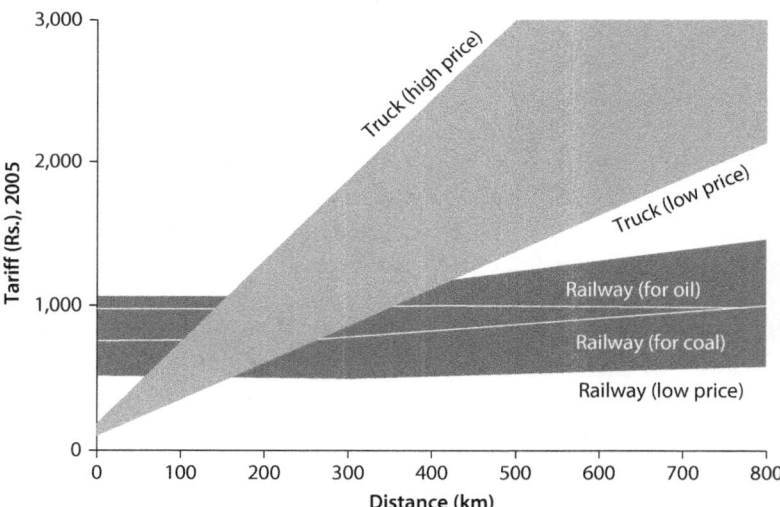

Source: JICA 2006.

Figure 6.2 Comparison of Tariffs between Trucks and Railways

Source: JICA 2006.

the atmosphere). The same example finds that emphasis on the freight sector would result in an annual reduction in the consumption of diesel fuels by the inland freight transportation sector in Pakistan, of about 1.06 million metric tons by the year 2025–26 (when compared to the current split mode between rail and road freight). These savings in diesel consumption would imply a yearly reduction of about 6,116 metric tons of sulfur burned in internal combustion engines in the country (Miglino 2011).

Efficiency gains (environmental and social) are to be realized as a result of fewer trucks operating on the road under the proposed multimodal transport system. The trucking sector is likely to be involved in a disproportionately high number of accidents because of practices such as overloading, modification and poor conditions of trucks, inadequate driving skills, and driver exhaustion caused by long hours behind the wheel (World Bank 2006). As trucks are more efficient in operating over short distances relative to trains, this will help clear up the excess amount of trucks operating on roads, hence decreasing road congestion, improving air quality and GHG emissions, enhancing road safety, diminishing the probability of road accidents and fatalities, and reducing noise pollution and hazardous material spills. On the social side, increased connectivity and the expansion of private-sector participation in freight (particularly railways) could help enhance spatial transformation and decrease the risk of HIV transmission.[2]

Finance from carbon markets and other international sources would be needed to promote a modal shift from roads to rail. GHG mitigation alone is not a sufficient reason to promote a modal shift in a country such as Pakistan, which contributes marginally to global emissions and faces significant socioeconomic challenges. However, if these reduced emissions are compensated through resources from programmatic operations of the Clean Development Mechanism or by international assistance for new instruments, such as National Appropriate Mitigation Actions, they could generate resources that could be invested in other priority areas. However, the competitivenss of rail freight for long distances strengthens the argument for a multimodal system, as rail freight transportation is likely to be a more effective means of transporting goods compared to trucks under the heavy precipitation and flooding events.

Railways

To allow for rail to operate on a commercial basis, Pakistan Railways (PR) might be split into two different organizations: one responsible for freight and the other for passenger services, without any sort of subsidization.[3] This will allow PR to be relieved of costs of operating the large noncommercial network of lines and services. PR should, over time, separate core and noncore activities with a view of having the company focus on its core function of providing rail transport rather than on management of its nonoperational land assets, such as factories and workshops. Investment in new rail lines for freight transport should be made based on public-private partnerships (PPPs) sharing risks and using the highest economic, financial, social, and environmental standards. Overall, such measures can help revitalize the rail freight sector, and enhance its reliability and performance, as well as its business reputation.

Private-sector involvement in rail services will open up opportunities for larger businesses in freight forwarding that will have the chance to explore opportunities in long-distance freight haulage. End users are likely to benefit in the long run, as rail freight is cheaper, less polluting, and more efficient than road haulage, provided it is managed properly and is instituted after significant investment in rail infrastructure.

Existing rail networks and the development of new transport infrastructure can facilitate the transport of underutilized natural resources. Pakistan is a country that is endowed with extensive natural resources. However, unlike other countries with extensive geological endowment, it has yet to exploit its natural resources optimally and sustainably to promote economic growth and reduce poverty. Large amounts of copper and gold are located in Saindak and Reko Diq in the Balochistan province. Some of the largest deposits of coal are in Badin, Lakhra, Metting, Sonda, and Thar; the Thar province alone contains one of the largest single coal deposits in the world. Currently, the mining sector constitutes only 0.4 percent of GDP. Based on the experiences of countries with similar geological endowments, under reasonable assumptions, these natural resources can generate up to 3 percent of GDP, stimulate secondary and tertiary economic activity, and increase employment opportunities. Furthermore, evidence from around the world demonstrates that if adequate institutional frameworks are put in place, tapping into these natural resources can stimulate inclusive economic growth while safeguarding the environment and local communities.

In addition, railways could also facilitate the transport of minerals, such as copper and iron, from Afghanistan to Peshawar and transport minerals and goods from Persian Gulf countries and territories to Central and East Asia. For the transport of these natural resources, it is cost-effective to use rail where the infrastructure already exists. Reko Diq in the Chaghai district, located in the northwest corner of Balochistan, is roughly 70 kilometers northwest of Nok-Kudi, which has a rail network. A multimodal system in which rail and road complement each other is cost-effective for the transport of these commodities.[4]

Modernization of the Trucking and Port Sectors

To remedy inefficiencies in the trucking sector (which arguably generate the lion's share of environmental and social problems in freight transport), the GoP might accelerate the implementation of its 2007 National Trucking Policy (GoP 2007b). The overall objective of modernizing the trucking sector is to encourage the use of large and modern fleet trucks (that meet minimum European emission standards), which can meet the country's transport demand at a lower cost. This reform is particularly important for the transport of heavy and bulk commodities (GoP 2007a). The 2- and 3-axle obsolete trucks that dominate the trucking sector are often assembled in backstreet operations, with no consideration to environmental quality standards. To adapt the truck fleet to the demand of faster and reliable transport of large quantities, the following measures need to be implemented:

- To encourage private-sector participation, all participants should operate within the same level playing field (regulatory environment) without privileges granted to public operators. Formal recognition of the trucking sector would

improve financing possibilities by facilitating access to insurance and foreign investment;
- Regulations to control vehicle overloading, including measures for trucks to adhere to established optimum axle load weights, as determined by vehicle types (GoP 2007b). This measure will help reduce the incidence of breakdowns, reduce damage caused to roads, and decrease road maintenance costs.
- Regular truck inspection and maintenance testing. This is to ensure truck safety, strict enforcement of environmental regulations, and testing of truck drivers for knowledge of traffic rules and physical and mental fitness. Routine truck technical inspections and maintenance help identify and fix polluting trucks that fail emissions standards. Inspection stations for trucks would be particularly desirable in larger cities (Faisalabad, Islamabad, Karachi, Lahore, Peshawar, Quetta, and Rawalpindi), where emissions from trucks contribute to overall emissions. Systems of vehicle registration, truck technical inspection, and driver tests can help improve the quality standards of the industry and sustain its long-term development.
- Import tariffs on new trucks should be relaxed to encourage the use of multi-axle heavy-duty trucks on long-distance hauls. This will help reduce the light-duty polluting trucks on the roads, thereby reducing GHG emissions.

The strategic location of the newly constructed Gwadar Port might be taken advantage of to facilitate regional and international trade. The city of Gwadar (located in the Balochistan province) is strategically located east of the Islamic Republic of Iran and south of Afghanistan, and has a seaport that is located at the entrance of the Persian Gulf. For Pakistan, the economic returns from Gwadar Port stems from its location near the Strait of Hormuz, a major conduit for global oil supplies in the region. Gwadar is of strategic importance to East and Central Asia (particularly Afghanistan and China) providing landlocked countries with access to the sea. However, Gwadar's strategic location for facilitating regional trade and alleviating poverty has yet to be fully capitalized to its greatest potential. The development and usage of the port has stalled because of a variety of issues ranging from a lack of infrastructure investment by the government, high costs of transport, and absence of any significant industry in Balochistan. Moreover, Gwadar serves as an important node for any Islamic Republic of Iran-Pakistan-India gas pipeline that could be developed, which could cross from the Islamic Republic of Iran to Pakistan's Balochistan province. Importation of natural gas from the Islamic Republic of Iran would address to some extent Pakistan's energy concerns, given that currently, natural gas demand in Pakistan has exceeded the available supply. There is a need to create a business climate prone to private-sector investment, including the identification of financing and risk management mechanisms to increase infrastructure investment and reduce high port entry charges, among others. The government needs to have a long-term vision of the development of this relatively new port sector, which occupies a critical location in the trade market.

Redefining the Role of Government and the Need for Private-Sector Participation

Promoting a multimodal transport system, which entails significant investment in the rail freight sector, might be supported with private-sector participation. Due to federal budget constraints, bringing in private participation to revamp PR, particularly its freight business, is advantageous given rail's competitive advantage for long distances over road freight transport. Private-sector participation in freight transportation in railways would be helpful in improving track utilization, which currently is only 42 percent. PR might increase private-sector participation in freight transportation—for example, outsourcing station management, letting suburban trains be run by separate companies, and allowing private companies to run their own container trains and rolling stock. Private-sector participation should be encouraged via opening of track access in which private operators are allowed to run freight services on selected routes, for which the legal and regulatory framework will be in place (GoP 2007a, 2007b, 2011).

A number of reasons support promoting the private sector in freight transport. Examples of public projects and policies that have generated significant inefficiencies include subsidies granted to passenger rail at the expense of freight rail, government protection of Pakistan International Airlines, government preference of road over rail, and high tariffs in ports. Even though the major share of trucking in Pakistan is private, the National Logistics Cell (NLC) is by far the largest trucking enterprise in Pakistan. The NLC, established in 1978 to transport public imports of wheat and fertilizer, operates some 1,400 trucks and employs more than 7,000 workers. The NLC subcontracts owner-operated trucks at very low rates, which hampers fleet modernization. The case for facilitating private-sector participation in the development of freight transport infrastructure is not only supported by the high costs and distortions generated by excessive governmental interference, but is also advocated by the 2011 *Framework for Economic Growth*.

To provide a level playing field, the government might consider developing a regulatory framework for ensuring free market competition in the rail and air transport sectors, including provisions for entry and exit of private operators. This regulatory framework could facilitate intermodal connectivity and private-sector participation. The regulatory structure should include responsibilities on cross-cutting issues such as environment and social management, project and concession contract development, and monitoring and evaluation. A regulatory organization could take over responsibilities such as regulatory policies and promotion of private-sector participation.

Currently, the responsibility for the construction, operation, and maintenance of Pakistan's transport infrastructure and policy setting for its freight transport sector is split across four governmental organizations (defense, communications, railways, and ports and shipping). None of these organizations has incentives to develop a modern, private-sector-driven, multimodal cargo transport industry. The recommendation here is for the GoP to consider a Freight

Transport Policy aimed at regulating and facilitating private-sector participation to develop transport infrastructure, strengthen intermodal connectivity, and contribute to Pakistan's spatial transformation. The regulatory framework would address the key obstacles for private participation in infrastructure development, while also ensuring that infrastructure projects are socially and environmentally sustainable and meet high-quality standards. Appendix B contains more information on this recommendation, the background and rationale for it, and a discussion of relevant political economy issues in the freight transport sector.

The regulatory framework proposed would enable an environment for private-sector participation in the transport sector, which requires strong political leadership. Excessive public interference in the transport sector has led to significant distortions that discourage productivity in the sector and has contributed to the poor performance of key freight sectors. Government privileges and subsidies such as those granted to passenger rail and ports have increased the cost of doing business and decreased export competitiveness. Private-sector participation, with adequate governmental regulation, not only helps free up the scarce public resources dedicated to infrastructure projects but helps provide much-needed capital investment, increases management expertise, helps enhance accountability and transparency, improves resource allocation, and increases the quality and reliability of delivery.

The proposed regulatory framework might give priority to promoting private-sector involvement in the freight transport sector, with the aim of helping Pakistan adapt to the era of co-modality, and to ensuring the social and environmental sustainability of transport infrastructure projects. In addition, the regulatory framework could include mechanisms for evaluating the use of best applicable technologies; overseeing that freight transportation investment projects and operations meet high-quality standards; and developing the institutional capacity to carry out streamlined and effective auditing, verification, and monitoring processes. A new organization could be created with a mandate to attract private-sector investment, including through the development of PPPs and development of concession contracts under schemes including "build, operate, transfer" and "build, own, operate," among others. The institutional framework should sustain the momentum for change by taking a holistic and integrated approach to identify and analyze the elements that significantly affect competitiveness and hamper private-sector participation in infrastructure development.

The design and implementation of the regulatory framework should include provisions to "ring-fence" (see page 151) regulatory agencies from regulatory capture. Regulatory capture can come about through corrupt means, but it can also come about through sympathy: regulators spend so much time working with the industry that they come to adopt the industry's viewpoint. In a regulatory organization, each freight sector actor will have comparatively less influence than it does currently; however, there will be a number of competing interests, including those of private-sector groups, attempting to capture it.

The Way Ahead

The two transformations currently taking place in Pakistan—one structural and one spatial—can be facilitated by investments to improve Pakistan's spatial connectivity, which include freight transport reforms in rail and road infrastructure. Such reforms are intended to help (i) serve as an impetus for enhancing industrial growth and allow millions of rural residents seeking better lives in urban areas to be absorbed into the labor force; and (ii) efficiently link sectors in the economy, contribute to both domestic and international trade, and help facilitate the overall spatial transformation occurring in Pakistan. Indeed, to expand effectively, the manufacturing sector will require improvements in the way sector inputs and outputs are transported in Pakistan, and improvements in urban-rural linkages through transport development. However, Pakistan's ability to enjoy the economic benefits by avoiding the external costs of increased urbanization and industrialization will be seriously hampered unless the GoP takes steps to manage social and environmental externalities. Industrial expansion and urbanization without attention to environment will lead to increased GDP figures that are inflated by high costs of environmental externalities.

Spatial transformation may prove to be a trend that helps Pakistan improve its GDP, and, at the same time, lift many out of poverty. Urban populations show better social indicators than their counterparts residing in rural regions. A growing population in urban areas has the potential to become a significant asset to economic growth, if adequate institutional, environmental, and transport policies are in place to facilitate industrial development. Pakistan suffers from significant problems linked to poor spatial connectivity that serves to hinder the spatial transformation of Pakistan, and hence urbanization, industrial development, and overall economic growth. To enhance the positive effects and reduce the negative effects of the spatial transformations facilitated by reforms and investments in the freight transport sector, the GoP might consider the following policy options:

- *Promote a development of freight transport that connects industrial clusters and facilitates the structural transformations taking place in Pakistan.* Agglomeration economies play a crucial role in supporting firms' competitiveness. In Pakistan, as in many other developing countries, within-industry externalities are much more important than inter-industry spillovers. Reforms and investments in the freight transport sector should therefore be developed in coordination with efforts to establish or strengthen industrial clusters in Pakistan. The synergies between the freight transport sector and an industrial policy that support the development of clusters would facilitate the structural and spatial transformations that Pakistan is undergoing and which could contribute significantly to the country's economic growth and poverty reduction goals.

- *Anticipate the potential effects of reforms in the trade and transport sector on urban centers.* Pakistan is rapidly urbanizing; reforms in the trade and transport sector are anticipated to contribute to this trend, particularly as investments and new employment opportunities will most likely materialize in urban areas. Evidence from around the world indicates that urbanization offers a number of benefits, but these can be offset by externalities such as congestion and pollution. Governmental policies should aim to harness urbanization, rather than contain it. The GoP should prioritize investments to improve slums, including aspects such as providing adequate water, sanitation, and waste management infrastructure, as well as establishing property rights. Appropriate actions for governments should take the following general forms (World Bank 2009, 229; italics added):

- In areas of *incipient urbanization*, the objective should be to facilitate a natural rural-urban transformation. The core policy instruments are spatially blind institutions that facilitate density in some locations. These instruments include secure land tenure and property rights, basic and social services, and policies that do not favor one productive activity (large industry) over another (small agriculture). Policy makers should aim for neutrality between rural and urban areas.

- In areas of *intermediate urbanization*, the rapid growth of some cities is associated with congestion and negative externalities. In addition to spatially blind policies to facilitate density, connective policies to tackle congestion and economic distance become necessary. They include investments in transport infrastructure (to enhance connectivity both within and between cities) and encouragement of socially efficient location decisions by firms.

- In areas with *advanced urbanization*, divisions within cities caused by formal settlements and slums, and by crime, add to the challenges of density and distance. In addition to spatially blind and spatially connective policies, spatially focused policies for addressing intracity divisions are necessary to target the difficulties of slums, crime, and the environment—and to improve livability.

- *Strengthen the institutional capacity of freight transport sector agencies and environmental agencies for environmental management.* Organizations in Pakistan's freight transport sector have limited capacity to address the environmental and social issues that arise during the construction and operation of transport infrastructure. As elaborated in the next chapter, strengthening their institutional capacity to incorporate environmental and social considerations at the earliest planning stages and address issues as they arise would generate significant benefits to Pakistan's population. In addition, given that reforms in the freight transport sector will have countrywide effects, they will put a burden on Pakistan's environmental management framework. Strengthening the institutional capacity of environmental agencies (particularly after the devolution of environmental responsibilities to the provincial governments as a result of the 18th Constitutional Amendment) and the Ministry of Climate Change should be of utmost priority, particularly as evidence indicates that the environmental externalities of the freight transport sector are already significant (see appendix B for more details).

- *Carry out a comprehensive package of reforms to unleash the potential of Pakistan's freight transport sector.* Pakistan's freight transport sector compares poorly with those of other competing economies and its inefficiencies represent 4–6 percent of GDP. Reforms to modernize the sector should give priority to the following actions:
  - Promoting the integration of different modes of transportation, giving preference to railways for transport involving long distances, where rail is more efficient and sustainable than road transport;
  - Redefining the government's role to focus on regulating and attracting private-sector investments in the sector and gradually eliminate current biases that distort the market; and
  - Fostering the adoption of new technologies and procedures that add value to the services provided by the trade and transport sector, including those that would help to move from the current focus on bulk cargo to containerized cargo.

Reforms, including some mentioned in this report, have been proposed or attempted before. In some cases, those proposals have been built upon, such as the recommendation to implement with high priority several elements of the 2007 National Trucking Policy. However, among a host of other challenges, Pakistan's "growth policy has been based on public-sector investments, incentives-subsidies and protection. The incentive structure has blunted the efficiency of infrastructure development while the system of incentives has not allowed the development of a competitive marketplace" (GoP 2011, 10).

In the post-18th Amendment milieu,[5] the Planning Commission will exercise control over the development process through

- Consultation, setting medium-term and annual development objectives for the government and for relevant ministries;
- Identification of key economic reforms that are required for these objectives, development of quantitative indicators (which can be monitored) for these reforms, and monitoring and reporting on them to government and the people;
- Specifying government- and ministry-level reporting requirements for development results and their costs to ensure accountability and track progress;
- Strengthening the capacity of ministries and, by interaction and evaluation, ensuring that their strategies and services support national development priorities; and
- Developing the capacity of the planning system to act as an institution that develops and oversees the government's reform agenda.

The Pakistan Planning Commission's *Framework for Economic Growth* was approved by the National Economic Council on May 28, 2011. The growth strategy advised in the *Framework* is "a new approach to accelerating economic growth and sustaining it." It aims to "improve the investment climate [and] reduce the cost of doing business, increasing the profitability of enterprises and encouraging them to expand." The *Framework* also "suggests deep and sustained reforms—in areas such as public-sector management, developing competitive markets, urban management and connecting people and places—as a way forward for accelerating growth to above 7 per cent" (GoP 2011, 10–11). Among its key thrusts is an emphasis on connectivity. It states, "Commercial activity requires dense well-connected cities and communities. Connectivity is a critical stratagem of the growth framework" (GoP 2011, 14).[6]

The *Framework* also highlights that "The new vision for economic growth will require periodic identification of emerging constraints to economic growth through research and dialog with all sectors and stakeholders" (GoP 2011). This report does just that, informing decision makers within the *Framework* target areas, and identifying a menu of options to avoid and minimize negative social and environmental externalities that could undermine spatial transformation and transport development gains.

Notes

1. Since only the multimodal transport operator is generally in charge of all matters relating to the transportation of the good, dealing with only one agency as opposed to many reduces the cost of doing business.
2. On the social side, increased connectivity and the expansion of private-sector participation in freight (particularly railways) could help decrease urban sprawl and the risk of HIV transmission.
3. The analyses of passenger transport in general and train passenger services in particular are beyond the scope of the strategic environmental, poverty, and social assessment.
4. A multimodal system might include transport of fuels, such as the proposed Islamic Republic of Iran-Pakistan gas pipeline and the Turkmenistan-Afghanistan-Pakistan (TAP) natural gas pipeline. The Islamic Republic of Iran-Pakistan project, signed in 2009, is expected to deliver gas from the Islamic Republic of Iran's South Pars gas field through Pakistan's Balochistan and Sindh provinces. The TAP project consists of a gas pipeline of approximately 1,700 kilometers that can transport up to roughly 20 billion cubic meters of natural gas per year from southeast Turkmenistan to Afghanistan, Pakistan, and India. The projects will not only link energy-deficit economies such as Pakistan to the relatively richer hydrocarbon Central Asian economies, but will also provide Pakistan with cheaper and cleaner energy sources. Furthermore, the projects will help meet current and future energy demands, and help overcome shortages in electricity. However, problems pertaining to political, security, technical, and funding challenges have stalled the TAP project from being implemented, and solutions for dealing with these issues have yet to be defined. Construction work on the Islamic Republic of Iran-Pakistan gas pipeline is currently in progress.

5. See appendix B for further details regarding the 18th Amendment and devolutions of responsibility.
6. See also appendixes A and B.

References

GoP (Government of Pakistan). 2007a. "National Transport Policy 2007–08." *Lahore Daily Times.* August 11, 2007. http://www.dailytimes.com.pk/default.asp?page=2007%5C08%5C11%5Cstory_11-8-2007_pg5_5.

———. 2007b. National Trucking Policy. National Trade Corridor Improvement Programme. Islamabad. http://www.ntcip.gov.pk/.

———. 2009. "Pakistan Economic Survey 2008–09." Ministry of Finance, Islamabad. http://www.finance.gov.pk/finance_survery_chapter.aspx?id=21. Accessed March 28, 2010.

———. 2011. *Pakistan: Framework for Economic Growth.* Islamabad: Planning Commission.

JICA (Japan International Cooperation Agency). 2006. *Pakistan Transport Plan Study in the Islamic Republic of Pakistan.* Final Report. http://www.ntrc.gov.pk/PTPS-reportSDJR06013FinalReport01.pdf.

Miglino, Luis. 2011. *SEPSA: Environmental Management Component.* Consultant report, Washington, DC: World Bank.

World Bank. 2006. *Transport Competitiveness in Pakistan: Analytical Underpinnings for the National Trade Corridor Improvement Program.* Report 36523-PK. Washington, DC: World Bank.

———. 2009. *World Development Report 2009: Reshaping Economic Geography.* Washington, DC: World Bank. http://www-wds.worldbank.org/external/default/WDSContentServer/IW3P/IB/2008/12/03/000333038_20081203234958/Rendered/PDF/437380REVISED01BLIC1097808213760720.pdf.

CHAPTER 7

An Agenda for Environmentally and Socially Sustainable Trade and Transport Reforms

Pakistan is currently undergoing two transformations: (i) a structural change in its economy, where the contribution of the primary sector to the country's economy is declining as that of industrial manufacturing increases, and (ii) a spatial transformation, with an increasing share of its population living in more densely populated urban centers. These two transformations are linked and are closely associated with reforms in the trade and transport sector. The proposed reforms would contribute to agglomeration economies in urban areas, thereby increasing job opportunities in those places, while also increasing mobility. Spatial transformation is associated with a country's economic development; however, in the case of Pakistan, the transformation is anticipated to take place within a short time frame, thereby increasing already severe problems, such as urban sprawl and negative social and environmental externalities. Thus, social and environmental policies addressing negative externalities and upgrading and improving public service delivery in urban settings should be given priority.

Reforms in the freight transportation sector are fundamental to enhance Pakistan's competitiveness and support inclusive and sustained economic growth. The previous chapter discussed the proposed overall approach to such reforms, particularly with regard to integrating different modes of transportation and strengthening their linkages with other sectors of the economy. This chapter discusses social and environmental policy options that could be adopted to enhance the positive effects of reforms and reduce the potential negative consequences of increases in productivity in the freight transport sector. The chapter provides recommendations to strengthen Pakistan's institutional

---

This chapter was prepared by Ernesto Sánchez-Triana, Ghazal Dezfuli, Zia Al Jalaly, and Santiago Enriquez, and draws from the analytical work prepared by IDS (2011), LUMS (2011), Hammad Raza, and Rahul Kanakia.

framework, including through the development of legal, regulatory, and management instruments that are inadequate or currently missing. The chapter also identifies opportunities to build the capacities of existing organizations to better identify, manage, and monitor and evaluate the consequences of trade and transport sector reforms on environmental, poverty, and social priorities.

Addressing Priority Social and Poverty Issues

While the benefits to be expected from increases in total factor productivity of freight transport are undeniable, some groups may nevertheless find themselves adversely impacted. Increases in transport productivity might affect rural nonfarm and urban poor households and might be correlated with negative social impacts such as social conflict, urban sprawl, transmission of HIV/AIDS, and involuntary resettlement.

Social Conflicts

Social conflicts in Pakistan are heightened by the country's demographic growth and manifest themselves as sectarian or ethnic strife. Given Pakistan's high sensitivity to ethnic tensions, such issues should be expected to arise in the context of any major freight transportation reform. Reforms in the freight transportation sector, for example, can be expected to affect one specific ethnic group disproportionately. Such a situation presents a potential for social unrest. In the case of the trucking sector, a mitigation strategy for potentially affected ethnic groups and owners of small and obsolete trucks likely to be negatively affected by the enforcement of the trucking policy needs to be concerned with two aspects: (i) how to provide a business climate that keeps such businesses profitable or finds alternative means of employment, and (ii) how to promote social inclusion. Access to vocational training and/or micro-loans to those workers should be considered as measures to facilitate the adjustment and limit the risk of social tensions. In addition, facilitating access to information about employment opportunities can ease the match between workers and new or growing private firms operating in the sector.

As discussed in chapter 3, increases in transport productivity might have negative impacts on rural nonfarm and urban poor households. Reforms in the trade and transport sector constitute a chance to address Pakistan's inequality of opportunities for these groups. Proactive measures are needed to counter structural inequalities that lead to inequality of opportunity for these groups. Structural inequalities are correlated with geographical and historical patterns of deprivation, market segmentation, and unequal access to public services. There are four key dimensions of structural inequality in Pakistan: (i) gender, (ii) region, (iii) economic class, and (iv) social identity (Gazdar 2009). While these forms of inequality contribute to poverty and socioeconomic inequality, the perceptions of those stark inequalities can also constitute a powerful tool for social unrest and militancy. Including inequality and redistribution concerns in the design of the trade and transport sector reforms and the modalities of their implementation could yield much benefit in sustaining growth, as well as in reducing poverty and social tensions.

Spatial Transformation

An econometric analysis completed by LUMS (2011) finds that infrastructure investments are likely to yield high payoffs in promoting localization economies and agglomeration. Industrial agglomerations form in districts with good market access, low transportation costs, and a skilled labor force. Agglomeration is fundamental to industrial competitiveness because it promotes (i) knowledge and information spillovers, and innovative ideas among firms; (ii) labor-market pooling; and (iii) input-output linkages. Industrial economic activity in Pakistan is highly concentrated around the metropolitan cities and urban centers with industrial clusters. Such concentration reflects the benefits that firms obtain from agglomeration economies, including both inter- and intra-industry spillovers. Econometric results reveal that there is a strong association between industrial clusters and markets, and poverty reduction.

Upgrading slums and improving service delivery in urban settings should be considered a priority to manage and take advantage of Pakistan's spatial transformation. As mentioned before, the envisioned reforms are likely to increase existing incentives for rural-to-urban migration. Under current circumstances, migrants will add to the urban population that already faces problems finding adequate housing and meeting their needs for municipal services, including water supply, sanitation, and waste management. Clearly designed programs to improve slums and service delivery, with adequate resources and political support, would not only improve the quality of life of most urban residents, but would also reduce the social risks identified in this report, including those related to social tensions and conflict.

Capacity building is required in at least two tiers of government (provincial and district) to better develop and implement urban development strategies that respond to Pakistan's spatial transformations. Pakistani cities have inadequate infrastructure to meet current needs, let alone an ability to respond to growing demand. In addition, cities are characterized by inefficient spatial structures (low-density ribbon development), restrictive land use regulations, rent control, and limited supplies of land for commercial, industrial, and residential development. As a result, land is relatively expensive and people and businesses tend to locate in distant locations and/or informal areas. This unplanned growth, coupled with high motorization rates, has resulted in significant congestion in urban areas. Within large cities, responsibilities for service delivery are fragmented, both spatially and institutionally, and fiscal capacity is limited. Addressing these challenges will be crucial to respond to the current urban population's needs, as well as to prepare for continued urbanization.

Reduced Opportunities Associated with Small Trucking Businesses

Small operators in the trucking sector have a high probability of losing business to new and larger enterprises due to implementation of the 2007

Trucking Policy and other freight transportation reforms. Ensuring that these businesses have access to credit and insurance, and are allowed a level playing field that allows their services throughout the country (including major routes), would help reduce the risks they might face. Business linked to the current trucking sector, particularly rural nonfarm and urban poor households, as well as women and youth, might benefit from the implementation of the trucking policy and the modernization of the railway and port sectors. Modernization will create new opportunities for smaller trucking firms, provided they have access to credit and are not forced to quit operating on major intercity routes.

To attain poverty reduction goals, increases in transport productivity need to be accompanied by reforms aimed at ensuring that vulnerable groups, particularly women and youth from nonfarm households and urban poor households, take advantage of employment opportunities. Reforms in the trade and transport sector represent an opportunity to include a proactive gender focus in a major sector, as well as in manufacturing activities.

Despite the constraints faced by Pakistani women, there are encouraging trends in the private and public sectors. Examples include the Pakistan International Freight Forwarders Association, in which women form approximately 15 percent of the workforce. They work at all levels of the freight forwarding industry, including management. The pharmaceutical industry reports that 50 percent of its employees are women; the shipping industry has approximately 25 percent women in all jobs except heavy physical labor; customs has 15–25 percent women (mostly all in the career-level cadre and as secretaries, with not many as junior officers); and women are active in the air freight industry. Women contribute significantly to Pakistan's main export engine, the textile and clothing sector. Apart from cotton-picking, women form about one-half of the workforce in the garment subsector. Furthermore, improving women's economic participation will also depend on progress made in service delivery in health and education, particularly for rural nonfarm households and poor groups in slums and areas of urban sprawl.

In the context of Pakistan's complex social context, youth, particularly from urban poor and nonfarm households, constitute a particularly vulnerable group that should receive special attention. Youth are a diverse social group with different characteristics and attitudes about work in different regions of Pakistan. The transition for both highly skilled and unskilled youth into the labor market is difficult. In the case of the highly skilled young people, the transition often ends in them taking a job beneath their skill level or expectations, or ending up inactive because they have given up hope of finding what they are looking for. A large share of the unskilled youth end up working as contributing family workers or in the informal sector. In both cases, the unsuccessful transition process leads to a waste of potential and increased risk of social unrest. To improve employability of the young labor force, an improvement in "human capital" through the reform of educational and vocational systems is needed.[1]

Transmission of HIV/AIDS

Modernization of the trucking sector and adaptation of a multimodal transport system will help curb the spread of HIV originating from the trucking sector. The introduction of newer and more modern trucks would decrease the probability of truck breakdowns and stopovers, which are places that sex workers frequent. Truck fitness testing stations to test the safety of trucks can help identify and repair trucks, thereby reducing the possibility that trucks break down unexpectedly. Moreover, the adoption of the multimodal transport freight system will reduce the number of truck drivers traveling long distances, thereby decreasing the frequency of risky behaviors. Efforts to control urban sprawl also can reduce the amount of truck traffic and travel time, thereby further decreasing risky sexual behavior. Improved connectivity could decrease the risk of HIV transmission, particularly if modernization of the trucking sector or increased participation of the railway sector takes place.

Public health initiatives to control the spread of HIV by changing behavioral risks of truck drivers are recommended. Important components would include the provision of services in geographically defined areas at greatest risk for HIV transmission (such as major trucking stopover locations). Experiences from other countries demonstrate that communication and condom distribution campaigns targeting vulnerable groups, including truckers, can be effective in changing risky behavior and reducing the risk of contagion. The services include information campaigns (Cornman et al. 2007) and behavior change communication aimed at improving vulnerable group's knowledge, attitudes, and behaviors regarding HIV; voluntary counseling and HIV testing; and proper management of sexually transmitted infections (STIs). Such a component has been found cost-effective in Pakistan if contracted with nongovernmental organizations (World Bank 2003). Another important component would be the development of linkages with local public and private institutions and other relevant stakeholders such as community healthcare workers, police, and community leaders. This would help to create an environment that facilitates dialogue with relevant stakeholders to introduce changes in the social and policy environment to encourage the community to engage in safe sexual behavior. Interpersonal communication is likely to be important in convincing truckers that STIs can be prevented.

Involuntary Resettlement

Since freight transport reforms and associated works are likely to require some resettlements, reforms need to address issues such as the resettlement and restoration of livelihoods of low-income people and the rights to proper compensation of tenants, squatters, and those with usufruct rights. The creation and implementation of a national resettlement policy that is enforced effectively and uniformly in all provinces and federal territories would help ensure that the rights of persons directly affected by transport programs are safeguarded. Resettlement plans also need to consider the fact that new roads can split communities and prevent access to social services, sources of water, and even divide agricultural lands. Chapter 4 has described the potential social effects associated with reforms in the freight transport sector focusing on issues of high socioeconomic salience for Pakistan and associated with mutually reinforcing impacts.

Prior to construction, effective safeguard measures and implementation mechanisms need to be put in place to ensure that people are promptly compensated in relation to resettlement and provided support for livelihood development along with appropriate and effective grievance-redress mechanisms at the local level. While resettlement is unlikely to be an issue in the first phase of the envisioned reforms, which are concerned with policy design and implementation, resettlement issues are likely to arise when work on the investment component for both road and rail gains momentum. Such resettlements may also take place in areas already disrupted by the 2010 floods and could thus increase the vulnerability of some affected households. Decisions should be based on considered, consultative, and inclusive planning. Regional and international policies and law precedents are available. In addition to measures for prompt compensation and support for livelihood development along with appropriate and effective grievance-redress mechanisms at the local level, transparent mechanisms for determining compensation, supported by effective and extensive public information campaigns, are critical.

Reforming the Land Registration Act to ensure security of land titles and mandate the complete computerization of all land records in the provinces with mechanisms for transparency and third party validation built in is crucial. The establishment of secure land and property rights and preventing malpractice in the real estate markets is not only vital for protection of existing land holders, but will provide incentives for new businesses and asset owners to invest in new lands. Such investment is an element of the increasing amount and geographical spread of market activity that trade and transport reforms are expected to stimulate.

Strengthening Pakistan's environmental impact assessment (EIA) as a tool to open governmental decisions to public scrutiny would support the adequate consideration of, and response to, the potential social effects of investments in the freight transport sector (table 7.1). While Pakistan's EIA system recognizes the importance of public participation, potentially affected groups are rarely consulted at an early stage of project development. The effectiveness of the EIA system should be bolstered by a reform that, among other things, opens up effective public participation mechanisms to

- Provide adequate opportunities to stakeholders to raise their concerns and influence decision making at early stages of a project;
- Obtain local and traditional knowledge;

Table 7.1 Policy Options to Manage Poverty and Social Priority Issues Associated with Freight Transportation Sector Reforms

Priority social issue	Description	Policy option
Social conflict in urban centers	Ethnic groups could be particularly affected.	Ensure adequate engagement of potentially affected groups in the design and implementation of proposed policies.
Urban poor and nonfarm households affected by increase in transport productivity	Urban poor and nonfarm households might lose their livelihoods because of reforms in the trade and transport sector.	Promotion of structural change to raise the contribution of industrial manufacturing to the economy, boost employment, and increase fiscal revenues. Strengthen connectivity between industrial clusters and domestic and international markets.
Urban sprawl	Creation of economic opportunities in urban areas may increase "pull" migration, increasing the demand for housing and public services.	Priority to slum upgrading and service delivery in urban settings. Capacity building required at least in two tiers (provincial and district) of government to better develop and implement urban development strategies that respond to Pakistan's spatial transformations.
Small operators in the trucking sector have a probability of losing business to new and larger enterprises due to trade and transport reforms. Truckers largely operate in the informal sector, and have little or no contact with government agencies. Programs directed at assisting them will have to reach out to a variety of truckers' associations, which cover truck manufacturers, drivers, adda owners, and goods companies.	Urban poor and nonfarm households might lose their livelihoods because of reforms in the trade and transport sector.	Community development organizations, which typically have experience in advising communities on small-scale enterprise development, to get involved in design and implementation. Community development organizations, might advise communities on small-scale enterprise development.
HIV/AIDS transmission	Growth in the road transport sector, under a business as usual scenario, is associated with increased spread of sexually transmitted infections, including HIV/AIDS. At the same time, increasing railway's participation and modernizing the trucking sector could significantly reduce the risk of HIV/AIDS transmission.	Strengthen the National AIDS Control Program in the freight transportation sector, including information campaigns targeting vulnerable groups.
Involuntary resettlement	Potential involuntary resettlement due to construction of freight transport infrastructure.	Create and implement a national resettlement policy that is enforced effectively and uniformly in all provinces and federal territories, with adequate grievance-redress mechanisms.

- Reduce conflicts among stakeholders;
- Make informed decisions by considering possible adverse impacts and mitigation measures in the EIA report and final decision;
- Educate and increase stakeholders' awareness about the project and its potential environmental impacts;

- Enhance transparency and accountability in decision making; and
- Build trust in the proponents and government institutions.

Public participation should be the basis of scoping efforts and should be mandatory for reviewing EIAs. Information on baseline environmental conditions, environmental impacts, analysis of alternatives, and environmental management plans must be disclosed publicly.

Addressing Priority Environmental Issues

As discussed in chapter 5, strategic environmental, poverty, and social assessment (SEPSA) identified a number of priority environmental problems associated with transport in Pakistan including (i) air and noise pollution, (ii) road safety, (iii) solid and hazardous wastes, (iv) habitat fragmentation and natural resource degradation, and (v) climate change. Freight transportation reforms might consider a number of environmental policy options to enhance the positive effects of increases in transport productivity and to mitigate negative consequences of trade and freight transport reforms.

Air and Noise Pollution Control

Adopting a multimodal transport system and accelerating the implementation of the 2007 Trucking Policy would lead to the replacement of the obsolete, poorly maintained, and highly polluting trucks by larger and modern trucks. These newer trucks, besides being technologically more efficient, cost effective, and less polluting, would reduce the number of trips required to move a given amount of cargo.

The maximum allowed content of sulfur for all fuels used in Pakistan originally was scheduled to drop from 10,000 parts per million (ppm) to 500 ppm by 2008, but the stricter standard was postponed until 2010, and then again until July 1, 2012. The main reason for the postponements was that companies needed more time to retrofit refineries. However, Pakistan can take advantage of ultralow sulfur fuels as they become increasingly available in international markets. Pakistan currently imports about 3.5 metric tons of diesel a year from Kuwait, whose content in sulfur is 2,000 ppm. Importing diesel from Bahrain, Oman, Qatar, or the United Arab Emirates could reduce sulfur contents of diesel used in urban centers to 500 ppm.

Systematic air quality monitoring in urban centers (especially of $PM_{2.5}$ and $PM_{1.0}$) helps track progress of the enforcement of vehicle emission standards. Air quality monitoring is essential to identify the changes in air quality over time, and to determine if vehicle standards are being properly enforced. Ambient air pollution in medium and large urban centers in Pakistan is very serious, and very little has been done to address the problem. The high levels of dangerous pollutants, such as fine particulate matter and sulfur dioxide, cause significant health risks to urban populations. The Government of Pakistan (GoP) needs to revise its strategy regarding ambient air quality management by regularly monitoring the most important pollutants, including $PM_{2.5}$, which according to available evidence plays the largest role in damaging human health.

Ambient air quality standards and vehicular emission standards have been recently adopted but need to be enforced. The enforcement of the recently approved National Environmental Quality Standards for Ambient Air (2010) and the National Environmental Quality Standards for Motor Vehicle Exhaust and Noise (2009) is necessary to help decrease the enormous mortality and morbidity costs associated with poor ambient air quality, particularly in urban areas such as Hyderabad, Karachi, Lahore, and Peshawar. These two standards provide the legal and foundational framework for federal, provincial, and local government programs to manage and mitigate ambient air quality in Pakistan.

Pakistan does need comprehensive legislation to control environmental noise pollution. The National Environmental Quality Standards for Motor Vehicle Exhaust and Noise only apply to noise generated from motor vehicles. There are no national standards for noise regulating limits for residential, industrial, and commercial areas. Road traffic noise is another major source of noise pollution in urban areas. Aircraft noise is a significant source of pollution primarily in the major airports that are located inside or very close to densely populated urban areas. Given that excessive noise is a health risk, there is a need to design, implement, and enforce a comprehensive regulation on noise pollution control that includes standards for controlling noise generated from sources such as airplanes and locomotives, as well as noise standards for residential, industrial, and commercial areas.

Road Safety

Pakistan's transport sector is associated with a significant accident rate that results in deaths, permanent and temporary disabilities, and other economic costs. Road conditions and human behavior are the most relevant variables affecting road safety. Available information indicates that risk factors include poor road quality and lack of appropriate signage. The trucking sector is likely to be involved in a higher proportion of accidents because of practices such as overloading, modifications and poor conditions of trucks, inadequate driving skills, and driver exhaustion caused by long hours behind the wheel. Until recently, obtaining a driver's license in Pakistan was relatively easy, as it did not require formal training and the process involved a few formalities with provincial authorities. The 2007 Trucking Policy should be implemented, as it contemplates measures to provide training to drivers and establish a new system enabling penalty points to be cumulatively counted, resulting in suspension or cancellation of driver's licenses. Additional measures that the GoP might consider include allocating a dedicated budget for road safety and building the capacity of police officers to enforce existing laws.

Transport of Hazardous Materials

Pakistan needs a national framework to manage the transport of hazardous materials. Different materials present hazards during shipment including toxic substances, explosives, compressed gases, flammable liquids and solids, oxidizers and organic peroxides, and radioactive and corrosive substances. The goal is to create and implement a regulatory framework that covers all aspects of hazardous material transport. Key measures that the GoP could adopt include

- Designing standards for the construction of vehicles used to transport hazardous materials;
- Updating information on new chemicals/substances that are transported on Pakistan's roads and railways;
- Enhancing institutional capacity and clarifying legal responsibilities for relevant agencies;
- Mapping of transportation routes and vulnerable points; and
- Providing resources to help the police and local fire departments to properly enforce regulations pertaining to the transport of hazardous materials.

Enhancing institutional capacity and clarifying legal responsibilities for relevant agencies is needed. Currently, the Pakistan Standards and Quality Control Authority (PS&QCA) acts on a demand-driven basis, only after receiving a specific request from a government agency regarding hazardous material spills. PS&QCA recognizes the seriousness of the problems related to a weak regulatory framework. As a result, the following measures can help enhance the institutional capability for relevant agencies: (i) designing training courses pertaining to the transport of hazardous material for personnel from the freight transport sector and government; (ii) training "master trainers" to instruct personnel from trucking companies, Pakistan Railways, law enforcement, and emergency response agencies; and (iii) training government officials in risk analysis and in developing contingency plans to deal with potential spills.

The GoP should consider international best practices in developing its national framework for hazardous materials management. Key examples include the technical guidelines for sound environmental management of various types of waste developed by the Basel Convention (to which Pakistan acceded in 1994),[2] the International Maritime Dangerous Goods Code,[3] and the Model Regulations on the Transport of Dangerous Goods prepared by the United Nations.[4] Part 7 of the UN document's "guiding principles" contains specific provisions concerning transport operations, including the conditions on classification, packing, marking, and issuance of a transport document on labeling, description, and certification that must be met before any dangerous good may be transported, as well as the general, marking, labeling, and placarding conditions with which transport units must comply.

Natural Habitat Fragmentation
The GoP should consider developing a new regulatory framework to avoid the fragmentation of natural habitats and protect biodiversity from the direct, indirect, and cumulative impacts of investments in freight transport

infrastructure. As discussed in chapter 5, Pakistan faces the highest deforestation rate in the region, and there is currently no policy in place to arrest deforestation, much of which is driven by governmental initiatives. The destruction of natural habitats not only affects biodiversity, but also reduces the capacity of ecosystems to provide critical services, such as protection against the floods that recurrently affect Pakistan.

To avoid or mitigate biodiversity loss and natural habitat fragmentation due to construction of new freight transportation infrastructure, Pakistan's EIA system could be reformed. While Pakistan's legal framework for EIA and the Guidelines for Preparation and Review of Environmental Reports have been in place for a number of years, a number of actions are needed to ensure their effective use as planning tools. An important first step would be requiring all public and private projects that require an EIA to comply with the existing guidelines.

Pakistan's EIA system faces a number of weaknesses that need to be addressed to reduce the potential negative effects of the expansion of transport infrastructure on natural habitats and ecosystems. Emphasis should be placed on the following activities:

- Improving the **screening** process to determine whether an EIA is needed based on the project's potential significant effects, instead of using criteria such as the project's cost or capacity;
- Enhancing the **scoping** of the EIA by involving stakeholders in the process;
- Bolstering the analysis of **alternatives**, including the "no project" alternative, so that it is not simply a discussion to justify decisions already made;
- Strengthening horizontal and vertical **coordination** including among sectoral agencies, different levels of government, and financial institutions, among others; and
- Allocating **sufficient resources** to ensure that authorities have the capacities needed to assess the EIA and monitor the implementation of the Environmental Management Plan.

Climate Change Mitigation

A modernized trucking sector and the use of railways for long hauling would help reduce greenhouse gas (GHG) emissions. If the split mode is changed for inland freight transportation to 30 percent rail and 70 percent road (currently it is 4 percent rail and 96 percent road), the annual greenhouse gas emissions would be reduced to 36.8 $TgCO_2eq$ (23.3 percent reduction or a reduction of about 11.2 million tons of GHG discharged into the atmosphere). Emphasis on the freight sector would result in an annual reduction in the consumption of diesel fuels by the inland freight transportation sector in Pakistan, of about 1.06 million metric tons by the year 2025–26. These savings in diesel consumption would imply a yearly reduction of about 6,116 metric tons of sulfur burned in internal combustion engines in the country (table 7.2).

Table 7.2 Policy Options to Manage Environmental Impacts Associated with Freight Transportation Sector Reforms

Priority environmental problem	Description	Policy option
Air pollution	Pakistan urban centers rank as some of the worst in particulate matter (PM) air pollution. Burning of high sulfur fuel leads to high quantities of fine and ultrafine PM, harming public health.	Stricter standards on sulfur content in diesel should not be delayed beyond the next target of July 2012. Low/ultralow sulfur fuels should be purchased from different suppliers, as they are available in international markets. Strengthen Pakistan's Environmental Protection Agency and provincial environmental protection departments and build their capacity to enforce recently adopted ambient air quality standards and vehicular emission standards. Accelerate implementation of the 2007 National Trucking Policy, particularly substitution of the obsolete, poorly maintained, highly polluting trucks for larger and modern trucks.
Noise pollution	Excessive noise levels in urban areas cause ear damage, sleep disturbance, psychiatric conditions, and cardiovascular disorders.	Develop a regulatory framework and enforcement capacity to control environmental noise pollution.
Road safety	Pakistan ranks as one of the most dangerous countries in the world in road safety.	Develop a regulatory framework and enforcement capacity on road safety.
Hazardous waste transportation	With further investment in trade and transport, and greater commerce, movement of hazardous materials and the probability of spills and other emergencies might increase.	Design and implement a national framework to manage the transportation of hazardous materials, based on international best practices.
Habitat fragmentation and natural resource degradation	Pakistan faces the highest deforestation rate in South Asia. Increases in road infrastructure could exacerbate this.	Strengthen the environmental impact assessment system to improve decision making for the development of freight transport infrastructure.
Climate change emissions of greenhouse gases (GHG)	Models showed that some modal shift from road to rail would significantly reduce GHG emissions.	Provide greater emphasis on railroads and on using existing railroads.

Addressing Institutional Change

The institutional capacity of the organizations directly involved in the trade and transport sector and responsible for natural resources protection, environmental management, and management of social aspects in Pakistan is, at best, deficient. The existence of a formal unit responsible for these areas, as well as the level of resources and expertise devoted to address environmental and social priorities varies notably from one organization to another (appendix B provides a description of environmental and social management structures in each key organization). However, even in those organizations that have devoted specific resources to create and staff a dedicated unit, such as the National Highways Authority, there is a lack of both technical capacity and ability to affect decisions within the agency. While the specific reforms advocated by SEPSA will do much to mitigate the impact of trade and transport reforms, they should be coupled with additional efforts to develop management systems to recognize, assess, and mitigate environmental and social issues as they arise.

The lack of environmental and social planning capacity at transport agencies should be rectified with a program of institutional strengthening and capacity building. Environmental and social units should be established in all those organizations that still lack them. These units should be integrated into the planning and decision-making process of their organization, so they possess the ability to influence construction and operation in such a way as to take into account environmental and social considerations (particularly early on in the planning process when such considerations can be dealt with more efficiently). The eventual aim of these environmental and social units should be to achieve certification as environmental management systems that meet international standards.

Establishment of dedicated environment and social units within Pakistan Railways, Civil Aviation Authority, and Gwadar Port Authority, and institutional strengthening for existing environment units might enhance environmental management of freight transport. Priority should be given to the creation of capabilities of environmental units to

- Integrate environmental and social aspects into early stages of planning/decision-making process within all organizations;
- Conduct analytical work on environmental priority setting for each transport organization;
- Align environmental expenditure with priorities;
- Monitor results of environmental interventions;
- Develop systems to monitor baseline environmental quality (and changes over time) as a result of freight transport reforms; and
- Achieve international certifications such as ISO 9001:2000 (Quality Management System), ISO 14001:2004 (Environmental Management System), and OHSAS 18001:2007 (Occupational Health and Safety Management System).

All environmental protection interventions should be accompanied by capacity-building efforts, which will help key environmental agencies in developing and enforcing environmental regulations. The stringency of the environmental regulatory framework and its effective enforcement are needed to improve environmental quality. Recent changes in Pakistan's Constitution have devolved major responsibilities for environmental management to subnational governments, which will have significant implications for environmental management. Capacity-building efforts are needed to train those involved in local governments for their new roles in enforcing environmental regulations. Since the adoption of the 18th Constitutional Amendment, provincial governments have devolved environmental management responsibilities in an ad hoc manner. In Punjab, for example, District Environment Officers have been appointed in most districts; however, in other provinces, the environment departments have set up regional offices. While decentralization of environmental management responsibilities offers a number of benefits, including the ability to respond more effectively to local environmental problems, differences in the capacity of environmental agencies or poor enforcement of environmental standards could lead to more severe environmental degradation in different parts of the country.

Enhancement of inter-agency and intersectoral coordination can also contribute to government effectiveness in environmental management. Institutionalized mechanisms should coordinate the role of other agencies involved in environmental management, whereas it is highly recommended that the newly created Ministry of Climate Change be strengthened to take a leading role in institutional coordination for the implementation of environmental protection interventions across different administrative levels through systematized agreements and coordinated actions.

Decentralization efforts may fail if they do not have a reasonable level of supervision and monitoring by central governments and a good level of coordination between environmental agencies. Even when local capacity to effectively address environmental issues such as urban air pollution is strong, the transfer of responsibilities may make the coordination of national environmental policies difficult, particularly in federative systems. Coordination is required both between economic and sector ministries, as well as across different tiers of government.

As a result of the 18th Amendment to the Constitution, Pakistan's Ministry of Environment (MoE) was formally dissolved in June 2011. The recently created Ministry of Climate Change has be given a mandate to carry out the functions of the former MoE, including developing national environmental policies, engaging in international environmental negotiations, dealing with transboundary environmental issues, and promoting interprovincial coordination. The apex environmental agency should also be given responsibility for coordinating the institutional strengthening and capacity building of provincial environmental protection agencies and environmental units to be created within transport agencies.

Notes

1. It should be noted that, in Pakistan, stark differences in educational attainment exist between regions and across ethnic groups. More than 50 percent of young people speaking Baluchi or Saraiki have less than four years of education, in contrast to roughly 10 percent of Urdu-speaking youth (UNDP 2010).
2. See Basel Convention Technical Guidelines at http://www.basel.int/TheConvention/Publications/TechnicalGuidelines/tabid/2362/Default.aspx. Accessed December 9, 2011.
3. International Maritime Dangerous Goods (IMDG) Code. See http://www.imo.org/blast/mainframe.asp?topic_id=158#1. Accessed December 9, 2011.

4. See UN Recommendations on the Transport of Dangerous Goods—Model Regulations. http://www.unece.org/trans/danger/publi/unrec/rev13/13nature_e.html.

References

Cornman, Deborah H., Sarah J. Schmiege, Angela Bryan, T. Joseph Benziger, and Jeffrey D. Fisher. 2007. "An Information-Motivation-Behavioral Skills (IMB) Model-based HIV Prevention Intervention for Truck Drivers in India." *Social Science & Medicine* 64 (8): 1572–84.

Gazdar, Haris. 2009. "Policy Responses to Economic Inequality in Pakistan Policy." Karachi, Pakistan: Collective for Social Science Research. http://researchcollective.org/Documents/Policy%20Responses_to_Economic_Inequality_in_Pakistan.pdf.

IDS (Innovative Development Strategies). 2011. *SEPSA: Poverty and Social Impact Assessment*. Consultant report prepared for the World Bank. Islamabad.

LUMS (Lahore University of Management Sciences). 2011. Abid A. Burki, Kamal A. Munir, Mushtaq A. Khan, M. Usman Khan, Adeel Faheem, Ayesha Khalid, and Syed Turab Hussain. *Industrial Policy, Its Spatial Aspects and Cluster Development in Pakistan*. Consultant report by the Lahore University of Management Sciences for the World Bank. Lahore, Pakistan.

UNDP (United Nations Development Programme). 2010. *The Real Wealth of Nations: Pathways to Human Development. Human Development Report 2010*. New York: UNDP.

World Bank. 2003. *Project Appraisal Document of a Proposed Credit in the Amount of SDR 20.2 Million and Grant in the Amount of SDR 6.7 Million to the Government of Pakistan for the HIV/AIDS Prevention Project*. Report 25109-Pak. Washington, DC: World Bank.

APPENDIX A

Key Issues for the Institutional Analysis of the Freight Transport Sector

Introduction

In the context of the strategic environmental, poverty, and social assessment (SEPSA), the institutional analysis presented here of the freight transport sector in Pakistan gives particular emphasis to environmental and social aspects to promote the adoption of a pragmatic approach for achieving an efficient, sustainable, and economical freight transport sector. The institutional analysis covers the four freight transport sectors in Pakistan—that is, road (mainly consisting of highways and trucking), rail (mainly consisting of Pakistan Railways (PR)), air (aviation-related services/industry), and water (mainly ports and shipping). It notes the limited institutionalization of environmental and social aspects in the transport sector, and how such institutionalization can be strengthened going forward.

This appendix reviews the organizational framework in place to address environmental and social priority issues associated with trade and transport reforms in Pakistan. It highlights gaps and inefficiencies in this framework and recommends proposals for remedying these gaps.

Since trade and transport sector reform is a large, national-level undertaking, the responsibility for mitigating its negative environmental and social impacts does not rest solely with transport-related departments and agencies. It is expected that freight transport reform will also place a burden on the environmental management agencies tasked with ensuring that trade and transport projects meet environmental standards. The scope of the institutional analysis presented in this appendix does not include Pakistan's environmental management framework and regulatory apparatus, which are discussed in appendix B.

This appendix was prepared by Ernesto Sánchez-Triana, Rahul Kanakia, and Hammad Raza. The findings, interpretations, and conclusions expressed in this appendix do not necessarily reflect the views of the staff or Executive Directors of the World Bank or the governments represented by the Executive Directors.

This appendix has four sections. The "Institutional Arrangements for Trade and Environmental Management" section describes freight transport institutions in Pakistan. The "Redefining the Role of Government in the Development of Freight Transport Infrastructure" section presents proposals for restructuring transport-related agencies and creating a new regulatory framework to better facilitate cross-sectoral planning and for raising the environmental management systems of transport agencies up to international standards. The "Summary of Conclusions and Recommendations Regarding the Freight Transport Sector" section summarizes this appendix's conclusions and recommendations.

Institutional Arrangements for Trade and Environmental Management

Road Transport Sector

The total road network in Pakistan is approximately 259,758 kilometers long, of which approximately 10,000 kilometers are national highways or federal motorways that are under the responsibility of the federal government's National Highways Authority (NHA) (GoP 2007a). As of March 2010, there were an estimated 216,119 trucks, which mostly plied approximately 180,000 kilometers of comparatively higher-quality roads (GoP 2010). The road freight industry has achieved remarkable growth since the mid-1970s and now dominates the domestic freight sector, with 96 percent of the market (GoP 2007b).

The Ministry of Communications functions as a central policy-making and administrative authority on the roads sector in Pakistan. The Ministry is headed by a Federal Secretary. It has been organized into two wings, the Administration Wing and the Roads & Road Transport Wing. There are a number of autonomous and attached/subordinate departments under the Ministry: (i) the National Transport Research Centre, (ii) the National Highways & Motorway Police, (iii) the NHA, and (iv) the Construction Machinery Training Institute.

Despite Pakistan's heavy reliance on the road sector for freight transportation, a massive financing gap in maintenance has caused the condition of major highways to deteriorate steadily. Poor funding for repairs and reconstruction has caused road users to complain about the poor state of the highway network. A survey in 2004–05 found that the pavement condition on 37 percent of the federal network was in *"poor to very poor condition"* (World Bank 2009). In recent years the budget allocation by NHA for road development and upgrade has shrunk. This will result in further road deterioration, which will eventually necessitate increased maintenance funding (World Bank 2009).

Monitoring of Environmental and Social Issues in Road Projects

In general, Pakistan's national/provincial environmental regulations require that road construction and rehabilitation projects prepare and submit an environmental impact assessment (EIA). Federal or provincial environmental protection agencies (EPAs) review and approve these EIAs. In some cases, the preparation of the EIA is carried out when the design work is well advanced and the main decisions regarding project alternatives (particularly alignment) have been determined based on their technical and economic merits. NHA has been working in the past few years to mainstream environmental considerations into its road projects (with certain environmental regulations to be followed). It has in its structure an environmental division comprising four areas: (i) environment, (ii) afforestation, (iii) land, and (iv) social (EALS). The division is headed by a General Manager, and has one Director of Environment, a Deputy Director of Environment, and two Assistant Directors. In addition, it has one Specialist in Environment, another in Afforestation, and one Environmental Inspector. The source of funding for the EALS division is the so-called "Establishment Charges," which consist of a charge of 1 percent of the total costs of all NHA projects. Although substantial advances have been made in the last five years at NHA, additional actions need to be taken to ensure proper consideration of environmental/social aspects.

While the NHA has traditionally only been responsible for highway construction and maintenance, it has of late expanded its functions to assess the environmental and social effects of highway development, a function that is handled by the EALS division, instituted in 2008.

An analysis completed under SEPSA, based on interviews and case studies, reflected on the lagging environmental management aspects of the NHA, which has not yet defined who is responsible for ensuring that road projects' design, construction, and operations are environmentally sound and comply with applicable environmental laws and regulations (Miglino 2011). Currently, this responsibility rests almost exclusively with the staff of the EALS division. Moreover, the experts from the environment division are not usually required to participate in the early phases of project planning (such as inception, pre-feasibility, and pre-design), although they might be invited to do so on a case-by-case basis. Nor do these environmental specialists generally participate in (i) preparation of bidding documents for hiring consultants to carry out designs or construction-supervision activities, (ii) preparation of bids for civil works' contractors, (iii) evaluation of the submitted technical proposals, or (iv) supervision of the work to be carried out by consultants and contractors.

Lack of road safety is caused mainly by (i) weak enforcement of traffic rules; (ii) problems with road design, construction, and maintenance; and (iii) the lack of training of drivers, who typically learn on the job and have not passed tests to obtain licenses. The National Road Safety Secretariat was created in 2006, under the Ministry of Communications. However, its recommendations have not been implemented due to a lack of resources. Average speeds for trucks on highways in Pakistan are about half the average speed for Europe. While road freight costs in Pakistan are among the lowest in the world, the trucking industry provides a low level of service, which is becoming a liability for export industries that need reliability to stay competitive (World Bank 2009). Due to the plethora of small operators in the sector, relative ease of entry, and poor regulation of the sector, truck operators/owners systematically overload their vehicles to maximize their profits. This overloading results in accelerated deterioration of roads

(World Bank 2009). Due to the lack of trained staff and funds, the NHA has not been effectively monitoring these issues.

Rail Transport Sector

The rail sector in Pakistan is operated by Pakistan Railways (PR), which is one of the largest organizations in Pakistan. It employed 86,669 workers in 2007–08 (GoP 2008). It has a network of 7,791 route-kilometers. In 2009–10, PR carried 4.6 million tons of freight, which was estimated at less than 5 percent of the total freight carried in the country (GoP 2008). Over the last decade, both freight and passenger traffic increased for PR, with the former registering an average annual increase of 4 percent and the latter of 3.2 percent (GoP 2010). However, business began to dwindle in 2008, as the economy slowed and internal security issues intensified.

PR is a state-owned rail transport service. Its headquarters are in Lahore, but its management is overseen by the federal Ministry of Railways in Islamabad. The Railway division of this ministry is responsible for overall control of PR, as well as for guiding its overall policy. There are four Directorates in this division: (i) the Administrative Directorate, (ii) the Technical Directorate, (iii) the Planning Directorate, and (iv) the Finance Directorate. In addition, the General Manager (Operations), the General Manager (Manufacture and Services), and the federal government Inspector of Railways also report directly to the Secretary of the Ministry of Railways.

The Railway Board is the highest body for technical matters in the railways. The general supervision and management of affairs of PR is vested in the Railway Board, which has been reconstituted. The new Railway Board consists of the Chairman and five Members, of whom three are from the private sector. The Secretary to the Ministry of Railways is the ex officio Chairman of the Railway Board, and the General Manager of Railways is the Chief Executive Officer.[1]

Presently, there is no railway regulatory framework in existence in Pakistan. However, because the Government of Pakistan (GoP) is considering limited privatization in the sector, a regulatory framework is under consideration. As per the Privatization Commission of Pakistan,[2] the broad objectives of the proposed Regulatory Policy are to

- Regulate the establishment, working, and provision of railway services in Pakistan;
- Promote and protect the interests of users of railway services;
- Promote competition in the provision of railway services;
- Encourage investment in railway infrastructure and rolling stock by the private sector;
- Promote efficiency and economy in the provision of railway services; and
- Resolve disputes arising in the industry.

Moreover, the Regulator is expected to have three major functions: (i) overseeing the rules and conditions establishing access to infrastructure and approving access contracts, (ii) licensing private train operations and resolving disputes of a regulatory nature, and (iii) managing public service obligations for the military and other passenger traffic.

Monitoring of Environmental and Social Impacts in the Rail Sector

The railway sector has made very little progress in considering the social and environmental aspects of rail projects. There is no formal structure within PR (properly staffed, with the necessary resources) that is tasked with addressing the environmental and social problems in the railways sector. The aforementioned analysis completed under SEPSA reported the low awareness of PR top management officials of potential environmental problems in Pakistan's rail sector (Miglino 2011). They considered these environmental issues to be meager and considerably smaller than those faced by sectors such as roads, ports, industry, and energy. In addition, they cited a lack of resources as a reason for not adopting sound environmental standards. With the exception of some projects of track rehabilitation and doubling of track, executed mainly in existing right-of-way, PR has not been involved in any major projects of expansion (new track construction) in the past few decades.[3]

It is understandable that the environment is not a top priority in an organization with enormous administrative, managerial, financial, political, and operational problems like PR. However, the organization needs to prepare itself to implement the institutional reforms and large investments required to become a major player in the freight transport sector in Pakistan, as it used to be in the past.

Aviation Sector

The Pakistan International Airlines (PIA) Corporation was established in 1955 and was for a long time the only airline in the country. It is a statutory body that comes under the administrative control of the Ministry of Defense. Pakistan adopted an Open Skies Aviation Policy in the early 1990s. Private airlines joined the civil aviation industry in Pakistan as a result of the policy.

Pakistan has 42 functional airports out of which 10 serve international flights. Two additional international airports are being constructed in Islamabad and Gwadar with the involvement of the private sector, under the policy of liberalizing the aviation industry in Pakistan. The Pakistan Civil Aviation Authority (CAA) was established to regulate the aviation sector in Pakistan and develops, maintains, and manages all civil aerodromes throughout the country. It is controlled by the GoP through the Ministry of Defense. To achieve its strategic objectives, the CAA has undergone a major restructuring process. The new organization now separates the three main functions of Regulatory, Airport Services, and Air Navigation Services.

The CAA Board is the highest body for technical matters in the airways. The general supervision and management of affairs of CAA is vested in the CAA Board. The CAA Board consists of a Chairman and 10 Members, of whom four are from the private sector. The Secretary of the Ministry of Defense is the ex officio Chairman of the CAA, and the Chief Financial Officer of the CAA is the Secretary to the CAA Board. Its other members include the Vice Chief of the Air Staff, the Secretary of the Planning and Development Division, the Additional Secretary of the Ministry of Defense, the Additional Secretary of the Ministry of Finance (MoF), the Director General of the CAA, and the Managing Director of the PIA.[4]

Management of Environmental and Social Impacts in the Aviation Sector

The aviation sector has made very little progress in considering the social and environmental aspects of its daily operations and new projects. There is no formal structure in the CAA that is tasked with addressing the environmental and social problems of the air transport sector. According to the CAA, their largest environmental initiative is "Bird Menace Control"—that is, controlling the population of birds on the airport grounds and in the vicinity that can be a potential hazard to aircrafts. The CAA considers its only environmental issue to be unwanted bird activity around airports, due to bird attraction sites (such as butcheries, slaughterhouses, and poultry farms). It has adopted measures to reduce bird activity in, or near, airports by discouraging development of garbage dumps and other sites or activities that can attract birds.

However, as of the recent restructuring, the CAA is now more focused on new initiatives, such as introduction of Enterprise Resource Planning; health, security, safety, and environment; Corporate Social Responsibility; Ethics Management Program; a customer feedback mechanism at the airports; Employees Performance Management System; benchmarking; and outsourcing of noncore and wasteful activities. The CAA is now also committed to acquiring international standards for the Integrated Management System such as the ISO 9001:2000 standards (Quality Management System), ISO 14001:2004 (Environmental Management System), and OHSAS 18001:2007 (Occupational Health and Safety Management System).[5] Achieving these standards would require substantial investments, reforms, and institutional strengthening, including those needed to address the environmental and social issues arising from its activities.

Recently, PIA launched the health, safety and environment (HSE) initiative. The objective of this program is to mature the airline's HSE systems to a level that will eventually lead to OHSAS 18001 and ISO 14001 certification. As part of this program, PIA plans to conduct organization-wide HSE trainings, development of HSE objectives, implementation of HSE system procedures, and management reviews to assess the continual effectiveness of the HSE system.[6]

Ports and Shipping Sector

In Pakistan, freight transported over water is almost always sea-based, since inland water channels do not have the infrastructure—nor, in many cases, the capacity—for freight transport. Pakistan has two main seaports through which much of the country's cargo moves. The Karachi Port (KP) and Port Qasim, both located in Pakistan's largest city and commercial center (Karachi), act as primary entry and exit points for imports and exports.[7] KP, which accounts for about 60 percent of the nation's sea trade, handles about 1.4 million twenty-foot equivalent units of cargo per annum.[8] The Port has two wharves (East and West Wharf with capacity of 17 and 13 vessel berths, respectively) and handles all forms of cargo. The Port can accommodate vessels of up to 75,000 deadweight tonnage (DWT).[9] Port Qasim, which handles about a third of total sea trade, can accommodate vessels of up to 75,000 DWT. The Gwadar Port, which was formally inaugurated in December 2008, currently has the capacity to handle vessels of up to 50,000 DWT.[10]

The Ministry of Ports and Shipping functions as the central policy-making and administrative authority for the country's shipping sector. The Ministry of Ports and Shipping consists of one division, the Ports & Shipping division, which takes care of all the ports in the country. The main responsibility of the ministry is to provide policy guidelines to the country's ports: the Karachi Port Trust (KPT), Port Qasim Authority (PQA), and Gwadar Port Authority.

A Board of Trustees, comprising a Chairperson and 10 Trustees, administers the KP. The federal government appoints the Chairperson, who is also the Chief Executive of the KPT. The remaining 10 Trustees are equally distributed between the public and the private sectors. The federal government nominates the five public-sector Trustees. Elected representatives of various private-sector organizations fill the seats for the private-sector Trustees. This way all port users find representation on the Board of Trustees.[11]

An act of Parliament on June 29, 1973, established the PQA. Like the other ports, it is under the administrative control of the Ministry of Ports and Shipping. The Chairman of the PQA Board is the Chief Executive of the port. All policy decisions are vested in the PQA Board, which consists of seven members. The Board is a blend of public- and private-sector participation.[12] The PQA is primarily a service-oriented organization. The port provides shore-based facilities and services to international shipping lines and other concerned agencies in the form of adequate water depth in the channel, berths/terminals, cargo-handling equipment, godowns, storage areas, and facilities for safe day and night transit of vessels.

The Gwadar Port Authority manages Gwadar Port, which is located in the western part of the country in the province of Balochistan. The Gwadar Port was developed to

- Capitalize on opportunities for trade with landlocked Central Asian states and Afghanistan;
- Promote trade and transport with Gulf States;
- Transship containerized cargo;
- Increase the socioeconomic development of Gwadar, the province of Balochistan, and the country;
- Reduce congestion and dependency on the country's existing ports; and
- Serve as a regional hub for major trade and commercial activities.[13]

Management of Environmental and Social Impacts in the Ports and Shipping Sector

Environmental management at the KPT is the responsibility of the Marine Pollution Control Department, which is headed by a Marine Chief Engineer. KPT also has a Karachi Port Operation Center, which, among other tasks, is responsible for (i) monitoring and controlling port operations, (ii) monitoring and controlling marine pollution in the harbor, and (iii) activating emergency response to handle crises. An analysis completed under SEPSA by a World Bank consultant identified that the knowledge of the officials is tacit rather than organizational. This can result in a significant loss of expertise at the KPT, since there is no succession planning or institutionalized approach. The KP suffers adverse effects from land-based pollution (domestic and industrial) in the harbor area. Due to its location, in the mouth of the Lyari River and in proximity to Karachi's downtown area, the port area receives the untreated wastes from millions of residents and thousands of industries. Port authorities have spent years trying to convince city, provincial, and federal authorities to address the wastewater pollution problem, but without any success, due to the large investment and operation costs involved in the proposed solution (a large wastewater treatment plant). However, KPT's technical capacity to prepare and/or evaluate cost-benefit analyses of large wastewater treatment facilities is very weak.

At PQA, the Environmental Department is responsible for all environmental management issues at the port. There are two Deputy Managers, one for Environment and Safety, and the other for Marine Pollution Control. PQA is presently working on two priority areas: wastewater treatment and solid waste disposal.

Port authorities have included environment on their agenda and have allocated some human resources to meet their environmental objectives. However, these efforts are not sufficient to meet the ever-increasing demands of better environmental and social conditions. The analysis completed under SEPSA found that these environmental units do not have the capacity to deal with complicated situations. Moreover, the knowledge is individual-specific rather than organizational. More needs to be done, particularly in the establishment of environmental and social standards, which are not currently the priority of any of the port authorities.

Other Government Organizations with Trade and Transport Responsibilities

Overall responsibility for providing a comprehensive national plan for development rests with the Planning Commission of Pakistan. This ten-member organization, which the Prime Minister chairs, is responsible for preparing Pakistan's Five Year Plans, whose aim is to provide strategic coherence to the disparate activities undertaken by the GoP. For several years, trade and transport sector reform has been an interest of the Planning Commission. Several reform activities were developed and bundled together as the National Trade Corridor Improvement Program. To design and implement this program, the Planning Commission created the National Trade Corridor Management Unit (NTCMU) to act as a coordinating body for collecting information from, and disseminating information to, the various trade and transport-related organizations. The NTCMU also includes technical advisory services: designing and administering studies to examine options for trade and transport reform and to assist sectoral agencies in managing environmental and social issues in their sectors.[14]

Trade and transport infrastructure is generally a federal responsibility; however, the provinces do play a role in several areas. First, more than 90 percent of Pakistan's roads are owned and maintained by subnational governments, and the majority of Pakistan's road freight does pass, for at least some portion of its journey, over nonfederal roads. The condition of these roads plays a role in affecting road safety and the condition of Pakistan's trucking fleet. In order for integrated multimodal planning to become a reality, there must be linkages between provincial and federal road and highway authorities. Second, with the recent devolution of environmental management responsibilities onto local authorities, the provincial EPAs will now have ultimate responsibility for designing and implementing the environmental requirements that transport-related projects will have to abide by. Provincial authorities will be setting environmental assessment requirements for projects, reviewing those assessments, and then monitoring the adequacy and implementation of mitigations. Given the number of infrastructure projects that are likely to be undertaken because of trade and transport sector reform, it might be useful to have linkages between transport organizations' environment cells and the provincial environmental protection agencies. However, no organizational liaisons of this nature currently exist.

Conclusions Regarding Pakistan's Freight Transport Institutions

Pakistan's transport sector is characterized by multiple agencies that fall under the purview of various ministries. Some of these agencies are responsible for infrastructure, others for operations, and still others for both. The Ministry of Communications is responsible for the National Highway, the Ministry of Ports and Shipping is responsible for shipping and ports, the Ministry of Railways for the railway subsector, the Ministry of Defense for the civil aviation subsector, and the provincial and district governments for the provincial and rural road subsectors. Enforcement of traffic regulations at the provincial level is the responsibility of the provincial police department and the Ministry of the Interior. For national highways, the National Highways & Motorway Police, under the Ministry of Communications, is responsible for enforcing highway regulations. The Railway Police performs this function in the railway subsector. This diversity of agencies promotes an environment in which coordination, intermodal planning, and enforcement are compromised. In addition, government organizations charged with responsibilities regarding the trade and transport sector have very little experience in adequately managing the environmental and social aspects of their activities.

Despite all the directives contained in the regulations stressing the importance of coordination among concerned agencies, at present no formal mechanisms exist for agencies involved in trade and transportation and environmental management to participate in a consultative process with other government agencies for priority setting, development of long-term action plans, and assessment of performance/impacts of specific initiatives. Intersectoral coordination for the oversight of cross-cutting issues is also nonexistent. Some attempts have been made in the past to establish focal points within other ministries, but interactions among these focal points have not yet been institutionalized. It is clear that one of the primary organizational problems facing both transport and environment agencies is a lack of formal mechanisms to promote and enforce coordination.

Redefining the Role of Government in the Development of Freight Transport Infrastructure

The institutional capacity of the organizations directly involved in the trade and transport sector, and responsible for natural resources protection and environmental management in Pakistan, is at best deficient. In addition, the GoP's traditional approach to financing the development of transport infrastructure and favoring public-owned transport enterprises has generated significant distortions that reduce competitiveness, while also allocating scarce public resources to activities that could be funded by other sources. Examples of public projects and policies that have generated significant inefficiencies include subsidies granted to passenger rail at the expense of freight rail, government protection of PIA, government preference of road over rail, and high tariffs in ports. The case for facilitating private-sector participation in the development of freight transport infrastructure is not only supported by the high costs and distortions generated by excessive governmental interference, but is also advocated by the 2011 *Framework for Economic Growth*.

In this regard, the analysis conducted under SEPSA recommends the establishment of a new regulatory framework for developing freight transport infrastructure in the road, railway, port, airport, and maritime modes, by structuring, adjudicating, and managing concession contracts with the private sector. The regulatory framework for developing freight transport infrastructure should also provide clear dispositions regarding the adoption of best environmental and social practices by private-sector contractors. Furthermore, the regulatory framework should provide clear dispositions for ensuring that services provided by the private sector meet high-quality standards and are aligned with the overarching goal of contributing to economic growth by integrating different modes of freight transport to strengthen connectivity and the country's competitiveness. The proposed regulatory framework will confer several benefits, including improving the allocation of public resources and facilitating private-sector participation to develop freight transport infrastructure more efficiently.

Rationale for Redefining the Government's Role

As the "Institutional Arrangements for Trade and Environmental Management" section of this appendix described, the responsibility for the construction, operation, and maintenance of Pakistan's transport infrastructure and policy setting for its freight transport sector is currently split across four ministries (defense, communications, railways, and ports and shipping). Each ministry has an incentive to seek rents by maximizing the power and influence of its portion of the freight transport sector. None of these ministries can acquiesce to the trade-offs involved in developing a modern, multimodal cargo transport industry without potentially losing resources and control. In particular, there is evidence that freight sector reform in Pakistan might result in increases in expenditure for rail transport and corresponding decreases in expenditure for road transport infrastructure. Unless there is a new regulatory framework that addresses Pakistan's overall needs in a dispassionate way, then these trade-offs will have to be imposed on the ministries politically, by parliament, since the ministries will be unwilling to see solutions that have the potential to negatively affect their resources. This kind of subsectoral focus should be avoided in the new regulatory framework, which should cover the entire transport sector.

Further, one of the recommendations of SEPSA is the development of a multimodal transport infrastructure that more closely links rail, road, and sea as transport modalities. The development of this structure will necessarily result in more intimate linkages between the three infrastructures. Given the structure of the GoP, it is unlikely that separate ministries will be able to successfully and efficiently coordinate their efforts in a manner that would efficiently enable this multimodal structure, unless a new regulatory framework that changes the current incentive structure is put in place. In its absence, the danger is that ministries will develop competing, parallel structures, or that ministries will seek to actively hamper cooperation because of a perceived danger that, for instance, linking national highways to rail hubs would eventually decrease the necessity for long-range interprovincial highways and end, in the long run, with decreasing funds for road construction. To the extent that the ministries see themselves as competitors for government funds, they will be unwilling to cooperate. Even when they are willing to cooperate, it is likely that the lack of direct authority over one another's operations will result in planning difficulties and priority-setting issues. It is difficult for any kind of organization to allow a substantial portion of its core mission to be dictated by external parties. Even if the ministries are required, by legislation, to mesh their operations, the differences in command structure are likely to make this cooperation somewhat inefficient and tenuous in practice.

Finally, the new regulatory framework for developing freight transport infrastructure should aim to minimize the risk of regulatory capture, which is the tendency of regulators eventually to come under the control of the industries that they are supposed to be regulating and, as a result, to create regulations that are designed to aid the industry, rather than the public. Regulatory capture can come about through corrupt means, but it can also come about through sympathy: regulators spend so much time working with the industry that they come to adopt the industry's viewpoint. Under the new regulatory framework for developing freight transport infrastructure, each freight-sector actor will have comparatively less influence than it does currently, since it will cover all modes of transportation. For instance, right now, there is a danger that the Ministry of Ports and Shipping could be captured by the port authorities, since these are the only major actors in the ports and shipping sector. However, under the proposed new regulatory framework, the ports would have to compete for influence with actors in air, rail, and road transport. This fear of regulatory capture is particularly relevant now, when Pakistan is considering partial privatization, as improperly conducted privatization can lead to giveaways for industry and a loss of possible gains for the government.

Nature of Consolidation

A key recommendation is for the GoP to integrate transport planning and programming under a Modern National Transport Policy and to establish a new regulatory framework for developing multimodal freight transport infrastructure through closely supervised concession contracts to private firms. A major weakness in the transport sector is that there is a lack of coordination among transport agencies, which prevents the consistent application of national priorities. The proposed regulatory framework, which approaches the development of freight transport infrastructure considering the country's (and not the sector's) needs, would need to create incentives to facilitate Pakistan's transit to the era of co-modality.

The new regulatory framework for developing freight transport infrastructure should enable an environment for private-sector participation in the transport sector, which requires strong political leadership. Excessive public interference in the transport sector has led to significant distortions that discourage productivity in the sector and has contributed to the poor performance of key freight sectors, as discussed above. Privatization, with adequate governmental regulation and oversight, not only helps free up the scarce public resources dedicated to infrastructure projects but helps provide the much-needed capital investment, increases management expertise, helps enhance accountability and transparency, leads to an optimal allocation of resources, and increases quality and reliability of delivery. The 2011 *Framework for Economic Growth* acknowledges that competition is a starting point toward increasing efficiency and sustaining economic growth.[15]

The proposed new regulatory framework for developing freight transport infrastructure could also establish coordination mechanisms to leverage carbon finance funds for the investment required to shift modalities from road to rail. Greenhouse gas mitigation alone is not a sufficient reason to promote a modal shift in a country such as Pakistan, which contributes marginally to global emissions and faces significant socioeconomic challenges. However, if these reduced emissions are compensated through resources from programmatic operations of the clean development mechanism or by international assistance for new instruments, such as National Appropriate Mitigation Actions, they could generate resources that could be invested in other priority areas. However, the competitiveness of rail freight for long distances strenghtens the argument for a multimodal system, as rail freight transportation is likely to be a more effective means of transporting goods compared to trucks under heavy precipitation and flooding events.[16]

For these reasons, important goals that the proposed regulatory framework should promote include, among others (i) facilitating private-sector involvement in the transport sector, particularly in the rail sector; and (ii) ensuring fair competition, in which agents are allowed to operate, compete, and interact with each other on a level playing field that creates the environment needed for private initiative to thrive and realize optimum productive efficiency. In some ways, the changes are already taking place. The momentum for change, however, needs to be maintained and possibly increased and extended to cover the entire transport system. The new regulatory framework should sustain the momentum for change by taking a holistic and integrated approach to identify and analyze the elements that significantly affect competitiveness.

It is important that the GoP carefully examine the rationale behind and consequence of *direct* involvement in the freight sector, and acts assertively to eliminate the special advantages or protection that is currently provided to certain companies. The prime examples are the National Logistics Cell and passenger rail services, the former dominating the road sector and the latter dominating rail services at the expense of freight rail transport. In the port sector, while each port has initiated development plans and some healthy competition has started between ports, the government needs to have a long-term vision of the development of the sector to make the best use of its port infrastructure, ensure that the best services are provided, and prevent duplication of investments and waste of resources. It also needs to restructure Pakistan Railways (PR) to translate into realities the objective of making it a more commercially oriented company.[17] As a top priority, the government needs to implement the new trade facilitation strategy, trucking policy, and civil aviation strategy, the latter of which calls for PIA to be restructured along commercial lines and eliminates cross-subsidies.[18] Eliminating harmful government intervention (albeit with competent regulation as required) and protection from anticompetitive practices is fundamental for enhancing the efficiency of the freight sector.

Due to federal budget constraints, bringing in private participation to revamp PR, particularly its freight business, is advantageous given rail's competitive advantage for long distances over road freight transport. Private-sector participation in freight transportation in railways would be helpful in improving track utilization, which currently is only 42 percent. PR might increase private-sector participation in freight transportation—for example, outsourcing station management, letting suburban trains be run by separate companies, and allowing private companies to run their own container trains and rolling stock. Private-sector participation should be encouraged via opening of track access in which private operators are allowed to run freight services on selected routes, for which the legal and regulatory framework will be in place.

The capacity of the new regulatory framework to facilitate private-sector investment and the integration of different modes of transport will require changing the ways in which resources are allocated, increasing accountability by relevant agencies and organizations, and creating a sound monitoring and evaluation framework that can inform progress on meeting Pakistan's goals of improving connectivity and stimulating economic growth. It will also require political support at the highest level, as powerful ministries and beneficiaries of the status quo are likely to resist the adoption of the new regulatory framework for developing freight transport infrastructure.

Scope of the Regulatory Framework

To address the key challenges faced by Pakistan with regard to its inefficient freight transport sector, which reduces the country's competitiveness and also generates significant environmental and social externalities, the new framework for developing freight transport infrastructure should regulate the following areas:

- *Project and Concession Contract Development.* The regulatory framework should clearly define responsibilities for identifying and proposing initiatives to attract private investment in the development of transport infrastructure and linked services, in accordance with policies defined by the Planning Commission and the MoF. Responsibilities should be explicitly allocated for

    (i) Developing plans, programs, and strategies for infrastructure development;
    (ii) Assessing the technical, financial, and legal feasibility of projects and the participation of the private sector in them;
    (iii) Unifying and streamlining the procedures for evaluation, elaboration of studies, negotiations, and other aspects of concessions for freight transport infrastructure development;
    (iv) Carrying out the studies needed to define tolls, charges, tariffs, and other financing mechanisms that would be charged for the use, construction, maintenance, or rehabilitation of infrastructure;
    (v) Assessing the risks of infrastructure development and proposing ways to manage them, distributing them clearly between the parties to the concession contracts; and
    (vi) Supervising, evaluating, and ensuring adequate contract execution.

- *Environmental and Social Management.* The regulatory framework should lead to the establishment of an integrated environmental and social management system (along the lines discussed in the next section), which would ensure that environmental and social concerns are addressed at every stage of the planning and implementation process. The regulatory framework should establish mechanisms to oversee contractors' compliance with applicable environmental and social norms and standards. In addition, it should provide mechanisms for ensuring that the resettlement and rehabilitation processes (both voluntary and involuntary) are consistent with international best practices.

- *Monitoring and Evaluation.* The regulatory framework should establish clear enforcement mechanisms and sanctions for breaches in procurement, financial management, human resources, or environmental and social policy. Ideally, the regulatory framework should create an independent reporting structure capable of intervening through layers of bureaucracy to provide rapid response to issues with potentially high economic and reputational risks. The framework should also enable the preparation of independent and periodic assessments to measure general institutional performance, first by collecting baseline performance data, and then determining indicators for measuring improvements in efficiency.

Attracting Private-Sector Investment

A new organization could be created with the mandate to attract private-sector investment, including through the development of public-private partnerships and the development of concession contracts under schemes including "build, operate, transfer" and "build, own, operate" among others. The institutional framework should sustain the momentum for change by taking a holistic and integrated approach to identify and analyze the elements that significantly affect competitiveness and hamper private-sector participation in infrastructure development.

Ring-Fencing

The new regulatory framework should include provisions to ring-fence agencies—providing an institutional shield to protect regulators from regulatory capture. At the very least, regulations should be enforced by independent units that do not report to, rely on, or have too much contact with those they are required to regulate (which will often include other divisions and departments of their own ministries). However, as the intermodality of Pakistan's transport system increases, the ability of ministries to self-regulate and to adjudicate conflicts between themselves will decrease. In the long run, an independent transport regulatory authority should enforce the new regulatory framework.

Strengthening Environmental Management in the Trade and Transport Sector

Of the primary agencies tasked with managing and regulating the nation's trade and transport systems, only the NHA and the port authorities have devoted significant attention to environmental issues. The NHA has an environment division whose responsibility is incorporating environmental considerations into road design, while the PQA and KPT have both devoted some level of staff and resources to monitoring and controlling marine pollution. However, even the environmental units of these three organizations are understaffed, lacking in technical capacity, and poorly integrated into the priority-setting and decision-making structures of their organizations.

Whether or not a new regulatory framework is established, all agencies and departments with transport-related responsibilities should have dedicated environmental units. These units should be responsible for

- Conducting environmental assessments that meet the standards of Pakistan's regulations;
- Designing and implementing proposals for enhancing the positive environmental and social impacts of transport programs;
- Measuring baseline environmental air, water, noise, and forest quality;
- Measuring the impact of freight activities on environmental quality;
- Conducting public hearings to gain feedback on transport-related proposals from affected populations—particularly the poorest and most vulnerable populations—as well as other stakeholders; and
- Affecting the decision-making process in their respective agency, not just at the mitigation phase (after major planning is completed) but also at the initial stages, where the environmental unit can influence the choice of possible alternatives.

Priority-Setting Role of Environment Units
Vulnerable populations and the overall society would benefit from the implementation of a priority-setting mechanism within each transport organization considering (i) the impacts of environmental degradation over the poor and most vulnerable groups, (ii) the most urgent needs as perceived by the population, (iii) the costs that environmental degradation impose on society, and (iv) a cost-benefit analysis of environmental measures. The creation of a group within each transport organization to conduct, in close collaboration with provincial environmental management agencies, the analytical work for priority identification would provide analytically sound foundations for environmental priorities and budget allocations in response to those priorities.

Creating the Capacity to Evaluate Results and Impacts and Learn from Experience
All the transport institutions would benefit from incorporating result and impact evaluations as part of their management routine. Without the capacity to evaluate, they will not be able to learn and build in institutional change. For this, they would need to systematically create baselines and entrust evaluations to independent consultants or organizations, researchers, think tanks, and academic institutions that could be contracted to conduct these evaluations. The creation of a competitive evaluation fund could be a good way of

encouraging an evaluation and learning culture in the system. The fund could also support the organization of learning activities, such as retreats to discuss evaluation results and workshops for cross-learning and analyzing international best practices. These learning activities should try to involve a broad audience of the institutions' staff, and participants from partner organizations, like nongovernmental organizations, research institutions, and universities.

Aligning Environmental Expenditures with Priorities
Public resources allocated to support environmental sustainability are scarce. Therefore, the effectiveness of environmental expenditure will increasingly depend on each transport organization's capacity to allocate resources according to environmental priorities. Therefore, it is suggested that a planning process be used to align the annual expenditures with environmental priorities identified through the priority-setting process. Additionally, given the number of environmental activities supported by donors, or implemented by regional and local governments, the transport organizations might consider efforts aimed at planning environmental roundtables involving public institutions, donor agencies, and civil society to discuss priorities, coordinate actions, and develop a joint strategy.

Creating Capacity to Monitor Environmental Expenditure
An adequate assessment of policy implementation requires reliable monitoring and evaluation of environmental expenditure according to results and impacts. The proposed environmental units at the transport organizations should conduct periodic monitoring. To do so, they would develop indicators of results and impacts for each of the priority issues, and incorporate data delivered by participatory monitoring mechanisms into the monitoring and evaluation system.

Measuring Environmental Quality
To measure the impacts of trade and transport reform, environmental units at transport organizations should create monitoring systems for environmental quality. This environmental information system should include air quality, water quality, waste handling/management, forestry, and biodiversity.

International Certifications
The eventual goal of these internal environmental and social management systems should be to achieve certification against international benchmarks. The ISO 14000 system of standards certifies that an organization's environmental management system is able to identify and control the environmental impact of its activities, continually improve its environmental performance, and implement a systematic approach to setting environmental objectives and targets.[19] These standards are seen as an international benchmark to which many private corporations and public utilities aspire. There are also equivalent certifications,

such as the ISO 9000 set of standards, covering quality management systems, and the OHSAS 18000 standards for occupational health and safety management systems.[20] The possession of international-quality environmental and social systems can often be a selling point for international donors and private partners, because they are seen as reducing the risk of environmental or social harms that might result in reputational losses for agencies and corporations that must bow to public opinion in the West. As a result, high-quality environmental management systems have the potential, in the long run, to pay for themselves in cheaper and more easily available financing for the organization as a whole.

Summary of Conclusions and Recommendations Regarding the Freight Transport Sector

In conclusion, one of the major challenges facing the fractured transport system in Pakistan is the lack of a unified planning structure. It is recommended that a new regulatory framework be adopted to develop the freight transport infrastructure in a way that facilitates intermodal connectivity and private-sector participation. For this new framework to effectively and efficiently facilitate private-sector involvement, promote integration of different modes of transportation, and address the freight transport sector's key challenges, it should have a broad scope covering environment and social management, project and concession contract development, and monitoring and evaluation. The framework should also create the mechanisms to leverage climate change mitigation funds for investment in cleaner freight transport modalities. This framework should avoid subsectoral focuses that can lead to perverse incentives, regulatory capture, and rent-seeking behavior that would inefficiently privilege one transport modality above the rest. The units responsible for enforcing this regulatory framework should be kept independent of the government agencies and private firms that they regulate. The current regulatory framework places transport in the hands of a number of different ministries and agencies. The new regulatory framework should provide a platform for them to engage in dialogue with each other to coordinate policies and investments.

Additionally, the lack of environmental planning capacity at transport agencies should be rectified with a program of institutional strengthening and capacity building. Environmental units should be established in all those organizations that do not currently possess them. These units should be integrated into the planning and decision-making process of their organization, so they possess the ability to influence construction and operation in such a way as to take into account environmental and social considerations (particularly early on in the planning process when such considerations can be dealt with more efficiently). The eventual aim of these environmental and social units should be to achieve certification as environmental management systems that meet international standards. Table A.1 presents a summary of recommended actions.

Table A.1 Recommended Actions for Improving Pakistan's Institutional Framework for Management of Trade and Transport

Recommended action	Time frame
Creation of a new regulatory framework	
A regulatory framework should be established to regulate private-sector participation in freight transportation infrastructure	Medium term
Establishment of clear mechanisms under the framework for project and concession contract development, environmental and social management, and monitoring and evaluation of the entire freight transport sector	Medium term
Creation of ring-fenced regulatory units within each transport-related ministry to enforce the regulatory framework	Medium term
Creation of an intersectoral transport regulatory authority to enforce regulatory framework and encourage dialogue/coordination	Long term
Strengthening environmental and social capabilities of transport agencies	
Establishment of dedicated environment and social units within Pakistan Railways, Civil Aviation Authority, and Gwadar Port Authority, and institutional strengthening for existing environmental units	Short term
Creation of capability for environmental units to (i) conduct analytical work on environmental priority setting for each transport organization, (ii) align environmental expenditure with priorities, and (iii) monitor results of environmental expenditure	Short term
Creation of systems to measure baseline environmental quality (and changes over time) as a result of freight transport reform, particularly changes to air and water quality	Short term
Integration of environmental and social units into early stages of planning/decision-making process within all organizations	Medium term
Achievement of international certifications: ISO 9001:2000 (Quality Management System), ISO 14001:2004 (Environmental Management System), and OHSAS 18001:2007 (Occupational Health and Safety Management System)	Long term

Notes

1. GoP Ministry of Railways. http://www.railways.gov.pk/. Accessed June 21, 2011.
2. GoP Privatization Commission of Pakistan. http://www.privatisation.gov.pk/Transport/Pakistan%20Railways.htm. Accessed June 20, 2011.
3. Aly, Javed Hasan, Abdus Sami Khan, Sheherbano Burki, and Faiza Ghaffar Khan. 2009. *Structural Analysis of Pakistan Railways. Study Conducted for Pakistan Railways Advisory and Consultancy Services (PRACS). Final Report.* Lahore, Pakistan. http://www.scribd.com/doc/27964121/Project-Warehouse-Design-Logistics-Sector-Report. Accessed June 20, 2011.
4. Civil Aviation Authority. http://www.caapakistan.com.pk/CAABoardView.aspx. Accessed June 22, 2011.
5. Civil Aviation Authority. http://www.caapakistan.com.pk/about_us.aspx. Accessed June 22, 2011.
6. Pakistan International Airlines. http://www.piac.com.pk/PIA_About/pia-about_HSEQP.asp. Accessed July 22, 2011.
7. Phase I of the deep-sea port at Gwadar in Balochistan province was inaugurated in March 2007, but port traffic has been relatively slow at Gwadar given available capacity at Karachi, and the fact that Gwadar does not yet have transport linkages up-country.
8. World Bank. 2006.

9. Karachi Port Trust. http://www.kpt.gov.pk. Accessed June 23, 2011. The Karachi International Container Terminal (KICT) opened the West Wharf in 1996 for specialized handling of container cargo. It has the capacity to handle 525,000 twenty-foot equivalent units (TEUs) of cargo per annum. Similarly, the Pakistan International Container Terminal (PICT), which opened at East Wharf in 2002, can handle up to 450,000 TEU of cargo per annum, with plans to expand capacity to 700,000 TEU per annum.
10. Gwadar Port Authority. http://www.gwadarport.gov.pk/PortProfile.aspx. Accessed June 23, 2011. Currently, it has three multipurpose berths and a 4.5 kilometer long approach channel, which has been dredged up to 14 meters. The second phase of port development is ongoing.
11. Karachi Port Trust. http://www.kpt.gov.pk/. Accessed June 23, 2011.
12. Port Qasim Authority. http://www.pqa.gov.pk/. Accessed June 23, 2011.
13. Gwadar Port Authority. http://www.gwadarport.gov.pk/Home.aspx. Accessed June 23, 2011.
14. National Trade Corridor Management Unit. http://ntcip.gov.pk/index.php?option=com_content&view=article&id=80&Itemid=69. Accessed October 9, 2011.
15. GoP Planning Commission. 2011.
16. Ibid.
17. World Bank 2009.
18. Government of Pakistan 2007b.
19. ISO (International Organization for Standardization). "ISO 14000 environmental management." http://www.iso.org/iso/iso_14000_essentials. Accessed September 13, 2011.
20. ISO (International Organization for Standardization). "ISO 9000 quality management." http://www.iso.org/iso/iso_9000_essentials. Accessed September 13, 2011.

References

GoP (Government of Pakistan). 2007a. "Road Safety in Pakistan." Ministry of Communication, National Road Safety Secretariat, Islamabad.

———. 2007b. "Trucking Policy for Modernization of the Trucking Sector of Pakistan under National Trade Corridor Improvement Programme." Ministry of Industries, Production & Special Initiatives. Islamabad. http://www.pakboi.gov.pk/pdf/Sectoral%20Policies/TruckingPolicy.pdf.

———. 2008. *Pakistan Railways: Yearbook 2007–08*. Lahore: Pakistan Railways.

———. 2010. "Pakistan Economic Survey 2009–10." Ministry of Finance, Islamabad. http://www.finance.gov.pk/survey_0910.html.

GoP (Government of Pakistan) Planning Commission. 2011. *Pakistan: Framework for Economic Growth*. Islamabad.

Miglino, Luis. 2011. *SEPSA: Environmental Management Component*. Consultant report, Washington, DC: World Bank.

World Bank. 2006. "Transport Competitiveness in Pakistan—Analytical Underpinning for National Trade Corridor Improvement Program." Energy and Infrastructure Operations Unit, World Bank, Washington, DC.

———. 2009. "Second Trade and Transport Facilitation Project. Project Appraisal Document." Report 48094-PK, Sustainable Development Unit, Pakistan Country Management Unit. Washington, DC: World Bank.

APPENDIX B

Pakistan's Environmental Regulatory Framework

Introduction

The strategic environmental, poverty, and social assessment (SEPSA) of trade and transport sector reforms primarily contains recommendations on how to strengthen the environmental planning capabilities of Pakistan's trade and transport organizations, so that these organizations will be better able to manage their own environmental impacts and priorities. However, it is expected that trade and transport sector reform in Pakistan will place a burden on Pakistan's environmental regulatory systems. For that reason, this appendix describes those systems and looks at policy options to strengthen Pakistan's environmental management framework to better accommodate the demands of trade and transport sector reform.

This analysis covers provincial environmental management agencies, the judicial system and Environmental Tribunals (ETs), and other ministries with environmental responsibilities. It also examines the recent devolution of federal environmental management responsibilities onto provincial governments.

Following the introduction above, this appendix has three additional sections. The first section provides a description of agencies tasked with environmental management. The second section contains recommendations for environmental coordination and institutional strengthening. The final section summarizes this appendix's conclusions and recommendations.

Environmental Management Agencies

Until recently, the responsibility for environmental priority setting and formulation in Pakistan rested with the federal Ministry of Environment (MoE), while the federal Pakistan Environmental Protection Agency (Pak-EPA) was the

---

This appendix was prepared by Ernesto Sánchez-Triana, Javaid Afzal, Rahul Kanakia, and Hammad Raza. The findings, interpretations, and conclusions expressed in this appendix do not necessarily reflect the views of the staff or Executive Directors of the World Bank or the governments represented by the Executive Directors.

organization mainly responsible for regulatory enforcement. However, the passage of the 18th Amendment to the Constitution of Pakistan resulted in the dissolution of the former ministry (in May 2011) and a downscaling of the latter's scope.

However, on October 26, 2011, the Government of Pakistan (GoP) established a Ministry of Disaster Management and assigned much of the MoE's environmental portfolio, including planning functions and control over the Pakistan EPA, to the new ministry. The Ministry was subsequently transformed into the Ministry of Climate Change (MoCC). Given the newness of this development, it is unclear how the new agency will fit into Pakistan's environmental regulatory framework, but it is likely that the agency will require institutional strengthening and technical assistance to meet its new responsibilities.

Environmental Management at the Federal Level

The 18th Constitutional Amendment devolved responsibilities for environmental management to subnational governments. Since the adoption of the 18th Constitutional Amendment, provincial governments have taken over environmental management responsibilities in an ad hoc manner. In Punjab, for example, District Environment Officers have been appointed in most districts. However, in the other three provinces, the environment departments have set up regional offices. While decentralization of environmental management responsibilities offers a number of benefits, including the capacity to respond more effectively to local priorities, there are also significant trade-offs and risks. For example, unequal definition and enforcement of environmental standards, as well as differences in the capacity of environmental agencies, could lead to more severe environmental degradation in different parts of the country.

With the creation of the MoCC, Pakistan has a new apex environmental ministry to aid in designing and implementing public policies, and enforcing regulations. Since environmental problems are typically felt locally, provinces and municipalities are often in a better position to address environmental problems, and thus would achieve superior outcomes if given the freedom to choose the most appropriate policies and instruments. This is the immediate rationale for decentralizing environmental management. However, without proper coordination, decentralization eventually leads to significant differences in environmental quality across regions. The MoCC is well suited to assume this coordination role.

Provincial Environmental Protection Agencies

Each of the four provinces possesses a provincial environmental protection agency, which is tasked with regulatory and monitoring functions such as enforcing environmental regulations, setting environmental priorities, developing policies, managing interventions to deal with environmental priority issues, collecting data on environmental quality, gathering environmental data on polluters, handling environmentally related complaints by stakeholders, developing new environmental regulations, and operating laboratories for testing samples. Generally, the role of these agencies has been limited in practice to the review of environmental assessment documents for large projects being undertaken within the province.

The ambit of each of these agencies increased considerably with the 18th Amendment and the resulting retreat of the federal government from the responsibility for environmental management. However, many environmental issues cut across geographical barriers, and systematized mechanisms for intersectoral coordination to tackle cross-cutting issues and harmonize common interventions have not been set in Pakistan (although hopefully the newly-created MoCC will take up the responsibility for these mechanisms). Despite all the directives contained in the regulations stressing the importance of coordination among concerned agencies, by June 2012, no formal mechanisms existed for agencies involved in environmental management to participate in a consultative process with other provincial or sectoral agencies for priority setting, design, and implementation of interventions; monitoring; and evaluation of effectiveness. Intersectoral coordination for the oversight of cross-cutting issues was also nonexistent. Some attempts were made to establish focal points within other nonenvironment ministries, but interactions among these focal points have not yet been institutionalized (World Bank 2011).

The provincial organizations charged with the implementation of the existing legal and regulatory framework have detailed and ambitious mandates, but in general, have insufficient staff, small budgets, low political prestige, little or no political/administrative autonomy, and high staff turnover rates. The agencies are rarely adequately staffed with experts to monitor and enforce ambient air, water, and soil quality standards; protect valuable natural resources; review environmental impact assessments (EIAs) of major and complex projects and monitor their implementation; carry out meaningful public consultations with affected communities, and so on. As a result, the enforcement of mandatory regulations is lax, and stricter penalties that are sometimes available in the laws are almost never imposed due to, among other reasons, the lack of technical capacity to provide sound evidence of infractions and the fear of political retribution. Furthermore, there is little priority setting for the use of their very limited resources based on sound analytical work, including social and cost-effectiveness criteria. The consequences for the country are, among others, (i) poor ambient quality; (ii) continuing destruction of valuable natural resources; (iii) disproportionate burden of disease on the poor and disadvantaged communities; (iv) ineffective review process of EIAs with long delays in the issuance of environmental permits, adding unnecessary costs to projects; and (v) an excessive judicialization of the environmental permitting process (Khan 2010; Miglino 2011).

A direct consequence of low levels of stakeholder accountability is the mixed quality of EIA reports. In many cases, the quality of reports submitted for highly visible megaprojects might be considered satisfactory, but often the level of research and information needed to evaluate project impact is lacking. Indeed, consultants have been known to submit reports without visiting affected sites to collect information. It is unlikely that this would be tolerated were there greater transparency, genuine public consultation, and social inclusion. According to data obtained from interviews with private consultants involved in the preparation of four EIAs for industrial projects, on average EIAs for such projects are carried out in a time frame of 1.5 months, and they charge project proponents from Rs 0.5 to Rs 1 million (about US$8,200–US$16,400). They complained that "black sheep" consultants conduct an industrial project's EIA even for Rs 0.05 million (US$820). This may explain the bad quality of a large number of EIAs in Pakistan. Based on the case studies of EIAs done for a chrome tannery, an ethanol manufacturing unit, a polyester cotton thread manufacturing unit, and a sugar mill, the authors showed that among other deficiencies, either no evaluation of alternatives was carried out (in the majority of cases), or just a statement was included saying that the alternative was selected based on maximum production efficiency and safety criteria (Miglino 2010).

Environmental Tribunals

In Pakistan, the judiciary has played an increasingly important role in the enforcement of environmental laws, and should continue to be strengthened through continued support for both judges and advocates. When regulatory avenues for environmental enforcement fail, the judicial system is often the only other recourse for resolving environmental conflicts. An independent judiciary and judicial process enhances implementation, development, and enforcement of air pollution control regulations. The Supreme Court of Pakistan has considered several cases regarding the degradation of the environment and the protection of a clean environment, and has concluded that the right to a clean environment is a fundamental right of all citizens of Pakistan, covered by the right to life and right to dignity under Articles 9 and 14 of the Constitution.

The High Courts in the provinces have also intervened and rendered decisions affecting future environmental management. One example of court policy intervention led to the establishment of the Lahore Clean Air Commission. The Lahore High Court appointed the Commission to develop and submit a report on feasible and specific solutions and measures for monitoring, controlling, and improving vehicular air pollution in the City of Lahore.

Section 20 of the Pakistan Environmental Protection Act of 1997 (PEPA) authorizes the federal government to establish as many ETs as it considers necessary, and to specify the territorial limits or class of cases under which each of them shall exercise jurisdiction. According to PEPA, ETs are staffed by Environmental Magistrates appointed by the federal and provincial governments among senior civil judges. ETs were empowered to sentence repeat offenders to up to two years imprisonment and to order the permanent closure of a factory. By January 2011, two ETs were based in Karachi and Lahore. These tribunals in Karachi and Lahore have jurisdiction over other provinces and areas (Khan 2010).

Other Government Agencies with Environmental Responsibilities

The Planning Commission of Pakistan contains an environment section, consisting of a Chief and Deputy Chief, under the Member, Infrastructure. The primary function of the environment section is to incorporate environmental concerns into national development policies. Similarly, all four provinces have an environment section in their Planning and Development Department. The aim of these departments is to incorporate environmental concerns into the overarching development policy of the province, and to ensure that environmental concerns are reflected in the schemes and projects that the province is developing.

Several federal sectoral ministries are important players in the design and implementation of environmental policies. The Ministry of Petroleum and Natural Resources (MoPNR) is responsible for combating adulteration of fuel and increasing standards, particularly by lowering sulfur content for fuel refined in the country. The Ministry of Industries (MoI) is responsible for regulating the types of vehicles that can be imported, potentially constraining imports of high-polluting vehicles at the gate. The MoI is also responsible for measures aimed at modernizing the fleet of public service vehicles and scrapping older vehicles. The Ministry of Finance and MoPNR are responsible for fuel pricing and subsidies. The Ministry of Energy is responsible for clean fuel imports and encouraging the use of compressed natural gas in vehicles. Finally, the Ministry of Agriculture is responsible for regulating burning of sugarcane fields and agricultural waste. However, no mechanism exists for these agencies to dialogue and coordinate with environmental management agencies—a problem that has worsened for these federal Islamabad-based agencies now that primary environmental management responsibilities have been dispersed to the four provincial capitals (World Bank 2011).

Environmental Coordination and Institutional Strengthening

While environmental management in Pakistan has been substantially decentralized, the GoP has recognized, with the creation of the MoCC, that certain responsibilities must be maintained by the central government, regardless of the level of decentralization. These responsibilities deal with (i) enacting environmental standards and policies; (ii) transboundary issues, including international agreements; (iii) coordination between local governments; and (iv) research into environmental issues, such as climate change adaptation and mitigation.

A prominent feature of environmental problems that fundamentally affects the environmental responsibilities of all countries is that they cut across a number of activities. Water pollution, for instance, involves industrial effluents, municipal discharges and agricultural runoff, and a wide range of economic sectors. Environmental regulation therefore is intimately related to the economic regulation of other sectors. Furthermore, while many environmental problems originate and are felt locally, others have a much broader regional or even global impact. The physical boundaries of environmental problems rarely coincide with those of existing political constituencies (districts, municipalities, and provinces), so the need for cooperation and coordination emerges, nationally and internationally, vertically and horizontally.

Specifically, the responsibilities that have been assigned to the MoCC are

- *Design and enactment of environmental policies and standards.* The MoCC has taken over the MoE's policy-making and planning functions for environmental protection and preservation.
- *Federal regulation.* The Pakistan EPA is now under the jurisdiction of the MoCC, and it will continue to be tasked with enforcing environmental regulations under the Pakistan Environmental Protection Act.
- *Handling transboundary issues.* The MoCC will represent the country at international negotiations and in international conventions and initiatives, such as the Montreal Protocol and the United Nations Framework Convention on Climate Change.
- *Coordination of regional agencies.* In the interest of efficiency, collaboration, and sharing of good practices, the role of coordination of efforts among the various regional institutions is maintained at the central government level. Monitoring and evaluating environmental programs that affect multiple regions and granting permits for activities that affect the environment in more than one geographic area are key functions done by the central government. The Global Environmental Impact Study Centre in Islamabad will continue to conduct federally supported research related to climate change, biodiversity, or water issues, such as glacial melting.

Strengthening Provincial Environmental Management Agencies

Trade and transport sector reform is expected to increase the burdens placed on provincial-level environment management agencies by devolution. Currently, the provincial EPAs suffer from (i) limited technical capacity and funding for conducting analytical work and priority setting, (ii) limited funding for designing and implementing programs to address environmental priority problems, and (iii) EIA systems that are too weak to fully address potential negative environmental impacts resulting from large infrastructure projects. The MoCC should be used as the coordinating agency for a program of institutional strengthening and capacity building directed at the provincial EPAs and provincial environmental planning divisions. This program would assist them in

- Acquiring baseline data and monitoring the impact of trade and transport reform on environmental quality in their provinces;
- Developing programs to address environmental priority problems resulting from trade and transport reform, such as: air pollution, hazardous waste transportation, water pollution, noise pollution, road accidents, and so on; and
- Strengthening EIA systems to increase technical capacity of reviewers, improve administrative framework, increase supervisory strength, and handle an increased caseload resulting from new responsibilities and new large infrastructure projects.

Strengthening the MoCC

The MoCC is a new agency that has been cobbled together from disparate bits and pieces. Its portfolio and role are currently unstable. Its staff members (often reassigned members of the defunct MoE) are being gathered up from their interim postings. Even the old MoE had considerable institutional gaps, and was unable to meet many of its constitutional responsibilities. It is highly likely that the MoCC will require considerable institutional strengthening and technical assistance before it is capable of addressing Pakistan's environmental priority problems. The agency should be subjected to a thorough needs assessment to determine what steps should be taken to strengthen its capabilities. Following this needs assessment, a technical assistance program could be developed, which might address the following areas:

- *Climate change research and negotiation.* The MoCC should have the capacity to produce high-quality analytical work on the possible effects of climate change for Pakistan, as well as mitigation/adaptation possibilities. They should have staff members capable of traveling with Pakistan's delegation to various global summits on climate change to provide the needed technical expertise to conduct efficient and informed negotiations regarding Pakistan's role in the emerging global climate change mitigation and adaptation frameworks.

- *Setting coordination incentives.* The MoCC should have the ability to set coordination incentives with subnational environmental units. These incentives include giving the MoCC the ability to cofinance investment projects at the regional level, linked to results agreements. In countries with a decentralized environmental structure, cofinancing is often the most important tool national authorities have to ensure national-regional coordination. A mechanism similar to the one described for budget allocation and disbursement could be applied to monitor compliance with results agreements. Conventional control mechanisms would be used to ensure that project funds are well spent. These mechanisms would help to bolster the federal government's ability to monitor environmental performance and could be used to finance environmental work related to freight transportation, such as air pollution control or projects to strengthen the EIA capacity of provincial EPAs.

- *Reduction of vulnerability to natural disasters.* Natural disasters pose a substantial risk to transport infrastructure. Earthquakes, mudslides, and flooding have the potential to cut vital rail and road links. Conversely, proper transport infrastructure is vital to disaster relief efforts. Is the MoCC capable of analyzing its disaster mitigation priorities and designing programs to address them?

- *Establishing accountability mechanisms.* The MoCC should be able to put in place a simple but effective accountability mechanism that consists of identifying a simple set of standards to measure the fulfillment of basic environmental rights, such as the right to clean air and water. Using simple language, these standards could be broadly disseminated among the population with the help of civil society organizations, making use of national and local media. Every year, report cards measuring the degree of fulfillment of those standards in each region or province could be produced, and town hall meetings could be called to discuss the ability to comply with authorities and civil society, and jointly find remedies and solutions.

- *Promoting public disclosure.* It is crucial that a systematic effort be made to raise awareness of environmental issues that could be a potential result of trade and transport sector reform. Examples of ways to improve public information, and promote transparency, accountability, and awareness are the publication of data in support of key environmental indicators (including health statistics or pollution loads), wider use of public forums to air development initiatives, and broader and more detailed review and discussion of environmental management tools. In Colombia and Indonesia, among other countries, the publication of key environmental performance indicators has been instrumental in raising environmental awareness and placing environmental issues in the national agenda. Mechanisms to disseminate information in a manner that is easily interpretable can allow communities to play a role as informal regulators, and promotes accountability on the part of those being regulated (World Bank 2005).

- *Strengthening the demand side of accountability.* Pakistan has active civil society organizations that play a crucial role in implementing projects, delivering services to poor sectors of the population, and those participating in policy debates. However, the capacity of civil society to participate in monitoring policy implementation and holding environmental institutions accountable is limited. International experience indicates that civil society can play a crucial role when citizens' organizations demand accountability from public institutions. The MoCC should be able to support the development of the technical capacity of civil society organizations to promote social accountability initiatives that could be independently implemented or in association with environmental agencies or with horizontal accountability institutions.

Conclusions and Recommendations

Pakistan's environmental management systems have been put into disarray by the recent reorganizations. Few, if any, provincial environment agencies are capable of enforcing the nation's environmental regulations within the borders of their provinces. None of them is capable of handling cross-boundary issues (which include air pollution and water pollution). Differential enforcement of environmental regulations has the potential to complicate large infrastructure projects—as well as trade and transport policy reform—and lead to areas of environmental degradation. Nor is it clear whether the MoCC is capable of assuming

Table B.1 Recommended Actions for Improving Pakistan's Environmental Framework

Recommended action	Time frame
Conduct needs assessment of MoCC	Short term
Develop institutional strengthening and technical assistance program for MoCC	Short term
Strengthen the capacity of provincial environment management agencies to handle burdens posed by trade and transport reform	Short term
Strengthen MoCC's ability to conduct climate change research and provide assistance to Pakistan's climate negotiations team	Short term
Set coordination incentives, possibly with a coordination fund to cofinance regional projects	Medium term
Strengthen disaster reduction functions of MoCC	Short term
Establish accountability mechanisms	Medium term
Promote public disclosure	Medium term
Strengthen demand side of accountability by strengthening civil society organizations	Medium term

its responsibilities as Pakistan's apex environmental body, in which role it should be able to conduct research on climate change adaptation and mitigation, set incentives for coordination, undertake initiatives to reduce vulnerability to natural disasters, promote public disclosure of environmental information, and strengthen civil society organizations. For recommended actions, see table B.1.

References

Khan, A. 2010. *Industrial Environmental Management in Pakistan*. Consultant report. Washington, DC: World Bank.

Miglino, Luis. 2011. *SEPSA: Environmental Management Component*. Consultant report. Washington, DC: World Bank.

World Bank. 2005. *World Development Indicators 2005*. Washington, DC: World Bank.

———. 2011. Policy Options to Address the Cost of Outdoor Air Pollution in Pakistan. Draft Report. August 2011. Washington, DC: World Bank.

APPENDIX C

Overview of Methodology

Introduction

Present patterns in transport and trade logistics in Pakistan generate inefficiencies that are costing Pakistan's economy roughly 4–6 percent of gross domestic product per year. The transport sector generates high economic losses because of the mismatch between the demand and supply for transport services and its support infrastructure. This substantially decreases the competitiveness of export industries. For example, lack of adequate roads, poor highway conditions, old and slow-running trucks, long customs clearance times at ports, and rudimentary supply chain systems reduce the speed and reliability of freight delivery. Consequently, exporters and importers of goods have to develop costly arrangements for transferring goods between locations while operating under time constraints. These setbacks in transport and logistics have a significant impact on the competitiveness of export products and hence export performance.

The World Bank's Economic and Sector Work "Pakistan Strategic Environmental, Poverty, and Social Assessment of Trade and Transport Sector Reforms" focuses on

- Analyzing the policy and institutional adjustments required to address environmental, social, and income effects of alternative trade and transport reforms;
- Developing recommendations to better serve the environment and the population; to enhance social cohesion, inclusion, and accountability; and to foster equitable benefit sharing with low-income or other vulnerable groups;
- Developing a broad participatory process to give a voice to stakeholders who could be affected by freight transport programs; and

---

This appendix was prepared by Ernesto Sánchez-Triana and Santiago Enriquez, and draws heavily on consultant reports prepared by IDS (2011). The findings, interpretations, and conclusions expressed in this appendix do not necessarily reflect the views of the staff or Executive Directors of the World Bank or the governments represented by the Executive Directors.

- Identifying policy options to strengthen governance and the institutional capacity of agencies to manage the environmental, social, and poverty effects of trade, infrastructure, and transportation.

This appendix discusses the methodology used as part of strategic environmental, poverty, and social assessment (SEPSA) to identify cost-effective opportunities for improving the efficiency of the freight transport system to meet the goals of alleviating poverty, mitigating social impacts, and reducing environmental degradation.

SEPSA—whose methodology is overviewed in this appendix—integrated a strategic environmental assessment (SEA), a poverty and social impact analysis (PSIA), and stakeholder consultations. Complementary studies relied on secondary information and data to assess institutional capacities related to trade logistics and freight transport policy, spatial disparities in transport, and determinants of industrial agglomeration. The overall findings were synthesized into an overarching strategy for improving the efficiency of the freight transport system to meet the goals of enhancing export competitiveness, decreasing spatial inequality and poverty, and reducing environmental degradation. Ex-ante analysis of the potential impacts and the likely consequences of proposed policy reforms, especially on the poor and vulnerable groups, are intended to inform dialogue and policy decisions.

Further information about SEPSA's methodology, in the form of technical notes for researchers and other technical specialists, is presented in appendix D.

Methodology

The methodology for this SEPSA incorporated a SEA,[1] a PSIA, and stakeholder consultations. Specifically, the SEPSA methodological framework combines the *two key elements of PSIA*[2]—namely, analysis of distributional impacts and engagement of stakeholders in policy making—with the *three key elements of the SEA* (Ahmed et al. 2008) *approach*: (i) analytical work that would provide a foundation for meeting SEPSA's objectives; (ii) public discussion to ensure meaningful exchange among relevant stakeholders, including vulnerable groups; and (iii) learning processes for strengthening the ability of institutions to adapt to changing conditions. More specifically, the PSIA is intended to assist policy makers to enhance the positive impacts of reforms and minimize their adverse impacts through

- Understanding the impact of policy reforms on poverty and social outcomes;
- Analyzing intended and unintended consequences of policy interventions (ex-ante, during implementation, or ex-post);
- Considering trade-offs between costs and benefits of reform by assessing opportunities, constraints, and risks; and
- Designing appropriate mitigation measures and risk management strategies for the reform program, when adverse impacts and risks are unavoidable, and

building country ownership and capacity for analysis and implementation of policy reforms.

Discussion among Key Stakeholders

The objectives of the stakeholder consultations are twofold. They not only raise public awareness and support for reforms in the trade and transport sector, but they also allow participation and involvement of unorganized or voiceless groups in the planning and implementation of such reforms. One means to achieve the second objective is to use the consultations to let stakeholders identify priorities for the sector's environmental and social development objectives and interventions.

To ensure meaningful discussion among key stakeholders in the identification of specific sustainability criteria that would be incorporated into transport reforms, the Government of Pakistan (GoP) and the World Bank held a series of workshops during 2009 to scope out the studies that would be completed using the SEA's methodology. The opinions and inputs provided by representatives from federal and provincial governments, as well as by nongovernmental organizations, were incorporated into SEPSA's concept note. These stakeholders helped to identify the priority environmental, poverty, and social issues that were assessed in the analytical work. In addition, each of the studies mentioned above was prepared in close consultation with relevant stakeholders. The methodology of some studies explicitly incorporated tools to obtain feedback from a broader range of stakeholders. In particular, structured and semi-structured interviews were carried out as part of the PSIA and the gender analysis to obtain feedback from vulnerable groups.

The Planning Commission and the National Trade Corridor Management Unit have undertaken a series of workshops to disseminate the findings of SEPSA. A major effort to reach additional stakeholders will be carried out to discuss the key findings and policy recommendations of the SEPSA, including a series of workshops planned to take place in Islamabad, Karachi, Lahore, and Peshawar during the second half of 2012.

Analytical Work as a Foundation for Meeting the GoP's Economic Objectives

To provide the analytical underpinnings for policy reform, consultants were engaged to conduct analytical studies. Studies were carried out that addressed the environmental, social, and poverty implications of freight transport programs. The SEA (Larsen and Skjelvik 2012; Miglino 2011) focused on the environmental aspects associated with trade and transport reforms. The potential environmental effects of three strategic alternatives were analyzed: (i) "no project" alternative in which no policy reforms are implemented, (ii) policies that emphasize reforms and investments in the road freight sector, and (iii) policies that emphasize reforms and investments in the rail freight sector. Each alternative was evaluated based on a set of priority issues (climate change, air quality, transport of hazardous materials, road and railway safety, urban sprawl and accessibility, and environmental management systems) to assess their potential environmental and social impacts.

A major component of the Lahore University Management Science (LUMS) 2011 study was to examine the impacts of infrastructure provision (schooling, health, and manufacturing) on poverty, inequality, population growth, and industrial cluster formation, as well as the impact of spatial inequality of road infrastructure on poverty. The objective of this component of the LUMS report was to determine the push and pull factors that influence demographic composition of districts, especially population growth and industrialization.

Impacts were evaluated using scatter plots relating district-level population with the following: district-level education, health, and manufacturing production. Secondary data came from 10 educational indicators from the Provincial Development Statistics, published by the Bureaus of Statistics of the four provincial governments and from the Census of Manufacturing Industries (CMI), 2005–06.[3] District-level road-density data of the districts of Punjab from the Punjab Highway Department for the period 1992–2006 were used to determine the impact of road density on poverty and firm location. Regression analysis was used to determine the causes of agglomeration based on CMI data for 1995–96, 2000–01, and 2005–06.

The Innovative Development Strategies (Pvt.) Ltd. 2011 study supporting SEPSA conducted a PSIA (IDS 2011) to identify possible ex-ante social and distributional impacts of stakeholder groups. The PSIA proceeded first by identifying—based on a literature review—the stakeholders in key sectors likely to be affected by freight transport sector reforms, and their possible interests and influences in policy reforms in the freight sector.

Policy reforms under freight transport programs were divided by sector as follows: (i) trade facilitation, (ii) ports and customs, (iii) highways and trucking, (iv) railways, and (v) aviation.

Based on the initial analysis, stakeholder groups within each sector were identified as constituting key groups likely to be affected by the proposed policy reforms, including from impacts resulting from upgrading the National Trade Corridor. A series of interviews and focus group discussions (FGDs) were arranged with identified stakeholders.

Vulnerable Groups and Stakeholder Identification

As part of the PSIA and stakeholder discussions, efforts were made to identify the groups that would be (directly, indirectly, positively, negatively) affected by the program, and to assess their interests, concerns, and influence in relation to transport policies. As part of the PSIA, the first step in this regard was to identify stakeholders within each freight transport sector (ports, aviation, highways and trucking, and rail). Within each sector, a number of stakeholder groups were identified as possible sources of information or groups to be contacted for interviews and discussions (table C.1). Substantial information has been generated throughout the course of the PSIA that identifies the range of

Table C.1 Stakeholder Identification

Sector	Stakeholders
Ports	Port authorities at Karachi, Gwadar, and Qasim Ports Pakistan Customs International and local terminal operators Federal Board of Revenue Karachi Dock Labor Board (working at Karachi Port) and other employee associations at the ports Private-sector stevedoring companies Logistics and freight forwarding companies as well as clearing agents Exporters and importers, in addition to the business community in general Fisherfolk communities
Highways and trucking	National Highways Authority Owners and employees of trucking companies (many are sole proprietorships) Owners and employees of auxiliary services Families and communities where the road transport sector is a major employer Logistics and freight forwarding companies as well as clearing agents Dry ports Truck manufacturing industry Standards and Quality Control Authority Exporters and importers, in addition to the business community in general
Railways	Pakistan Railways Railway Workers Union Logistics and freight forwarding companies as well as clearing agents Exporters and importers, in addition to the business community in general
Aviation	Civil Aviation Authority Pakistan International Airlines Management of at least one private airline
Cross-cutting	Communities living along the main trade corridor Families of those employed in the trade and transport sector (including women and children)

stakeholders (both organized and unorganized groups) that are likely to be affected by reforms.

Participatory Processes: Stakeholder Consultations

Participatory approaches for identifying the impacts of freight policies on social and poverty indicators included a set of preliminary discussions held in Islamabad with the key members of the National Trade Corridor Task Force in May 2010.[4] Field-visit teams to the cities of Islamabad, Karachi, Lahore, Peshawar, and Quetta carried out interviews and conducted FGDs with the stakeholders identified in each sector.[5] In addition, teams were dispatched to hold grassroots-level discussions with communities likely to be directly affected in the future by the upgrading or new construction of road and rail links.[6] Ten separate central towns/hubs were chosen along the routes of the proposed rail and road links, and field teams branched out from the hubs to hold FGDs in rural and/or semi-urban communities within a day's journey of each hub location. Table C.2 lists the communities visited, and table C.3 lists the persons and institutions interviewed.

Table C.2 List of Communities Visited

Province	District	Tehsil	Mauza	Name of settlement
Khyber-Pakhtunkhwa	Haripur	Haripur	Saraisala	Mohalla Haji Imam Pir
	Haripur	Haripur	Panian	Mohalla Monwala
	Peshawar	Jamrud	Soor Kamar	Soor Kamar Baguri
Punjab	Toba Tek Singh	Gojra	Kathor	304 JB Kathor
	Toba Tek Singh	Toba Tek Singh	Bhlair	Chak No. 327 JB
	Khanewal	Mian Chunnu	128/15	128/15
	Gujranwala	Wazirabad	Ladhe Wala Chema	Ladhe Wala Chema
Sindh	Sukkur	Sukkur	Deha	Deha
	Dadu	Dadu	Khudabad	Khudabad
Gilgit-Baltistan	Gilgit	Gilgit	Danyore	Danyore
	Gilgit	Gilgit	Jutal	Jutal

Table C.3 List of Persons Interviewed

City	Name	Organization
Islamabad	Mr. Himayatullah Khan	Senior Joint Secretary, Ministry of Commerce
	Mr. Maqbool Elahi	Project Director, NTCMU, Planning Commission
	Mr. Irtiqa Zaidi	Project Director, Trade and Transport Facilitation, Ministry of Commerce
	Mr. Mumtaz Haider Rizvi	Member, Federal Board of Revenue
	Mr. Zahid Ali Baig	Secretary, Customs Reform and Automation, Federal Board of Revenue
	Brig. Laiq Ali Khan	General Manager (Improvement), National Highway Authority
	Dr. Hasan Raza	Former Program Manager, NACP
	Dr. Qudsia	NACP
	Dr. Imran	NACP
	Dr. Faran Emmanuel	NACP
	Dr. Khurram Shahzad	Family Health International
	Dr. Sajra Abbas	UNICEF
	Ms. Bushra Rani	Consultant to UNICEF
	Dr. Irfan	Plan Pakistan
	Mr. Mohsin Khalid	Managing Director, ITC Logistics
Karachi	Mr. Hasan Zaidi	Director General, Ports and Shipping Directorate
	Mrs. Nasreen Haque	Chairperson, Karachi Port Trust
	Mr. Miran Mohiuddin	Secretary, Port Qasim Authority
	Capt. Zafar Iqbal Awan	CEO, Pakistan International Container Terminal
	Mr. Changez Niazi	CEO, Qasim International Container Terminal
	Mr. Anjum Sajjad	CEO, Karachi International Container Terminal
	Brigadier Syed Jamshed Zaidi	General Manager P&D, Karachi Port Trust
	Mr. Alqera Atiq	Director SQMS Civil Aviation Authority (CAA)
	Mr. Khawaja Tanveer Ahmed	Commissioner, Inland Revenue, Federal Board of Revenue
	Mr. S.M. Tariq Huda	Additional Collector PACCS, Federal Board of Revenue
	Mr. Tariq M. Chaudhry	Chairman, Pakistan International Freight Forwarders Association (PIFFA)

table continues next page

Table C.3 List of Persons Interviewed *(continued)*

City	Name	Organization
	Mr. M. Nadeem Khan	CEO, Raaziq Group
	Mr. Mansoor Alam	Deputy General Manager, Hinopak Motors Limited
	Mr. Jahanzeb Khan	Deputy General Manager, Master Motor Corp. Ltd.
	Mr. Aqil Maniar	Managing Director, Nashrah Shipping & Logistics Pvt. Ltd.
	Mr. Saeed Baloch	General Secretary, Pakistan Fisherfolk Forum
	Ms. Tahira	Social Organizer, Pakistan Fisherfolk Forum
	Mr. Noor Muhammad	President, Port Workers Federation Pakistan
	Mr. Tariq M. Chaudhry	CEO, Dynamic Shipping Agencies Pvt. Ltd.
	Mr. Abdul Majeed	President, Karachi Chambers of Commerce & Industry (KCCI)
	Mr. Javed Ahmed Vohra	Vice President, Karachi Chambers of Commerce & Industry (KCCI)
	Haji Noor Mohammad	Port Workers Federation of Pakistan
	Mr. M. Safdar	Secretary, Karachi Dock Labor Board (KDLB)
	Mr. Muhammad Khaqan Khan	Secretary, Pakistan Stevedores Conference
	Mr. Haji Gul Muhammad Afridi	President, Karachi Harbors & Dock Workers Union
Lahore	Mr. Irfan Jehangir Wattoo	Director, General Audit, Pakistan Railways
		Lahore Chamber of Commerce
Quetta	Mr. Maqbool Ahmed Magsi	Divisional Superintendent, Railways
	Mr. Niaz M. Khan	Former President, Quetta Chamber of Commerce
	Mr. Kamran Ajmal	Vice President, Quetta Chamber of Commerce
	Mr. Sahibzada M. Khan	Member, Executive Committee, Quetta Chamber of Commerce
	Haji Noor M. Shahwani	President, Balochistan Truck Driver's Association
	Mr. Noor ul Amin Mengal	AFS Budget, Finance Department

A set of FGD questions was prepared for each stakeholder meeting, while a detailed questionnaire was prepared for use in the communities.

In all cases, the focus of the exercise was to identify the potential direct and indirect social and distributional impacts—including impacts on income, employment, assets, power relations, and social cohesion—that the proposed freight transport reforms, through their influence on trade and the logistics sector, would have on stakeholder groups, classified by gender, socioeconomic status, age, ethnicity, and religious conviction.

The findings of the social assessment were presented as elements in a social analytical framework, which includes a vulnerability analysis, an analysis of sustainable livelihoods, and an assessment of empowerment. Table C.4 describes the key issues that each of these tools seeks to address. The social impact assessment uses the analytical framework embodied in the three tools specified to see how freight transport reforms can affect the lives of different stakeholder groups, with particular emphasis on the possible effects on vulnerable groups as defined earlier. Table C.4 also defines the channels through which effects can manifest themselves.

Table C.4 Key Features of Social Analytical Tools

Tool	Issues addressed	Possible transmission channels for impacts
Vulnerability analysis	To find out: What shocks people may face and their capacity to respond Whether a policy has decreased or increased existing shocks, or introduced new ones, or whether it has changed people's capacity to respond	Access to employment and services Cost of doing business Inflationary pressures Changes in asset values Possibility of social conflict or increases in conflict Possibility of resettlement/ rehabilitation
Sustainable livelihoods analysis	To assess: How people are likely to adjust their livelihood strategies in response to shocks Whether people have assets or other resources (human, financial) that they can draw down on if faced with adverse circumstances	Employment opportunities or potential for job loss Cost of doing business Access to markets Potential for asset/land acquisition or transfer
Empowerment analysis	To assess: The extent to which policy change will increase or decrease a stakeholder group's capacity to make effective choices	Institutional reforms that may or may not allow space for stakeholder groups to voice their needs

Source: Adapted from World Bank 2007.

Notes

1. The SEA is a tool used to incorporate environmental and sustainability considerations at an early stage of policy making.
2. SEPSA's PSIA was based on the Poverty and Social Impact Analysis (PSIA) approach developed by the World Bank in 2002 (www.worldbank.org/psia). The general elements of the PSIA approach, as outlined in the User's Guide, were adjusted and tailored to the political, social, cultural, economic, and security situation in Pakistan at present and to the situation in the trade and transport sector in particular.
3. Fifty-six districts in the 1990–91 district classification were retained and district-level data were accordingly adjusted on value of production obtained from CMI (LUMS 2011).
4. Meetings were held with the World Bank on May 24, 2010, and then on June 2, 2010. Meetings were also held on May 28, 2010, with the Trade and Transport Facilitation Unit of the Ministry of Commerce; June 10, 2010, with the Planning Commission's NTCMU; and June 11, 2010, with the Federal Board of Revenue's Member for Customs Revenue (IDS 2011).
5. Field teams were to be sent to Dalbandin, Gwadar, Khuzdar, and Panjgur to conduct interviews with Port authorities and FDGs with communities on proposed rail and road links, but the murder of a prominent Baloch political leader in mid-July 2010 instigated a series of strikes and disturbances in the province; as a result of the security concern, field work had to be canceled (IDS 2011).
6. While the PSIA was concerned with policy reforms, the community outreach exercise was still conducted to get a better understanding of the possible localized effects of transport and logistics facilitation (IDS 2011).

References

Ahmed, Kulsum, and Ernesto Sánchez-Triana, eds. 2008. *Strategic Environmental Assessment for Policies: An Instrument for Good Governance*. Washington, DC: World Bank. https://openknowledge.worldbank.org/bitstream/handle/10986/6461/446390PUB0Stra101OFFICIAL0USE0ONLY1.pdf?sequence=1.

IDS (Innovative Development Strategies). 2011. *SEPSA: Poverty and Social Impact Assessment*. Consultant report, Islamabad, Pakistan: World Bank.

Larsen, Bjorn, and John Magne Skjelvik. 2012. *Environmental Health Priorities in the Province of Sindh, Pakistan*. Consultant report prepared for the World Bank. Washington, DC.

LUMS (Lahore University of Management Sciences). 2011. Abid A. Burki, Kamal A. Munir, Mushtaq A. Khan, M. Usman Khan, Adeel Faheem, Ayesha Khalid, and Syed Turab Hussain. *Industrial Policy, Its Spatial Aspects and Cluster Development in Pakistan*. Consultant report by the Lahore University of Management Sciences for the World Bank. Lahore, Pakistan.

Miglino, Luis. 2011. *SEPSA: Environmental Management Component*. Consultant report, Washington, DC: World Bank.

World Bank. 2007. *Tools for Institutional, Political, and Social Analysis of Policy Reform: A Sourcebook for Development Practitioners*. Washington, DC: World Bank. https://openknowledge.worldbank.org/handle/10986/6652.

APPENDIX D

Technical Notes Regarding Methodology

Introduction

This appendix presents technical notes on the social accounting matrix (SAM) and computable general equilibrium (CGE) model used as part of strategic environmental, poverty, and social assessment's (SEPSA) analytical work *to assess the poverty and distributional impacts of potential reforms in Pakistan's trade and transport sector*. (See figure D.1 for a general structure of a SAM, and table D.1 for a listing of SAM accounts.) This appendix draws heavily from the analytical work conducted by Innovative Development Strategies (IDS 2011), including economic analysis prepared jointly with Paul Dorosh, Dario Debowiz, and Sherman Robinson of the International Food Policy Research Institute (IFPRI). A SAM (2007–08) was developed to examine the effects of productivity enhancement of the transport sector and its subsectors on different subsectors and household categories. A simulation analysis was undertaken, and three simulation scenarios were conducted: (i) impact of a 10 percent increase in the productivity of road transport, (ii) impact of a 10 percent increase in the productivity of rail transport, and (iii) a simultaneous increase in the productivity of the road and rail sector by 10 percent. A CGE model was used to estimate how the economy might react to changes in policy, technology, or other external factors. The poverty impact assessment was conducted by analyzing data from the Federal Bureau of Statistics Household Income and Expenditure Surveys of 2005–06 and 2007–08 (the last two years for which these data are publicly available). Poverty incidence was computed for the National Trade Corridor (NTC) and non-NTC agro-climatic zones to highlight the disparity between the regions through which the NTC runs and those that are further away (see tables D.2–D.6).

This appendix draws heavily on consultant reports prepared by IDS (2011). The findings, interpretations, and conclusions expressed in this appendix do not necessarily reflect the views of the staff or Executive Directors of the World Bank or the governments represented by the Executive Directors.

Figure D.1 General Structure of a Social Accounting Matrix

	Sectors	Products	Factors	Households	Government	Investment	Rest of the world	Total
Sectors		Marketed supply (PD, D)						
Products	Intermediate demand $(io)^b$			Private consumption $(C)^{c,d}$	Public consumption $(G)^{b,c,e}$	Investment demand $(N, e)^{b,c}$	Export demand $(PE, E)^a$	Total demand
Factors	Value added $(V, W, Z)^{c,d}$							Factor income
Households			Income distribution $(\delta)^d$				Transfers $(hw)^{f,d}$	Household income (Y)
Government	Indirect tax $(te)^{a,e}$	Indirect tax $(tc, tm)^{a,e}$	Factor tax $(tf)^e$	Income tax $(ty)^{d,e}$			Transfers $(rw)^{e,f}$	Total revenues (R)
Savings				Private savings $(s)^{c,d}$	Public savings $(FB)^{c,e}$		Foreign savings $(FS)^f$	Total savings (S)
Rest of the world		Import supply $(PM, M)^a$						Total foreign payments
Total	Gross output (PP, X)	Total supply (P, Q)	Factor payments	Total household spending	Recurrent spending	Total investment (I)	Total foreign receipts	

Note: Main data sources used to populate the SAM.
a. customs data and tax revenue authorities; b. input-output tables and industrial surveys; c. national accounts, regional production data; d. household and labor force surveys; e. government budgets; f. balance of payments.

Table D.1 Social Accounting Matrix Accounts

A-WHTI	Wheat irrigated	A-PERSV	Personal services	C-ESERV	Education
A-WHTN	Wheat non-irrigated	A-OSERV	Other private services	C-HSERV	Health care
A-PADI	Rice IRRI (irr)	A-PUBS	Public services	C-PERSV	Personal services
A-PADB	Rice basmati (irr)	C-WHT	Wheat	C-OSERV	Other private services
A-COTT	Cotton (irr)	C-PADI	Unmilled rice IRRI (irr)	C-PUBS	Public services
A-CANE	Sugar cane (irr)	C-PADB	Unmilled rice basmati (irr)	LA-AGL	Labor-agric (own)-large
A-OCRP	Other field crops	C-COTT	Cotton (irr)	LA-MF1	Labor-agric (own)-med Sindh
A-HORT	Fruits/vegetables	C-CANE	Sugar cane (irr)	LA-MF2	Labor-agric (own)-med Punjab
A-CATT	Livestock (cattle, milk)	C-OCRP	Other field crops	LA-MF3	Labor-agric (own)-med OPak
A-POUL	Livestock (poultry)	C-HORT	Fruits/vegetables	LA-SF1	Labor-agric (own)-sm Sindh
A-FOR	Forestry	C-CATT	Livestock (cattle, milk)	LA-SF2	Labor-agric (own)-sm Punjab
A-FISH	Fishing	C-POUL	Livestock (poultry)	LA-SF3	Labor-agric (own)-sm OPak
A-MINE	Mining	C-FOR	Forestry	LA-AGW	Labor-agric (wage)
A-VEGO	Veg oils	C-FISH	Fishing	LA-SKU	Labor-non-ag (unsk)
A-WHTF	Wheat milling	C-MINE	Mining	LA-SK	Labor-non-ag (skilled)
A-RICI	Rice milling (Irri)	C-VEGO	Veg oils	LN-LG1	Land-large-Sindh
A-RICB	Rice milling (Bas)	C-WHTF	Wheat milling	LN-LG2	Land-large-Punjab
A-SUG	Sugar	C-RICI	Milled IRRI rice	LN-LG3	Land-large-OthPak
A-OTHF	Other food	C-RICB	Milled basmati rice	LN-MD1	Land-irrigated-med Sindh
A-LINT	Cotton gin (lint)	C-SUG	Sugar	LN-MD2	Land-irrigated-med Punjab
A-YARN	Cotton spin (yarn)	C-OTHF	Other food	LN-MD3	Land-irrigated-med OthPak
A-CLTH	Cotton weave (cloth)	C-LINT	Cotton lint	LN-SM1	Land-irrigated-sm Sindh
A-KNIT	Knitwear	C-YARN	Cotton yarn	LN-SM2	Land-irrigated-sm Punjab
A-GARM	Garments	C-CLTH	Cotton cloth	LN-SM3	Land-irrigated-sm OthPak
A-OTXT	Other textiles	C-KNIT	Knitware	LN-DR1	Land non irrig-sm/m Sindh
A-LEAT	Leather	C-GARM	Garments	LN-DR2	Land non irrig-sm/m Punjab
A-WOOD	Wood	C-OTXT	Other textiles	LN-DR3	Land non irrig-sm/m OthPak
A-CHEM	Chemicals	C-LEAT	Leather	WATER	Water
A-CEM	Cement, bricks	C-WOOD	Wood	K-LVST	Capital livestock
A-PETR	Petroleum refining	C-CHEM	Chemicals	K-AGR	Capital other agric
A-MANF	Other manufacturing	C-CEM	Cement, bricks	KFORM	Capital formal
A-ENRG	Energy	C-PETR	Petroleum	KINF	Capital informal
A-CONS	Construction	C-MANF	Other manufacturing	H-LF1	Large farm Sindh
A-TRADW	Trade-wholesale	C-ENRG	Energy	H-LF2	Large farm Punjab
A-TRADR	Trade-retail	C-CONS	Construction	H-LF3	Large farm Other
A-TRADO	Trade-other	C-TRADW	Wholesale trade	H-MF1	Med farm Sindh
A-RAIL	Transport-rail	C-TRADR	Retail trade	H-MF2	Med farm Punjab
A-ROAD	Transport-road	C-TRADO	Other trade	H-MF3	Med farm Othpak
A-TRWAT	Transport-water	C-RAIL	Rail	H-SF1	Small farm Sindh
A-TRAIR	Transport-air	C-ROAD	Road transport	H-SF2	Small farm Punjab
A-TROTH	Transport-other	C-TRWAT	Water transport	H-SF3	Small farm OthPak
A-HSNG	Housing	C-TRAIR	Air transport	H-OF1	Landless farmer Sindh
A-OWNH	Imputed rent	C-TROTH	Other transport	H-OF2	Landless farmer Punjab
A-BSERV	Business services	C-HSNG	Rented housing	H-OF3	Landless farmer OthPak
A-ESERV	Education	C-OWNH	Own housing	H-AGW1	Rural landless Sindh
A-HSERV	Health care	C-BSERV	Business services	H-AGW2	Rural landless Punjab

table continues next page

Table D.1 Social Accounting Matrix Accounts *(continued)*

H-AGW3	Rural landless OthPak	ENT	Enterprises	EXPTAX	Exports tax (inexistent)
H-NFNP	Rural non-farm non-poor	GOV	Government	ROW	Rest of world
H-NFP	Rural non-farm poor	TINDDOM	Domestic taxes	S-I	Capital
H-URNP	Urban non-poor	IMPTAX	Import tariffs	DSTK	Changes in stocks
H-URPR	Urban poor	TDIR	Direct taxes	TOTAL	Total

Table D.2 Poverty by Agro-Climatic Zone, 2005–06

Region	Agro-climatic zone	Poverty status (no.)			Poverty status (%)	
		Nonpoor	Poor	Total	Nonpoor	Poor
Urban	Rice-wheat Punjab	6,084,177	781,867	6,866,044	88.61	11.39
	Mixed Punjab	2,232,386	141,797	2,374,183	94.03	5.97
	Cotton-wheat Punjab	1,175,836	180,926	1,356,762	86.66	13.34
	Low-intensity Punjab	724,310	145,332	869,642	83.29	16.71
	Barani Punjab	1,927,382	30,221	1,957,603	98.46	1.54
	Cotton-wheat Sindh	1,526,536	198,189	1,724,725	88.51	11.49
	Rice—other Sindh	8,658,930	446,688	9,105,618	95.09	4.91
	Khyber-Pakhtunkhwa	2,319,416	682,712	3,002,128	77.26	22.74
	Balochistan	1,033,920	495,893	1,529,813	67.58	32.42
	Other Punjab—urban	8,536,381	1,608,291	10,144,672	84.15	15.85
	Other Sindh—urban	4,209,294	1,078,170	5,287,464	79.61	20.39
	Total	38,428,568	5,790,086	44,218,654	86.91	13.09
Rural	Rice-wheat Punjab	9,582,581	2,742,282	12,324,863	77.75	22.25
	Mixed Punjab	8,320,141	2,430,110	10,750,251	77.39	22.61
	Cotton-wheat Punjab	12,005,016	3,501,104	15,506,120	77.42	22.58
	Low-intensity Punjab	4,978,829	1,756,413	6,735,242	73.92	26.08
	Barani Punjab	4,108,739	320,372	4,429,111	92.77	7.23
	Cotton-wheat Sindh	5,998,411	2,519,103	8,517,514	70.42	29.58
	Rice—other Sindh	5,169,807	2,796,199	7,966,006	64.90	35.10
	Khyber-Pakhtunkhwa	11,374,557	4,696,544	16,071,101	70.78	29.22
	Balochistan	2,137,327	2,789,009	4,926,336	43.39	56.61
	Total	63,675,408	23,551,136	87,226,544	73.00	27.00
Pakistan	Rice-wheat Punjab	15,666,759	3,524,149	19,190,908	81.64	18.36
	Mixed Punjab	10,552,527	2,571,907	13,124,434	80.40	19.60
	Cotton-wheat Punjab	13,180,853	3,682,030	16,862,883	78.16	21.84
	Low-intensity Punjab	5,703,139	1,901,745	7,604,884	74.99	25.01
	Barani Punjab	6,036,121	350,593	6,386,714	94.51	5.49
	Cotton-wheat Sindh	7,524,947	2,717,292	10,242,239	73.47	26.53
	Rice—other Sindh	13,828,737	3,242,887	17,071,624	81.00	19.00
	Khyber-Pakhtunkhwa	13,693,973	5,379,256	19,073,229	71.80	28.20
	Balochistan	3,171,247	3,284,903	6,456,150	49.12	50.88
	Other Punjab—urban	8,536,381	1,608,291	10,144,672	84.15	15.85
	Other Sindh—urban	4,209,294	1,078,170	5,287,464	79.61	20.39
	Total	102,103,978	29,341,223	131,445,201	77.68	22.32

Table D.3 National Trade Corridor (NTC) Districts

Road construction	Road upgradation	New railway track	Rehabilitation of track	Doubling of track
Faisalabad	Rawalpindi	Bhakkar	Bhakkar	Rawalpindi
Toba Tek Singh	Jhelum	Jhelum	Peshawar	Jhelum
Khanewal	Gujranwala	Karachi	Khyber Agency	Gujranwala
Dera Ghazi Khan	Gujrat	Peshawar	Dera Ismail Khan	Gujrat
Sukkur	Khanewal	Khyber Agency	Quetta	Lahore
Shikarpur	Lodhran	Kohat	Mastung	Shaikhupura
Larkana	Bahalwalpur	Karak	Zhob	Karachi
Dadu	Rahim Yar Khan	Dera Ismail Khan	Qila Saifullah	Peshawar
Karachi	Sukkur	Abbotabad	Naseerabad	Batagram
Peshawar	Ghotki	Mansehra	Pishin	Charsadda
Khyber Agency	Mansehra	Haripur	Khuzdar	Mardan
Khuzdar	Abbotabad	Lakki Marwat	Kalat	Swabi
Turbat	Haripur	Mastung		
Gwadar	Gilgit	Khuzdar		
Kech	Batagram	Awaran		
Panjgur	Kohistan	Turbat		
Kharan	Shangla	Gwadar		
Kalat		Kech		
		Kalat		
		Gilgit		
		Batagram		
		Kohistan		
		Shangla		

SAM Definition

As noted earlier in the SEPSA, a SAM represents the flow of all economic transactions and transfers between different production activities, factors of production (land, labor, and capital), and institutions (households, enterprises, and government) within the economy and with respect to the rest of the world (ROW). The basic structure of this SAM can be explained as follows: production requires intermediate goods and the primary factors of production (for example, labor and capital), which are contributed by institutions (for example, firms, households, and government). In return, these institutions receive factor payment (value added) and income from other sources, such as transfers (for example, remittances and social assistance) and from the ROW. The income is spent as consumption expenditure on goods and services, for payment of taxes, and for purchase of investment goods. The total supply in the economy is matched by the demand made by the institutions and the purchase of investment goods. All the transactions in the economy are presented in the form of a square matrix in a SAM, where columns represent buyers (expenditures) and rows represent sellers (receipts). The SAM is read from column to row—that is, each entry in the matrix comes from its column heading, going to the row heading. The sum of each column equals the sum of each corresponding row. The columns and rows

Table D.4 Districts Falling in Agro-Climatic Zones

Zone	Districts		
Rice-wheat Punjab	Gujranwala	Mandi Bahauddin	Sialkot
	Lahore	Hafizabad	Sheikhupura
	Narowal	Kasur	Gujrat
Mixed Punjab	Sargodha	Khushab	Faisalabad
	Jhang	Toba Tek Singh	Okara
Cotton-wheat Punjab	Vehari	Multan	Pakpattan
	Bahawalpur	Rahim Yar Khan	Sahiwal
	Khanewal	Lodhran	Bahawalnagar
Low-intensity Punjab	Mianwali	Dera Ghazi Khan	Muzaffargarh
	Bhakkar	Rajanpur	Dera Ismail Khan
Barani Punjab	Islamabad	Rawalpindi	Chakwal
	Attock	Jehlum	
Cotton-wheat Sindh	Khairpur	Nawabshah	Ghotki
	Tharparkar	Mirpurkhas	Sukkur
	Naushero Feroz	Hyderabad	Sanghar
	Tando Mohammad Khan		
Rice—other Sindh	Jacobabad	Dadu	Thatta
	Karachi-South	West Karachi	Larkana
	Karachi East	Central Karachi	Shikarpur
	Badin	Malir	
Khyber-Pakhtunkhwa	Lower Dir	Buner	Nowshera
	Kohat	Hangu	Mansehra
	Haripur	Kohistan	Swabi
	Lakki Marwat	Malakand	Chitral
	Charsadda	Peshawar	Karak
	Tank	Abbotabad	Batagram
	Mardan	Bannu	Upper Dir
Balochistan	Quetta	Sibi	Makran
	Nasirabad	Qila Abdullah	Khuzdar
	Mastung	Turbat	Kalat
	Zhob	Pishin	Ziarat
	Lasbela	Punjgur	Kharan

of SAM indicate that all institutional agents (for example, firms, households, government, and ROW) are both buyers and sellers.

Economic Impact of Increase in Total Factor Productivity: Conceptual Framework

A supply-demand framework can be used to show the economic benefits of increase in total factor productivity (TFP) of a commodity in a partial equilibrium framework. Figure D.2 presents a simple static model with the assumptions of linear demand D and supply S. Assuming a closed economy and parallel supply shift, an increase in TFP reduces the cost of production and shifts the supply curve from S to S'. Output increases from Q_0 to Q_1 and price declines from P_0

Table D.5 Poverty Bands by Agro-Climatic Zone

	Occupation of head of household								
	Legislators, senior officials, and managers (%)	Professionals (%)	Technicians and associate professionals (%)	Clerks (%)	Service workers and shop and market sales workers (%)	Skilled agricultural and fishery workers (%)	Craft and related trade workers (%)	Plant and machine operators and assemblers (%)	Elementary occupations (%)	Total (%)
---	---	---	---	---	---	---	---	---	---	---
Rice–wheat Punjab	2.6	4.9	4.6	2.1	20.7	21.7	16.2	7.2	19.9	100.0
Mixed Punjab	1.3	3.7	2.5	3.1	20.8	31.7	7.0	5.5	24.3	100.0
Cotton–wheat Punjab	0.7	3.1	3.4	1.6	19.6	30.7	9.6	4.1	27.2	100.0
Low intensity Punjab	0.6	2.1	2.2	1.5	12.0	44.2	8.3	4.7	24.5	100.0
Barani Punjab	4.5	5.1	7.4	6.8	9.3	22.8	7.8	8.5	27.9	100.0
Cotton–wheat Sindh	1.7	4.4	4.8	4.4	13.0	21.1	10.0	4.7	35.8	100.0
Rice—other Sindh	0.2	2.5	3.8	1.6	9.3	44.5	10.4	4.1	23.6	100.0
Khyber-Pakhtunkwa	0.7	7.8	4.7	3.0	18.6	28.1	10.2	7.7	19.2	100.0
Balochistan	1.0	3.3	8.2	4.0	12.2	27.2	3.5	7.8	32.8	100.0
Total	1.4	4.3	4.7	3.1	15.6	28.8	9.4	6.0	26.7	100.0

Table D.6 Basic Facts Regarding Pakistan's Transport Sector

	GDP (constant factor cost) million Rs	Value added of transport sector (million Rs)	Share of transport sector in GDP (%)	Annual growth rate (%)	Share of transport sector in total employment (%)	Investment in transport sector (at constant factor cost) (million Rs)			Total investment (all sectors) (million Rs)	Share of transport sector investment in total investment (%)	Investment in transport sector as percent of GDP (%)
						Public	Private	Total investment transport sector			
'99–2000	3,562,018	326,052	9.2	n.a.	4.1	45,709	19,408	65,116	607,410	10.7	1.8
2000–01	3,632,091	343,300	9.5	5.3	4.1	57,271	24,874	82,145	634,422	12.9	2.3
2001–02	3,745,118	347,448	9.3	1.2	4.8	41,642	23,882	65,524	632,133	10.4	1.7
2002–03	3,922,104	362,292	9.2	4.3	4.8	22,908	37,387	60,295	658,070	9.2	1.5
2003–04	4,534,149	375,078	8.3	3.5	4.7	35,723	50,347	86,071	617,731	13.9	1.9
2004–05	4,881,796	388,003	7.9	3.4	4.7	34,576	74,345	108,921	701,392	15.5	2.2
2005–06	5,183,371	403,373	7.8	4.0	4.7	33,513	130,766	164,279	840,976	19.5	3.2
2006–07	5,477,948	422,411	7.7	4.7	4.4	28,763	131,567	160,330	955,141	16.8	2.9
2007–08	5,565,375	438,520	7.9	3.8	4.4	30,250	133,189	163,439	1,024,696	16.0	2.9
2008–09	5,767,536	450,568	7.8	2.7	4.2	19,550	106,485	126,035	908,856	13.9	2.2
2009–10	6,018,865	470,776	7.8	4.5	4.2	18,527	89,777	108,304	890,301	12.2	1.8
Average	4,753,670	393,438	8.4	3.7	4.5	33,494	74,730	108,224	770,103	13.7	2.2

Source: Pakistan Economic Survey 2009–10.
Note: Transport and communication appear as one category in the reported national accounts. Transport has been separated above using ratios from FBS (2004), the 1999–2000 rebasing exercise. n.a.= not applicable.

Figure D.2 Effect of Increase in Total Factor Productivity on Economic Surplus

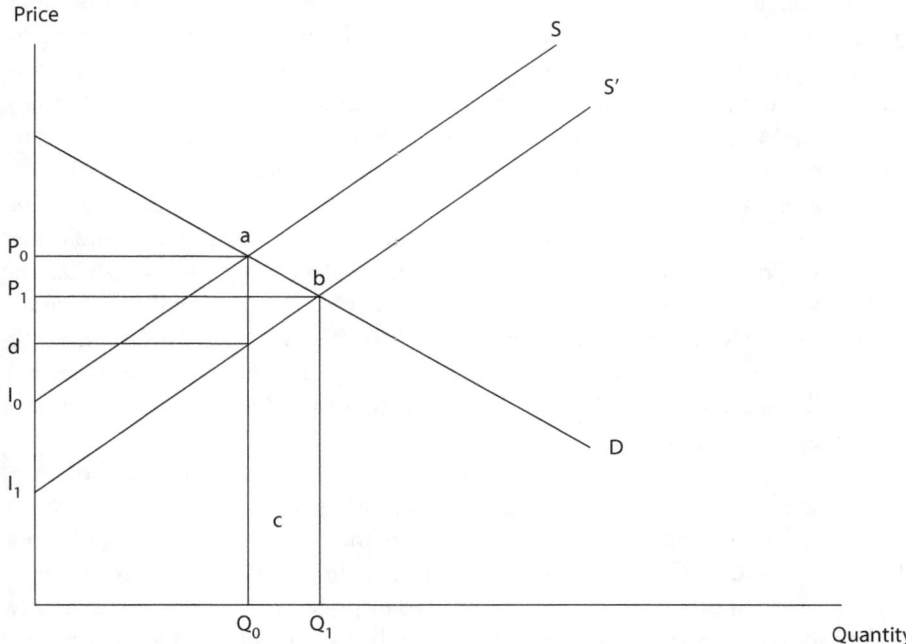

to P_1. Consumers can benefit from a decline in price, and producers can gain from selling greater quantities. The change in total economic surplus is measured by the cost saving on the original quantity ($I_0 ac I_1$), and the economic gains (abc) due to the increment to consumption ($Q_0 ab Q_1$) minus the total cost of the increment to production ($Q_0 cb Q_1$). Therefore, the change in total economic surplus is $\Delta TS = I_0 ab I_1$. The change in consumer surplus is $\Delta CS = P_0 ab P_1$, and the change in producer surplus is $\Delta PS = P_1 b I_1 - P_0 a I_0$.

The sections below summarize the work that has been done to build an updated SAM for Pakistan, explain how households are classified into representative household groups in the SAM, and show the incidence of poverty among them and their income composition. Also briefly described is the CGE used to inform the SEPSA.

Building an Updated Social Accounting Matrix for Pakistan

The SAM used in SEPSA's analytical work was developed by updating and disaggregating the Pakistan SAM 2001–02 developed by Dorosh, Niazi, and Nazli (Dorosh et al. 2006), which utilized the available input-output table for 1990–91, and distinguished four accounts in 34 domains: (i) activities; (ii) commodities; (iii) factors of production; and (iv) institutions (households, government, and the ROW), including an aggregate institutional savings-investment account. The SAM 2007–08, which provided the basis for SEPSA's economic analysis, uses 2007–08 as base year, since the last nationally representative household survey was conducted in that year.

In addition, the new SAM expanded the SAM 2001–02 from 34 to 49 activities and included 48 commodities, 27 factors, and 19 representative household groups. With regard to activities, wheat was split between irrigated and nonirrigated, and rice was split between IRRI and basmati. In view of the importance of the cotton-textile sector, the two activities (cotton lint/yarn, and cotton textile) given in SAM 2001–02 were further disaggregated into six activities (cotton ginning, cotton yarn, cotton clothing, knitwear, garment, and other textiles). In services, commerce is disaggregated into wholesale trade, retail trade, and other trade. Five categories of transport were introduced (rail, road, water, air, and other transport). Private services were divided into five categories (business, education, health, personal, and other services). The number of service activities increased from six in SAM 2001–02 to 17 in SAM 2007–08, while activities related to agriculture, and all other accounts (factors of production and institutions) remained the same as in SAM 2001–02. Factors of production and households were disaggregated by regions.

After disaggregating the SAM, the share of labor in the value added of each activity was imposed. The SAM was balanced using the cross-entropy software developed by Prof. Sherman Robinson, controlling for the 2008 values of gross domestic product (GDP), private consumption, final investment, government expenditure, exports, and imports, all at market prices. In this process, a variety of data sources was used, including data on public expenditure, macroeconomic accounts, and household surveys.

Once the SAM was disaggregated and updated, the IFPRI standard model was used to check that the SAM was exactly replicated by the model in the base simulation, run a set of simulations to test the model workings, and check that the model provided sensible results for a set of supply shocks affecting the different transport activities in Pakistan.

Household Classification, Income Sources, and Incidence of Poverty

Households were split into 19 groups, as follows. Large farms are those owning more than 50 acres, medium ones are those owning more than 12.5 but not more than 50 acres, and small ones are the rest of those owning land. Landless farmers are farmers who cultivate, but do not own, land. Rural landless are those hired in agricultural activities. The rest of the households are divided into rural and urban and, among them, into poor and nonpoor with a poverty line of Rs 1,140.05 of per capita per month expenditure. Tables D.7 and D.8 provide a snapshot of the poverty rates in the different household groups—both at household and individual levels—as well as the composition of their incomes.

Table D.7 shows that 27.9% of Pakistan's population is below the poverty line, and that the incidence of poverty is especially high for landless farmers and rural agricultural workers. The classification of incomes suggests that the bulk of household income comes from factor income, that the rural households rely much more on capital income than their urban counterparts, and that labor income is concentrated in agricultural workers, the rural nonfarm, and urban households.

Table D.7 Population, Poverty Rates, and Monthly Expenditures by Household Groups

Household group	Number of households (000)			Household size			Population (000)			Population below poverty line	Households below poverty line	Household expenditure (million Rs)	Household expenditure/ person (Rs)
	Poor	Nonpoor	Total	Poor	Nonpoor	Total	Poor	Nonpoor	Total				
Large-farm Sindh	—	6	6		9.5	9.5	0	57	57	0.0	0.0	115	2,026
Large-farm Punjab	1	32	33	8.0	7.7	7.7	10	246	256	3.9	3.7	1,615	6,308
Large-farm other Pakistan	1	5	6	9.3	8.4	8.6	9	42	51	17.2	15.8	110	2,150
Medium-farm Sindh	13	66	79	11.9	8.3	8.9	159	548	706	22.5	16.7	1,127	1,596
Medium-farm Punjab	25	262	287	10.9	7.2	7.5	274	1,880	2,154	12.7	8.7	5,230	2,428
Medium-farm other Pakistan	21	29	50	11.3	9.3	10.2	239	271	511	46.9	42.0	744	1,458
Small-farm Sindh	158	225	383	9.8	7.1	8.2	1,551	1,594	3,145	49.3	41.3	3,883	1,235
Small-farm Punjab	478	1,844	2,321	8.7	6.4	6.9	4,156	11,811	15,967	26.0	20.6	27,576	1,727
Small farm other Pakistan	147	526	673	10.9	7.6	8.3	1,609	3,988	5,597	28.7	21.8	8,794	1,571
Landless farmers Sindh	160	173	333	9.3	5.9	7.6	1,494	1,033	2,527	59.1	48.1	2,887	1,142
Landless farmers Punjab	155	353	507	7.8	6.7	7.0	1,203	2,353	3,557	33.8	30.5	4,925	1,385
Landless farmers other Pakistan	78	112	190	10.7	7.9	9.1	835	890	1,725	48.4	40.9	2,312	1,340
Rural agro-laborer Sindh	182	311	494	8.5	5.2	6.4	1,547	1,614	3,160	48.9	36.9	3,851	1,219
Rural agro-laborer Punjab	341	278	619	7.3	4.9	6.2	2,473	1,364	3,837	64.5	55.1	4,133	1,077
Rural agro-laborer other Pakistan	29	44	72	9.2	6.0	7.3	263	261	525	50.2	39.7	638	1,215
Rural nonfarm nonpoor	—	5,190	5,190		5.7	5.7	0	29,735	29,735	0.0	0.0	58,038	1,952
Rural nonfarm poor	1,801	—	1,801	7.9		7.9	14,195	0	14,195	100.0	100.0	12,960	913
Urban nonpoor	—	6,081	6,081		6.0	6.0	0	36,505	36,505	0.0	0.0	96,759	2,651
Urban poor	714	—	714	8.9		8.9	6,374	0	6,374	100.0	100.0	6,059	951
Total	4,304	15,536	19,840	8.5	6.1	6.9	36,391	94,191	130,583	27.9	21.7	241,754	1,851

Source: Authors' calculation based on HIES 2007–08.
Note: — = not available.

Table D.8 Composition of the Total Income by SAM Household Group
Percent

	Labor	Land	Water	Capital	Enterprises	Government	Foreign sector	Total
Large-farm Sindh	13.6	38.4	12.3	30.2	0	0	5.4	100
Large-farm Punjab	9.7	34.4	8.7	41.8	0	0.1	5.4	100
Large-farm other Pakistan	10.4	33.8	0	50.1	0	0.1	5.6	100
Medium-farm Sindh	18.4	38.1	0	38.0	0	0.0	5.4	100
Medium-farm Punjab	16.0	28.0	0	50.5	0	0.1	5.4	100
Medium-farm other Pakistan	18.6	38.2	0	37.6	0	0.2	5.4	100
Small-farm Sindh	16.9	22.1	0	55.0	0	0.6	5.5	100
Small-farm Punjab	22.8	21.0	0	50.4	0	0.6	5.2	100
Small-farm other Pakistan	18.5	13.7	0	61.3	0	1.0	5.4	100
Landless farmers Sindh	31.6	16.6	0	45.8	0	0.4	5.5	100
Landless farmers Punjab	30.0	16.6	0	47.4	0	0.5	5.5	100
Landless farmers other Pakistan	25.7	15.6	0	52.7	0	0.4	5.6	100
Rural agro-laborer Sindh	50.4	0	0	43.1	0	0.9	5.6	100
Rural agro-laborer Punjab	49.8	0	0	44.5	0	0.2	5.5	100
Rural agro-laborer other Pakistan	19.9	0	0	74.4	0	0.1	5.7	100
Rural nonfarm nonpoor	42.5	0	0	50.4	0	1.9	5.1	100
Rural nonfarm poor	30.3	0	0	62.6	0	1.7	5.5	100
Urban nonpoor	48.2	0	0	11.7	35.7	0.8	3.6	100
Urban poor	74.9	0	0	19.1	0	0.5	5.5	100

Source: Social Accounting Matrix, Pakistan 2008.

SAM Relationship to the CGE Model

CGE models are a class of economic models that use actual economic data to estimate how an economy might react to changes in policy, technology, or other external factors. A CGE model consists of equations describing model variables and a detailed database consistent with the model equations. The values of almost all variables and parameters in the CGE model are drawn from a SAM.[1] The SAM contains a number of "accounts" (see, for example, table D.1) representing different agents in the model, including sectors (producers) and households (consumers). The rows and columns of the SAM represent incomes and payments, respectively, from one account to another. As with double-entry accounting, the SAM is a *consistent* economy-wide database because row and column totals must be equal. In other words, a payment from one account always becomes an income for another. The SAM therefore provides the base-year equilibrium state for the CGE model.

The International Food Policy Research Institute's CGE model[2]

This description of the CGE model closely follows chapter 2 of Xinshen Diao, James Thurlow, Samuel Benin, and Shenggen Fan (Diao et al. 2011).

Consumer Behavior

Following general equilibrium theory, representative consumers (that is, households) and producers in IFPRI's model are treated as individual economic agents. Representative consumers maximize their welfare or utility subject to a budget constraint. IFPRI employs a Stone-Geary utility function in which the consumer problem can be represented mathematically as follows:

$$\text{Max}_i U_h = \prod_i (C_{hi} - \gamma_{hi})^{\beta hi}$$

$$\text{subject to} \quad \sum_i (P_i \cdot C_{hi}) = (1 - s_h - ty_h) Y_h$$

Each representative household h in the model has its own utility function, in which C is the level of consumption of good i, γ is a minimum subsistence level of consumption of good i, and β is the households' marginal budget share (that is, share of the next "dollar" of income spent on each type of good). Consumption-based utility is maximized subject to a budget constraint, in which P is the market price of each good, Y is total household income, and s and ty are marginal savings and direct income tax rates, respectively. Maximizing the above utility function generates the following set of demand functions:

$$C_{hi} = \beta_{hi} \left[(1 - S_h - ty_h) Y_h - \sum_{i'} (P_{i'} \cdot \gamma_{hi'}) \right] P_i^{-1} \quad \text{where } i' \approx i \quad \text{(D.1)}$$

This is the well-known linear expenditure system (LES) of demand.

Producer Behavior

Producers are defined at the sector level. Each representative producer maximizes profits subject to a given set of input and output prices. Following neoclassical theory, IFPRI assumes constant returns to scale. Accordingly, a constant elasticity of substitution (CES) function is used to determine production:

$$X_i = \Lambda_i \left(\sum_f \alpha_{if} \cdot V_{if}^{-\rho i} \right)^{-1/\rho i} \quad \text{(D.2)}$$

where X is the output quantity of sector i, Λ is a shift parameter reflecting TFP, V is the quantity demanded of each factor f (that is, land, labor, and capital), and α is a share parameter of factor f employed in the production of good i.[3] The elasticity of substitution between factors σ is a transformation of ρ (that is, $\sigma_i = 1/(1 + \rho_i)$. Profits π in each sector i are defined as the difference between revenues and total factor payments:

$$\pi_i = PV_i \cdot X_i - \sum_f (W_f \cdot V_{if})$$

where PV is the value-added component of the producer price, and W is factor prices (for example, labor wages and land rents). Maximizing sectoral profits subject to Equation (D.2) and rearranging the resulting first-order condition provides the system of factor demand equations used in the model:

$$V_{if} = \Lambda_i^{-\frac{\rho i}{1+\rho i}} \cdot X_i \left(\alpha_{if} \cdot \frac{PV_i}{W_f} \right)^{1/(1+\rho i)} \quad \text{(D.3)}$$

Intermediate inputs are also used in the production process. IFPRI's model assumes Leontief technology when determining intermediate demand of individual goods and when combining aggregate factor and intermediate inputs. Thus, demand for intermediates is based on fixed input-output coefficients $io_{i'i}$ defining the quantity of good i' used in the production of one unit of good i. Thus, the complete producer price PP is

$$PP_i = PV_i + \sum_{i'} P_{i'} io_{i'i} \quad \text{(D.4)}$$

Behavioral Functions Governing International Trade

Given observed two-way trade between countries for similar goods, IFPRI assumes imperfect substitution between domestic goods and goods supplied to and from foreign markets. An Armington specification (that is, CES function) (Armington 1969) is used to define the relationship between domestically produced and imported goods:

$$Q_i = \Omega_i [\mu_i \cdot D_i^{-\theta_i} + (1+\mu_i) M_i^{-\theta_i}]^{-1/\theta_i} \quad \text{(D.5)}$$

$$(1 - tc_i) P_i \cdot Q_i = PD_i \cdot D_i + PM_i \cdot M_i \quad \text{(D.6)}$$

$$PM_i = (1 + tm_i) pwm_i$$

where tc is an indirect sales tax, Q is the composite good consumed domestically, D and M are domestically supplied and imported quantities, and PD is the price of domestic good D. Import price PM is determined exogenously by world imports prices pwm and import tariff rates tm under the small country assumption.

A constant elasticity of transformation function determines the relationship between the quantity of goods produced for domestic and foreign export markets:

$$X_i = \Gamma_i [\tau_i \cdot D_i^{\varphi i} + (1+\tau_i) E_i^{\varphi i}]^{1/\varphi i} \quad \text{(D.7)}$$

$$PP_i \cdot X_i = PD_i \cdot D_i + PE_i \cdot E_i \quad \text{(D.8)}$$

$$PE_i = (1 - te_i) pwe_i$$

where E is the quantity of good i that is exported, te is the export tax rate, and pwe is the exogenous world export price.

Maximizing $P_i Q_i - PD_i D_i - PM_i M_i$ subject to Equation (D.5) and rearranging the resulting first-order condition gives the following equation defining the ratio of D and M:

$$\frac{D_i}{M_i} = \left(\frac{\mu_i}{1-\mu_i} \cdot \frac{PM_i}{PD_i} \right)^{1/(1+\varphi_i)} \quad \text{(D.9)}$$

Similarly, minimizing $PP_i X_i - PD_i D_i - PE_i E_i$ subject to Equation (D.7) gives the ratio of D and E:

$$\frac{D_i}{E_i} = \left(\frac{\tau_i}{1-\tau_i} \cdot \frac{PD_i}{PE_i} \right)^{1/(\varphi_i - 1)} \quad \text{(D.10)}$$

Equilibrium Conditions

With full employment and factor mobility across sectors, the following factor market equilibrium conditions hold:

$$\sum_i V_{if} = VS_f \quad \text{(D.11)}$$

where VS is fixed total factor supply. Assuming all factors are owned by households,[4] household income Y is determined by

$$Y_h = \sum_{if} \delta_{hf} \left(1 - tf_f \right) W_f \cdot V_{if} \quad \text{(D.12)}$$

where δ is a coefficient matrix determining the distribution of factor earnings to individual households, and tf is the direct tax on factor earnings (for example, corporate taxes imposed on capital profits).

Finally, commodity market equilibrium requires that the composite supply of each good Q equals total demand, as shown below:

$$Q_i = \sum_h C_{ih} + N_i + G_i + \sum_{i'} \left(io_{i'i} \cdot X_i \right) \quad \text{(D.13)}$$

where N is investment demand and G is government recurrent consumption spending.

The relationship between savings and investment demand N, and taxes and government spending G, will be specified below. However, in the absence of taxes or savings (that is, when ty, tf, s, N, and G are all zero), the above 13 equations simultaneously solve for the values of the 13 endogenous variables (that is, Y, C, X, V, Q, D, M, E, P, PV, PP, PD, and W). The general equilibrium solution defined by the equations only holds if there are no foreign transfers—implicitly a zero trade balance. This assumption is often made in simple theoretical general equilibrium models, but it is rarely used in CGE models, which need to be calibrated to observed data for a country. Foreign transfers and current account imbalances are introduced later. Before doing this, however, government G and investment demand N are defined.

Government and Investment Demand

The government is treated as a separate agent with income and expenditures, but without any behavioral functions. Total domestic revenues R is the summation of all individual taxes:

$$R = \sum_i (tc_i \cdot P_i \cdot Q_i + tm_i \cdot pwm_i \cdot M_i + te_i \cdot pwe_i \cdot E_i) \\ + \sum_h (ty_h \cdot Y_h) + \sum_{if} (tf_f \cdot W_f \cdot V_{if})$$ (D.14)

Tax rates are typically exogenous in a CGE model so that they can be used to simulate policy changes. The government may also receive income from abroad, such as via foreign grants/borrowing and from holding assets. These additional income sources will be discussed below when the macroeconomic closure is introduced.

The government uses its revenues to purchase goods and services (that is, recurrent consumption spending) and to save (that is, finance public capital investment), as shown below

$$R = \sum_i (P_i \cdot G_i) + FB$$ (D.15)

where G is consumption spending from Equation (D.13) and FB is the recurrent fiscal surplus (or deficit if negative). IFPRI assumes that G is determined exogenously, implying that an increase in government revenues causes the fiscal surplus to expand (or deficit to contract). In reality, the government also makes transfers to (and receives incomes from) households and firms (for example, social grants and contributions). These may be fixed values or in proportion to household populations or incomes. While the final CGE model includes such transfers, they are excluded here to simplify the equations.

There is also no behavioral function determining the level of investment demand for goods and services (that is, N from Equation (D.13)). The total value of all investment spending must equal the total amount of investible funds I in the economy. The model therefore assumes that the value of N for each good i is in fixed proportion to the total value of investment, as seen below

$$I \cdot \varepsilon_i = P_i \cdot N_i$$ (D.16)

where ε is the value share for each good i, and P is the market price determined by the equilibrium condition in Equation (D.13). Macroeconomic closure must be defined to determine the value of I.

Current Account and Macroeconomic Closure

A CGE model is an empirical tool based on neoclassical general equilibrium theory in which there is no room for current account imbalances. However, CGE models are often calibrated to observed data for a country. Hence, Walras's law no longer holds unless real financial flows are introduced into the model, such as incomes from holding foreign assets or the government's foreign borrowing. Current account imbalances must be accounted for, since they affect the real side of the economy via the relationship between exports and imports, and between savings and investment. The model starts from the well-known identity linking a country's current account balance CA to national savings S and investment I:

$$CA = TE - TM - NFI = S - I = \Delta NFA \qquad (D.17)$$

where $TE = \sum_i (pwe_i \cdot E_i)$ and $TM = \sum_i (pwm_i \cdot M_i)$

The left-hand-side of the identity states that a country's current account balance is equal to its trade balance (TE–TM) less net foreign incomes NFI. A country is therefore running a current account surplus whenever the sum of its trade balance and NFI is positive, in which case national savings exceed national investment and there is an accumulation of net foreign assets NFA. Total savings in the economy is the sum of all household savings and the government's recurrent fiscal balance, as shown below

$$S = \sum_h (s_h \cdot Y_h) + FB \qquad (D.18)$$

Macroeconomic balance in a CGE model is determined exogenously by a series of "closure rules." The most important of these is the current account balance. While this is a substantive research topic within macroeconomics, it is treated as an exogenous variable within this single-country open economy CGE model. For example, one area of macroeconomics focuses on the dynamics of exports and imports, and explains how growth in *total* exports is the result of export-led growth strategies and undervalued exchange rates. In the same vein, it is possible to introduce a nominal exchange rate into a CGE model to act as a *numéraire* to convert international prices measured in foreign currency (for example, dollars) into domestic currency units. However, the nominal exchange rate is unlikely to be chosen as a policy instrument to determine trade patterns. Instead, as discussed above, the behavioral function determining trade flows in the CGE model is at the sector level (see Equations (D.5)–(D.8)), and the focus of the model is on the structure of exports and imports, rather than their totals.

Before discussing the adopted closure rules, two of the previous equations are expanded to include the foreign incomes received by households and the government. Accordingly, Equations (D.12) and (D.15) can be rewritten as

$$Y_h = \sum_{if} (\delta_{hf}(1-tf_f)W_f \cdot V_{if}) + hw_h \qquad (D.12')$$

$$R + rw = \sum_i (P_i \cdot G_i) + FB \qquad (D.15')$$

where hw are foreign transfers received by households (for example, remittances from members working abroad), and rw are incomes earned by the government through its holding of foreign assets. If transfers are negative, they would denote net foreign payments. Given the new Equations (D.12′) and (D.15′), the value of NFI in Equation (D.17) can therefore be defined as

$$NFI = \sum_h hw_h + rw$$

Since the model is for a single country, hw and rw cannot be modeled endogenously using behavioral functions. These two variables (and hence NFI) are exogenous in the model, either as fixed values or in proportion to endogenous variables, such as household or government incomes. CA may not be equal to NFI if there is a trade surplus/deficit observed in the country's data. When CA is greater (less) than NFI, the country runs a trade surplus (deficit) and total exports are greater (less) than total imports plus NFI. For the external account, the closure rule is to treat CA as an exogenous variable, thus controlling its effect on the macroeconomic behavior of the model.

In practice, when NFI is not zero, then instead of fixing CA the trade surplus (deficit) FS can be fixed such that FS = CA−NFI. The size of FS determines the *difference* between total exports and imports, but it does not determine their individual *levels*. At a given FS, the level of total exports and imports can change, but they have to change simultaneously. For example, CGE models are frequently used to simulate trade liberalization by reducing import tariffs. This affects relative prices for different sectors/commodities, which in turn affects imports and exports at sectoral and national levels. In this case, total imports usually increase at a given FS, which in turn affects relative prices and exports at the sector level. At the national level, total exports would have to increase to maintain FS.

The choice of current account closure influences how we select our second closure rule, which is the identity on the right-hand-side of Equation (D.17). By fixing CA, the model also fixes the value of ΔNFA, which means that either total savings S or total investment I (but not both) should be determined exogenously. This choice is called the "savings-investment" closure, which is a term borrowed from macroeconomics. If the CGE model is "savings-driven," then I is automatically determined by the level of total available savings (that is, $I = S - \Delta NFA$). Consistent with Equation (D.1) in which s is a fixed parameter, the model specification is savings-driven. Were an "investment-driven" closure to be chosen, then total investment I would have been exogenously set at a fixed value or in proportion to a macroeconomic indicator (for example, GDP), and total savings would be made endogenous by allowing marginal savings rates s to adjust proportionally for all households.

Finally, the treatment of the government balance in Equation (D.15′) is in fact the third closure rule in the model. IFPRI chose to make recurrent consumption spending G exogenous and allow the fiscal balance FB to adjust to changes in revenues R. An alternative would have been to allow recurrent spending to adjust to changes in revenues, while holding FB constant. In this case, government spending on individual commodities G would be in proportion to total spending (that is, analogous to investment demand in Equation (D.16)).

Through the introduction of the government, investment demand, and macroeconomic closures, IFPRI included five new equations into the model (Equations (D.14)–(D.18)) and five new endogenous variables (R, FB, N, I, and S).[5] Together, the 18 equations and variables describe a static single-country model. The current account closure fixes the national trade balance. The government closure implies that changes in revenues alter the fiscal balance (and hence public investment) rather than recurrent spending. Finally, in the savings-driven closure, total investment adjusts to the level of total savings.

Model Calibration

One of the main advantages of CGE models over (more complex) theoretical models is their calibration to detailed empirical data. "Calibration" refers to the process of assigning values to the model's parameters and variables, typically using observed country data. Some of the assumptions that were made when specifying the CGE model were done to ease its calibration, since in many cases the data needed for more complex functional forms are unavailable in developing countries. For example, the LES function that was used to determine consumer demand assumes that income elasticities remain constant. Functions that are more elaborate often drop this assumption, such as in the "Almost Ideal Demand System." However, this model retains the LES function because it requires data that can readily be obtained from household surveys (that is, expenditure shares and income elasticities). Calibrating the behavior of more complicated functional forms often just involves making more assumptions where data are unavailable. In this appendix, the data sources and estimation procedures used to calibrate the CGE models are described.

Social Accounting Matrices

The values of almost all variables and parameters in the CGE model are drawn from a SAM (see Pyatt and Round 1985; Reinert and Roland-Holst 1997; see also figure D.1). Constructing a SAM is therefore a fundamental part of developing a CGE model. A SAM is constructed in two stages. During the first stage, data from different sources are entered into each of the SAM cells. As with the CGE model, the SAM allows for multiple sectors and households. Thus, the "sector," "product," and "household" rows and columns actually contain many sub-accounts. The three main data sources for constructing a SAM are national accounts, input-output tables (or supply-use tables), and nationally representative household budget surveys. As shown in the table, national accounts provide information on the composition of GDP at factor cost (that is, sectoral value added) and by broad expenditure groups at market prices (for example, $C + I + G + E - M$). The technical coefficients in the input-output table are used to estimate intermediate demand based on sectors' level of GDP or gross output. It also disaggregates government and investment demand across products. The household survey is used to segment labor markets (that is, disaggregate labor income into different groups, such as by education). The survey also defines households' expenditure patterns and the distribution of factor incomes to representative household groups. The survey data are therefore the main determinant of differential income and distributional effects across household groups in the CGE model.

Other databases are used to complete specific cells within the SAM. Government budgets provide information on tax rates, revenues, and expenditures. Although not shown in the table, government budgets (and household surveys) also determine the level and distribution of social transfers. Customs and revenue authorities provide data on imports and exports and their associated tariffs and subsidies. The balance of payments, usually compiled by a country's central bank, is used to populate the external or "rest of the world" account, including information on transfer receipts and payments and the current account balance. Finally, sectors in our SAMs are usually disaggregated across subnational regions using information on regional production and technologies from agricultural and industrial surveys. Trade margins, which are not shown in the table, are estimated using information on producer and consumer prices. Trade margins may also be drawn from input-output or supply-use tables.

There are inevitably inconsistencies between data from different sources, which lead to unequal row and column totals in SAMs. The second stage of constructing a SAM is therefore to "balance" these totals. This reconciliation of data from disparate sources is similar to a "rebasing" of national accounts. Cross-entropy econometric techniques were used to estimate a balanced SAM (see Robinson, Cattaneo, and El-Said 2001). This is a Bayesian approach that uses a cross-entropy distance measure to minimize the deviation in the balanced SAM from the unbalanced prior SAM containing the original data. Constraints are imposed during the estimation procedure to reflect narrower confidence intervals around better-known control totals (for example, total GDP). Figure D.1 shows which cell entries in the balanced SAM are used to calibrate the model's variables and parameters. From this, it is clear that the SAM and its underlying data sources provide almost all of the information needed to calibrate the CGE model. Only the behavioral elasticities remain (that is, β, ρ, θ, and φ).

Behavioral Elasticities and Other External Data

Behavioral elasticities are needed for the consumption, production, and trade functions. The LES demand function requires information on income elasticities and the Frisch parameter (see Frisch 1959). Income elasticities were econometrically estimated using the same household survey data on which the SAM is built, and following the approach described in King and Byerlee (1978). Marginal budget shares (that is, β in Equation (D.1)) are derived by combining the estimated income elasticities with the average budget shares drawn directly from the SAM.

Trade elasticities determine how responsive producers and consumers are to changes in relative prices when deciding to supply goods to, or purchase goods from, foreign markets. Higher elasticities are expected when substituting between more homogenous products, such as maize and copper. Lower elasticities are expected for more differentiated product categories, such as chemicals and machinery. In most developing countries, the data needed to econometrically estimate country-specific elasticities do not exist—at least in an appropriate form (see Arndt, Robinson, and Tarp 2002). Therefore, the values for the two trade elasticities (θ and φ in Equations (D.5) and (D.7)) were assigned using global estimates from Dimaranan (2006).

The elasticities governing factor substitution in the production functions (that is, ρ in Equation (D.2)) rarely exist for developing countries. In the absence of reliable country-specific estimates, elastic factor substitution is assumed for most activities (that is, $\sigma > 1$: σ is a transformation of ρ). This is consistent with recent meta-analyses of econometrically estimated elasticities (see, for example, Boys and Florax 2007) and cross-country econometric analysis (see Behar 2009).

Finally, the SAM provides information on values but not quantities. Therefore, external data sources were used to calibrate the model's production output X and factor quantities V. For example, crops' land use and gross output are calibrated to match agricultural data on harvested areas (in hectares) and production quantities (in tons). Observed labor employment numbers are also used to determine sector-specific wages. In such cases, factor and product prices in the model are not normalized to one, but rather reflect observed prices.

Baseline Dynamics

The model is calibrated to the base year reflected in the SAM. It is then run forward over time to create a baseline growth path—normally a series of years. The baseline scenario is therefore determined by annual growth in factor supplies and productivity. With the exception of capital, factor, and productivity, growth rates are calibrated to observed historical trends. For example, changes in labor supply are usually based on population projections for rural and urban areas, and on labor force participation rates for workers with different education levels. Similarly, agricultural land either expands alongside rural populations or is calibrated to long-term trends in total harvested land area from historical data (for example, FAO 2010). The annual growth capital stocks are targeted so that it grows at a relatively smooth rate in relation to GDP. This is done either by assigning base-year capital-output ratios or by adjusting the price of capital.

After a suitable baseline scenario has been calibrated, it is possible to conduct counterfactual simulations. Alternative growth paths are evaluated by changing exogenous variables in the model from baseline levels. The model is resolved and deviations from the baseline are attributed to the simulated change in policies or external factors. The model is therefore an ideal tool for ex-ante evaluation of development options in countries where historical evidence is lacking and ex-post analysis is impossible. While the model's general equilibrium specification is based on economic theory, its detailed calibration to observed data provides a "quasi-empirical" laboratory for conducting complex experiments within a consistent modeling framework.

Notes

1. For detailed discussions on SAMs, see, for example, Pyatt and Round (1985), and Reinert and Roland-Holst (1997).
2. The model assumes that all factors are mobile in the simulations, except for physical capital, which is fixed at the sector level. The macro closures are those in the IFPRI standard model as described in IDS (2011).
3. Given the existence of byproducts (for example, multiple goods from a single sector) and the fact that the same good can be produced in different sectors, the model distinguishes between sectors (activities) and goods (commodities). However, the exposition is simplified by using the two interchangeably (IDS 2011).
4. In reality, part of factor incomes (that is, the return to capital) can be owned by the government or foreign institutions. While this is allowed in the model implemented in each case study, nonhousehold factor ownership is ignored in order to simplify the discussion (IDS 2011).
5. Note that the third closure rule in the model made G exogenous in Equation (D.15).

References

Armington, Paul S. 1969. "A Theory of Demand for Products Distinguished by Place of Production." *IMF Staff Papers* 16 (1): 159–78. http://www.jstor.org/sici?sici=0020-8027(196903)16:1<159:ATODFP>2.0.CO;2-5&origin=crossref.

Arndt, C., S. Robinson, and F. Tarp. 2002. "Parameter Estimation for a Computable General Equilibrium Model: A Maximum Entropy Approach." *Economic Modeling* 19 (3): 375–98.

Behar, Alberto. 2009. "Directed Technical Change, the Elasticity of Substitution and Wage Inequality in Developing Countries." Economics Series Working Paper 467. Oxford, U.K.: University of Oxford, Department of Economics.

Boys, Kathryn A., and Raymond J. G. M. Florax, 2007. "Meta-Regression Estimates for CGE Models: A Case Study for Input Substitution Elasticities in Production Agriculture." Paper presented at the 2007 Annual Meeting of the American Agricultural Economics Association (new name 2008: Agricultural and Applied Economics Association), Portland, OR, July 29–August 1.

Diao, Xinshen, James Thurlow, Samuel Benin, and Shenggen Fan. 2011. *Agricultural Strategies in Africa: Evidence from Economywide Simulation Models*. Manuscript (January 25, 2011). Washington, DC: IFPRI (International Food Policy Research Institute).

Dimaranan, Betina V., ed. 2006. Global Trade, Assistance, and Production: The GTAP 6 Data Base. Center for Global Trade Analysis, Purdue University, West Lafayette, IN. https://www.gtap.agecon.purdue.edu/databases/v6/v6_doco.asp.

Dorosh, Paul A., Muhammad Khan Niazi, and Hina Nazli. 2003. "Distributional Impacts of Agricultural Growth in Pakistan: A Multiplier Analysis." *Pakistan Development Review* 42 (3): 249–75.

———. 2006. "A Social Accounting Matrix for Pakistan, 2001–02: Methodology and Results." PIDE Working Paper 2006:5. Islamabad: PIDE (Pakistan Institute of Development Economics).

FAO (Food and Agricultural Organization of the United Nations). 2010. *The State of Food Insecurity in the World: Addressing Food Insecurity in Protracted Crises.* Rome: FAO. http://www.fao.org/docrep/013/i1683e/i1683e.pdf.

Frisch, R. 1959. "A Complete Scheme for Computing All Direct and Cross Demand Elasticities in a Model with Many Sectors." *Econometrica* 27 (2): 177–96.

IDS (Innovative Development Strategies). 2011. *SEPSA: Poverty and Social Impact Assessment.* Consultant report, Islamabad: World Bank.

King R. P., and D. Byerlee. 1978. "Factor Intensity and Locational Impacts of Rural Consumption Patterns in Sierra Leone." *American Journal of Agricultural Economics* 60: 197–206.

Pyatt, G., and J. I. Round, eds. 1985. *Social Accounting Matrices: A Basis for Planning.* Washington, DC: World Bank.

Reinert, K. A., and D. W. Roland-Holst. 1997. "Social Accounting Matrices." In *Applied Methods for Trade Policy Analysis: A Handbook*, ed. J. F. Francois and K. A. Reinert, 94–121. Cambridge, U.K.: Cambridge University Press.

Robinson, S., A. Cattaneo, and M. El-Said. 2001. "Updating and Estimating a Social Accounting Matrix Using Cross Entropy Methods." *Economic Systems Research* 13 (1): 47–64.

Glossary

Civil Aviation Authority (CAA). The CAA was created on December 7, 1982, under the Pakistan Civil Aviation Authority Ordinance Act of 1982, to regulate Pakistan's aviation sector. The Authority develops, maintains, and manages all civil aerodromes throughout the country. The Government of Pakistan, through the Ministry of Defense, controls it. To achieve its strategic objectives, CAA has undergone a major restructuring and now separates its three main functions: regulatory, airport services, and air navigation services.

Computable general equilibrium (CGE). CGE models are a class of economic models. This class uses actual economic data to estimate how an economy might react to changes in policy, technology, or other external factors. A CGE model consists of two components: (i) equations describing model variables and (ii) a detailed database consistent with the model equations. The values of almost all variables and parameters in the CGE model are drawn from a social accounting matrix. This type of matrix is an economy-wide representation of a country's economic structure. It captures all income and expenditure flows between producers, consumers, the government, and the rest of the world during a particular year.

Disability-adjusted life year (DALY). A measure of the overall disease burden. This measure is expressed as the number of years lost due to disability, illnesses, or premature death.

Economic and Social Commission for Asia and the Pacific (ESCAP). The regional development arm of the United Nations for the Asia-Pacific Region. It has a membership of 62 governments, 58 of which are in the region. ESCAP's geographical scope stretches from Turkey in the west to the Pacific island nation of Kiribati in the east, and from Russia in the north to New Zealand in the south. ESCAP is the most comprehensive of the United Nations five regional commissions. It is the largest United Nations body serving the Asia-Pacific

---

This glossary was prepared by Ghazal Dezfuli. The findings, interpretations, and conclusions expressed in this glossary do not necessarily reflect the views of the staff or Executive Directors of the World Bank or the governments represented by the Executive Directors.

region with over 600 staff. For more information, see http://www.unescap.org/about.

Elasticity of poverty. The percentage change in poverty rates associated with a percentage change in the opposite direction in mean (per capita) income. Standard estimates of elasticity of poverty for developing countries range from 1.5 to 5. The average estimate is around 3. This implies that a 1 percent increase in per capita income is associated with a 3 percent decrease in the poverty rate (proportion of people living on less than US$1 per day). This implies that economic growth is crucial for decreasing poverty rates, especially in low-income countries.

Gwadar Port. Gwadar Port was formally inaugurated in December 2008. It currently has the capacity to handle vessels of up to 50,000 deadweight tonnage. It is managed by the Gwadar Port Authority. The key objectives for developing the Gwadar Port are to

- Capitalize on opportunities for trade with landlocked Central Asian states and Afghanistan;
- Promote trade and transport with gulf states;
- Provide transshipments of essentially containerized cargo;
- Increase the socioeconomic development of Gwadar, the province of Balochistan, and the country;
- Reduce congestion and dependency on the country's existing ports; and
- Serve as a regional hub for major trade and commercial activities.

See http://www.gwadarport.gov.pk/.

Karachi Port. This port is located in Pakistan's largest city and commercial center (Karachi). Karachi Port is one of the two primary entry and exit points for imports and exports. The port, which accounts for about 60 percent of the nation's sea trade, handles about 1.4 million twenty-foot equivalent units of cargo per year. The port has two wharves (East and West Wharf, with a capacity of 17 and 13 vessel berths, respectively) and handles all forms of cargo. The port can accommodate vessels of up to 75,000 deadweight tonnage. See http://www.kpt.gov.pk/.

Karachi Port Trust (KPT). A Board of Trustees, comprising a Chairperson and 10 Trustees, administers Karachi Port. The federal government appoints the Chairperson, who is also the Chief Executive of KPT. The remaining 10 Trustees are equally distributed between the public and the private sector. The federal government nominates the five public-sector Trustees. Elected representatives of various private-sector organizations fill the seats for the private-sector Trustees. See http://www.kpt.gov.pk/.

Katchi Abadi (Plural: Katchi Abadis). Informal settlements created through squatting or informal subdivisions of state or private land. The *katchi abadis* are of two types: The first type comprises settlements established through unorganized invasion of state lands at the time of partition. Most of these settlements were removed and relocated during the 1960s or have been regularized. The second type comprises informal subdivisions of state land. This second category of informal settlements is further divided into (i) notified *katchi abadis*, which are settlements earmarked for regularization through a 99-year lease and local government infrastructure development and (ii) nonnotified *katchi abadis*, which are settlements that are not to be regularized because they are on valuable land required for development, or on unsafe lands. Informal settlements do not fall under the realm of responsibility of city administrations and as such tend to be un-serviced or critically under-serviced.

Katchi Abadi Improvement and Regularization Program (KAIRP). Introduced in 1978, KAIRP aims to provide basic amenities to residents living in *katchi abadis*. The process has been painfully slow, with the pace estimated at 1 percent of *abadis* regularized per year in the 1990s. Data that are more recent (2007) suggest this has not speeded up, and net progress is particularly slow because new settlements keep coming up. KAIRP has been hampered by poor record keeping of land records, which typically leads to land disputes and prolonged legal arbitration.

Ministry of Ports and Shipping. Created on September 2, 2004, the Ministry functions is a central policy-making and administrative authority on the ports and shipping sector in Pakistan. It consists of one division, Ports and Shipping Division, which takes care of all the ports in the country. The Ministry's main responsibility is to provide policy guidelines to all the country's ports: Karachi Port Trust, Port Qasim Authority, and Gwadar Port Authority. The Ministry aims to rationalize port tariffs/freight rates including terminal handling charges, promotion of private investments, and public engagement in the port and shipping sector.

Mohajir. Refugees who arrived in Pakistan in the aftermath of Partition. It derives its origin from the term *Hijr*, the flight of the Islamic prophet Muhammad from Mecca to Medina, a journey that was undertaken to escape persecution due to religious beliefs.

National AIDS Control Program (NACP). Established in 1990 with a focus on diagnosis of cases in hospitals, NACP progressively began to shift toward a community-wide focus. Its objectives are the prevention of HIV transmission, promotion of safe blood transfusions, reduction of STI transmission, establishment of surveillance, training of health staff, research and behavioral studies, and development of program management. The NACP has conducted studies on HIV transmission and the trucker community, and also devised a program for the control of HIV/AIDS, but such initiatives have not been sustained. See http://www.nacp.gov.pk/programme_components/nacp_projects/national_truckers_project/.

National Trade Corridor Improvement Program (NTCIP). The Program, included in the Medium Term Development Framework period (2005–10), comprised policies intended to lead to modern and streamlined trade and transport logistics practices; improve port efficiency, reduce the costs for port users, and enhance port management accountability; create a commercial and accountable environment in Pakistan Railways and increase private-sector participation in operation of rail services; modernize the trucking industry and reduce the cost of externalities for the country; sustain delivery of an efficient, safe, and reliable National Highways system; and promote and ensure safe, secure, economical, and efficient civil aviation operations, and boost air trade.

National Trade Corridor (NTC). The ports, roads, and railways along the corridor that stretches from the southern city of Karachi to the northern Punjabi cities of Lahore and Peshawar. The NTC handles approximately 95 percent of the country's external trade and 65 percent of total land freight.

NEET. Government acronym for people currently not in education, employment, or training.

Pakistan Customs Computerized System (PACCS). Under the Customs Administration Reforms Program introduced in 2002, PACCS allows for electronic documentation and clearance of imports and exports. It was introduced in April 2005 on a pilot basis at the Karachi International Container Terminal. As a result, customs clearance time has decreased from 4–5 days to less than 24 hours. PACCS is being progressively expanded to the rest of Karachi Port and elsewhere. See http://www.unescap.org/tid/projects/da6_symposium_s5khan.pdf.

Pakistan Environmental Protection Act (PEPA). Enacted on December 6, 1997, PEPA is the cornerstone of environmental legislation in Pakistan. The Act provides a comprehensive framework for regulating environmental protection, including air pollution. PEPA established the general conditions, prohibitions, penalties, and enforcement to prevent and control pollution and to promote sustainable development. The Act delineated the responsibilities of the Pakistan Environmental Protection Council, Pakistan Environmental Protection Agency, and provincial environmental protection agencies.

Pakistan Environmental Protection Agency (Pak-EPA). Established under Section 5 of PEPA, the Pak-EPA is an executive agency managed by the Ministry of Climate Change. Its basic functions include preparing, revising, and establishing the National Environmental Quality Standards with approval of the Pakistan Environmental Protection Council. For more information, see http://www.environment.gov.pk/ABOUTUS.HTM.

Pakistan Environmental Protection Council (PEPC). The apex decision-making body on environmental issues in the country. PEPC was established under the Pakistan Environmental Protection Ordinance (1983), and it was later reconstituted based on Section 3 of PEPA. The Prime Minister of Pakistan heads the Council, and the Federal Minister of Environment serves as the Vice Chairman. Membership of the Council consists of multiple stakeholders: Chief Ministers of four provinces, Provincial Environmental Ministers, 35 ex officio representatives (industry, technical, professional, trade unions, and nongovernmental organizations (NGOs)), and the Secretary of the Ministry of Climate Change (MoCC). The MoCC serves as the Council's secretariat. Major functions of the PEPC are to supervise implementation of the Pakistan Environmental Protection Act (PEPA), coordinate and supervise enforcement of PEPA, approve comprehensive national environmental policies, approve the National Environmental Quality Standards, provide guidelines for the protection and conservation of natural resources and habitats, integrate sustainable development into national development plans and policies, instruct relevant institutions to prevent and control pollution, undertake research activities, and execute sustainable development and research projects. The PEPC has the powers to establish issue-specific committees and invite any technical expert, government representative, or NGO to assist in supporting the implementation of its functions.

Pakistan International Airlines (PIA). The government-owned, national airline of Pakistan. PIA operates scheduled and charter services to more than 65 destinations throughout Asia, Europe, and North America. PIA was created in 1955 through the merger of the privately owned Orient Airways with the proposed Pakistan government-sponsored airline. Currently the airline has its main hubs in Islamabad, Karachi, and Lahore. See http://www.historyofpia.com/list_main.htm.

Pakistan Railways (PR). The government-owned rail transport service of Pakistan, headquartered in Lahore and administered by the federal government under the Ministry of Railways. PR's main focus is on improving passenger rather than freight services, despite freight being more profitable. In 2009–2010, PR carried 58.97 million passengers and only 4.6 million tons of freight.

Port Qasim. Located in Pakistan's largest city and commercial center (Karachi), Port Qasim acts as one of the two primary entry and exit points for imports and exports. It handles about a third of Pakistan's total sea trade and can accommodate vessels of up to 75,000 deadweight tonnage.

Port Qasim Authority (PQA). Established through an act of parliament on June 29, 1973, PQA is under the administrative control of the Ministry of Ports and Shipping, Government of Pakistan. A Chairman is the Chief Executive of the port. All policy decisions are vested in the PQA Board, comprising seven members headed by the Chairman. The Board is a blend of public- and private-sector participation. PQA is primarily a service-oriented organization. The port provides shore-based facilities and services to international shipping lines and other concerned agencies in the form of adequate water depth in the channel, berths/terminals, cargo-handling equipment, godowns, storage areas, as well as facilities for safe day and night transit of vessels.

Poverty and social impact analysis (PSIA). An ex-ante analysis of impacts used to "predict" impacts before a policy actually takes effect. PSIA analyzes the distributional impacts of public policies, with particular emphasis on poor and vulnerable groups. The PSIA is one among several World Bank tools to generate evidence that can inform dialogue, debate, and decisions on policy.

Slums. Settlements of villages absorbed in the urban sprawl or the informal subdivisions created on community and agricultural land. In Pakistan, slums can be divided into two types. The first type comprises inner-city, traditional preindependence working-class areas now densified and with inadequate infrastructure. The second type comprises goths or old villages now part of the urban sprawl. Those within or near the city center have become formal—others have developed informally into inadequately serviced high-density, working-class areas. While tenure security may be greater in slums than in *katchi abadi*, they are not usually concerned with programs to improve living conditions. More than 55 million people, or 71.7 percent of Pakistan's urban population, lived in slums in 2005.

Social accounting matrix (SAM). It represents the flow of all economic transactions and transfers between different production activities; factors of production (land, labor, and capital); and institutions (households, enterprises, and government) within the economy and with respect to the rest of the world (ROW). The basic structure of the SAM used for the SEPSA can be explained as follows: production requires intermediate goods and the primary factors of production (for example, labor and capital), which are contributed by institutions (for example, firms, households, and government). These institutions, in return, receive factor payment (value added) and income from other sources, such as transfers (for example, remittances and social assistance), and from ROW. The income is spent as consumption expenditure on goods and services, for payment of taxes, and purchase of investment goods. The total supply in the economy is matched by the demand made by the institutions and the purchase of investment goods. All the transactions in the economy are presented in the form of a square matrix in a SAM, where columns represent buyers (expenditures) and rows represent sellers (receipts). The SAM is read from column to row—that is, each entry in the matrix comes from its column heading, going to the row heading. The sum of each column equals the sum of each corresponding row. The columns and rows of SAM indicate that all institutional agents (for example, firms, households, government, and ROW) are both buyers and sellers.

Strategic environmental assessment (SEA). A tool used to incorporate environmental and sustainability considerations at an early stage of policy making. There are three key elements in the SEA approach. The first element is analytic work to facilitate the influence of SEA on policy design and implementation, including the identification of environmental priorities, technical analyses, and institutional analyses. The second element is participatory approaches, including public discussion to ensure meaningful exchange among relevant stakeholders, including weak and vulnerable groups. The third element is enhancement of social learning processes to periodically reevaluate policy direction and implementation to improve the quality of life for people.

Total factor productivity (TFP). The portion of output not explained by the amount of inputs used in the production process. If all inputs are accounted for, then TFP is the measure of an economy's long-term technological change or technological dynamism.

Environmental Benefits Statement

The World Bank is committed to reducing its environmental footprint. In support of this commitment, the Office of the Publisher leverages electronic publishing options and print-on-demand technology, which is located in regional hubs worldwide. Together, these initiatives enable print runs to be lowered and shipping distances decreased, resulting in reduced paper consumption, chemical use, greenhouse gas emissions, and waste.

The Office of the Publisher follows the recommended standards for paper use set by the Green Press Initiative. Whenever possible, books are printed on 50% to 100% postconsumer recycled paper, and at least 50% of the fiber in our book paper is either unbleached or bleached using Totally Chlorine Free (TCF), Processed Chlorine Free (PCF), or Enhanced Elemental Chlorine Free (EECF) processes.

More information about the Bank's environmental philosophy can be found at http://crinfo.worldbank.org/crinfo/environmental_responsibility/index.html.

www.ingramcontent.com/pod-product-compliance
Lightning Source LLC
Chambersburg PA
CBHW081215230426
43666CB00015B/2735